Printmaking & Picture Printing

A Bibliographical Guide to Artistic & Industrial Techniques in Britain 1750-1900

GAVIN BRIDSON
and
GEOFFREY WAKEMAN

The Plough Press
Oxford
1984
The Bookpress Ltd
Williamsburg

Published by The Plough Press, 2 Manor Way
Kidlington Oxford
ISBN 0 902813 12 9
and The Bookpress Ltd, Post Office Box KP
Williamsburg Virginia 23187
ISBN 0 916271 00 5
Printed in England by Parchment (Oxford) Ltd
60 Hurst Street Oxford
Bound by Woolnough Bookbinding Wellingborough

Addenda et corrigenda Pages:

26 A77 Add to entry: also letter from W. Day, p.43.
45 A243 Amend end of line 6 to read: London, 1969.
55 A323 Amend date to read: [1882.]
59 A351 Amend title to read: Copies as originals.
80 B42 Delete: with pls. Not seen.
Add: 3 pls.
Frontis. is a silhouette, pl. 2 is a landscape vignette on t.p., pl. 3 shows 6 grounds. Describes, in simple terms, resin and spirit grounds.
83 B61 Add: Bodleian Lib. copy has 3 pls.
" Add: B61** Bradbury, H. 1860. Specimens of banknote engraving designed & executed by Henry Bradbury. London. 7pp. & 48 pls., 10pp. & 2 pls.
The pages at the end are descriptions of the engraving machines shown in the pls. Paper samples.
97 B175 Amend pagination to read: ii+100+12pp.
106 C13* Amend title to read: Woone's patent method ...
108 C42 Amend date to read: [1882.]
112 C85 Amend author to read: G., R.
135 D58 Add to 3rd edn: 46pp.
155 Section Dj, last line of intro. Amend date to read: 1850's
161 E35 Amend to read: 6 pls.
162 E36 & E42 Amend to read: 6 pls.
165 E65 Amend author to read: Woodbury, W.E.
166 Line 8 from end. Before Anon. (E101) insert: Dawson (E99*).
167 Last line of introduction. Amend to read: ... see also Huson (E112) & Wilmer (E115).
169 Add: E99* Dawson, A. 1889. The limits of photogravure. Photographic News 33: 340-343.
185 E268 Add to entry (as first periodical ref.): Journal, Photographic Society 15: 78-84, & specimen.
194 E363 Add: 2nd edn., n.d.
" E364 Add: 4th edn., 1898. 89pp. & 1 pl.
" Line 16 of Eh intro., before Hodson add: Anon. (E366*)
195 Add: E366* Anon. 1882. Hoeschotype, a new photo-chromic printing process. Printing Times & Lithographer N.S.8: 190-191.
204 Amend A458 & A459 to read: E458 E459
205 E477 Add: Also pub. in British Printer 8: 68-70, 1895.
208 E498 Amend author to read: Swan, D.C.
221 Aquatinta ... Specimens ...
aquatinta grounds ... Add: B42
222 Bank-note engraving ... Add: B61**
Specimens ... Add: B61**
226 Hoeschotype ... Add: E366*
235 Bradbury, H. Add: B61**
237 Add: Collas, A. B56
" Add: Day, W. A77
" Add to Dawson, A.: E99*
239 Add: G., R. C85
241 Add: Isert, T. A. B76 B188
248 Swan, D. G. Amend to read: Swan, D.C.
250 Woodbury, W. B. Delete: E65
" Add: Woodbury, W. E. E65

CONTENTS

Section B: Intaglio plate processes

Section C: Relief block processes

Section D: Planographic (lithographic) processes

Section E: Photo-mechanical processes

Section F: Periodicals consulted

Introduction

Richard Godfrey's history, "Printmaking in Britain", opens a survey of the late eighteenth century with the comment

> Throughout the eighteenth century, reproductive prints must outnumber those which were designed and executed by a single hand in a proportion of at least fifty to one. As the century progressed this trend increased, and the various techniques that were introduced were the result -- not of some chalcographic self-generation -- but of the desire to find more accurate means of simulating the appearance of paintings, watercolours and drawings. The second half of the century thus saw the successive introduction of the crayon manner, stipple, aquatint and soft-ground etching, to augment the existing techniques of mezzotint and line engraving. This predominantly "servile role" of the engraver was emphasized on the foundation of the Royal Academy in 1768 by the exclusion of engravers from membership, to their bitter fury and chagrin. See (A270).

In consequence of this new trend a briskly active print trade developed amongst which the large firms of John Boydell and John Raphael Smith were preeminent. Once a fashion had been nurtured and a market created the commercial pressure to satisfy this demand led to the debasement of originality in printmaking; easy production methods and increased output became the most significant factors. The numbers of illustrated books also increased greatly at this time and they became more ambitious and elaborate. Soon, a graphic arts industry had grown up to provide all the printed pictures that the public demanded. Developments in reproduction techniques and production methods continued without pause for another hundred years.

By the end of the following century the photo-mechanical revolution had entirely changed the face of the whole world of commercial graphic arts and had even filtered into the more sophisticated field of artistic printselling. Mass produced illustrated newspapers, periodicals and books were filled with chromo-printed artwork and photographic images, the advertising industry had adopted all the advances in graphic arts technology for products ranging from giant wall posters to tiny pictorial packages, and the Printseller's Association -- guardians of excellence in their trade -- even registered photogravure and other similar prints in limited editions.

The provision of such quantities of illustrations and prints had caused great factories to grow up, often employing labour forces of several hundreds. They ran busy "artistic" departments or photographic studios, were equipped with serried ranks of power-driven printing machines and other related appliances, and required large numbers of skilled graphical and printing personnel to man them. Their output was colossal. For example, a regular annual event in the later 19th century was the distribution of immense numbers of pictorial trade almanacs and calendars, often colour printed, and serving as much to demonstrate the progress of printing as to advertise the tradesman with whose "compliments" they were given away. This created a large branch of the industry in itself and in 1888, for instance, we are told by a reviewer in the British Printer that

> 2,000,000 Picture Calendars are printed every year by Messrs Taylor Brothers of Leeds. When it is remembered that there are an average of thirteen or fourteen printings in each of these calendars, and that the two million are the production of one firm alone, some idea may be formed of the extent

of the trade in this branch of printing. Messrs Taylor Brothers' connexion extends to all parts of the world and the large demand necessitates extensive preparations long before they are actually required for use. This is how it is that one year has scarcely commenced before new subjects are ready and on the market for the next. Messrs Taylor Brothers submit no less than forty-four designs -- in three sizes -- for the year 1889. (British Printer 1 (2): 28, 1888.)

Meanwhile, the Society of Painter-Etchers and Engravers, distressed by the debasement of printmaking, strove to keep creative printmaking alive and appreciated. Their Founder-President, F.S. Haden, was busy lecturing, writing, and etching in support of his conservative ideals in painter-etching, which he regarded as the highest artistic expression of original printmaking. The Society's self-conscious creative output was printed, not in factories like that of Taylor Brothers, but on the simple hand presses of such master craftsmen as Frederick Goulding.

This bibliography is concerned with the processes for preparing printing surfaces, and the means of printing from them, as practised in Britain. Literature extending from 1750 to 1900 is recorded with a little occasional overlap at both ends. Some standard older manuals in regular use in 1750 are included, as also are a few works published after 1900 which illuminate end of century developments. The first commercially published book to be illustrated throughout with tri-chromatic process-engraved reproductions of water-colour illustrations was published in 1900. Works illustrated with colour photographs from life soon followed. Thus, by 1900, virtually the whole range of modern graphic reproduction processes had been developed and were in production.

The technical literature accompanying these graphic arts developments, which extend from self-conscious creative printmaking to impersonal mass-produced picture printing, is extensive and widely scattered. It comprises many specialised manuals and treatises, a considerable quantity of encyclopaedia articles, and some hundreds of contributions to specialised artistic and trade periodicals. The present bibliography forms an introductory guide to this literature and, by presenting the contents of each section in chronological order, illustrates the development of each speciality. About 1760 titles are included in this work. For contemporary titles published between 1750 and 1900 we have tried to be as comprehensive as possible, only excluding some inconsequential trifles.

Each section, covering a major graphic art medium, is accompanied by a subsection which includes a selection of relevant historical and bibliographical studies published to date. Since the emphasis of the whole bibliography is on the technical history of printmaking and picture printing, works on the artistic history of prints and the aesthetics of print collecting are generally excluded.

The great quantity of articles in trade and other periodicals have not previously been included in a bibliography of printmaking. Their research and examination involved making a systematic page-by-page perusal of all the major printing-trade, and several photographic, periodicals. Some of these appeared weekly and recorded -- often with great excitement -- the announcement of technical innovations and improvements within days of their happening. Weeklies, by their nature, were obliged to keep their content brief and "newsy" and their articles are often very short. In consequence (particularly in the photo-mechanical section) we record numerous, individually slight, contributions which are nevertheless important source material for the historian.

From time to time details of recent innovations, together with the established methods, were synthesised in a technical manual providing both a basic instructional text and a "state-of-the-art" survey. Several such works first appeared as regular series of articles in printing or photographic periodicals before acquiring a separate existence in book form. As a result the reader who kept up-to-date with periodicals had this information a year or so before the title-page date of the book. We have recorded both forms of the text for several such instances.

Copyright was much more relaxed in the 19th century and periodicals were regularly filled with articles reprinted from the pages of their rivals, sometimes with only a week between. These alternative appearances of articles have been reported when they are known. This practice was not limited to borrowings from British periodicals. Continental and American articles were regularly translated or reprinted in British periodicals so that the the home trade was apparently much more familiar with foreign developments than one might have supposed. A selection of relevant articles from overseas sources has been included herein.

The regular inclusion of articles on printmaking in the general encyclopaedias made a concise but useful body of information available to the public at large. In their efforts to be up-to-date the editors of encyclopaedias often took pains to ensure that the latest developments were mentioned. Unfortunately, these were sometimes "nine day wonders" but, nevertheless, we can be grateful, for some of the ephemeral byways thus recorded might not otherwise have found a place in print. Encyclopaedia editors frequently chose writers who were acknowledged experts in their fields so that, even when unsigned, these articles may provide singularly authoritative information. It has not been possible to search all the encyclopaedias of our period, but the selection provided should indicate the value of this field of research. The many smaller technical encyclopaedias may reveal nuggets that we have yet to discover.

The bibliography is classified under six broad headings -- A Printmaking & picture printing in general; B Intaglio plate processes; C Relief block processes; D Planographic (lithographic) processes; E Photo-mechanical processes; F Periodicals consulted. Section E is subdivided according to photo-mechanical processes that correspond to sections A to D.

In order to keep this work within reasonably handy proportions we have confined our annotations to selected works and have prefaced each section with some introductory notes which highlight "key" works in that field. For less familiar processes we have also given an outline of the principal techniques and their development. A fully annotated bibliography remains a desideratum and the present work is offered as a contribution towards that goal.

Collations are kept to a minimum and text illustrations are not generally mentioned. Plates, however, are always noted and, in the happy event that they represent actual examples of graphic processes described, we have recorded their details.

Contemporary examples of individual processes are essential for an understanding of the "look" of the print produced by that means. Modern books on the study and identification of older printmaking processes, whilst giving admirable descriptive accounts of studio techniques, often underemphasise the important fact that the "print" only becomes one when the printing surface has been applied to paper. Thus, the way the ink sits on the print and the alteration which printing produces in the surface of the paper are of the greatest significance to identification. Only then do the methods employed for preparing the printing surface become meaningful. "Model" examples are essential if one wishes to learn to identify processes used for prints or for illustrations in 18th and 19th century books and magazines. Fortunately, plenty are provided in the contemporary literature of printmaking and we have been careful to note all that we know of.

Two indexes conclude the work. One lists authors and all others who contributed to any publication, whether translators, editors, or even correspondents. The other is a subject index and includes contemporary names, patent titles, and popular terms for individual graphic processes, with cross-references from alternative terms. The structure of the index segregates the contemporary technical literature from subsequent historical studies. To assist those who are looking for examples of the many graphic processes the index provides, for each process, the sub-heading, "specimens" (where they exist).

Entries are serially numbered within the sections A to F. The preparation of the detailed subject index, which, of course, followed the numbering of all entries, necessitated the re-location of certain items and at the same time some late addenda had to be incorporated. As a result of accommodating these some asterisked sequence numbers had to be inserted, rather than re-number and re-index the whole again. All the asterisked insertions follow the corresponding plain number, are indexed, and should not prove a hindrance to the user. The senior author's move to the United States of America at this crucial stage was largely responsible for this problem.

This guide is intended for print curators, printing historians, bibliographers, and librarians, as well as all who wish to know something of the literature of old prints and book illustrations, items that are so avidly collected today. However, the bibliography is intended as a guide to reading, rather than collecting, and we make no mention of special-paper issues or other "points" that the collector might seek.

The compilation of this work was based, in the first instance, on our own private collections. However, the services of the Victoria & Albert Museum Library, Science Museum Library, Society of Antiquaries, and especially the St. Bride Printing Library were essential to us. We warmly thank their respective staffs for their cheerful provision of library services and photocopies and even, in one case, periodic refreshment! Although the St. Bride Printing Library is clearly the most comprehensive, there is no single library that holds all the literature we record herein and, for some titles, we were unable to trace a copy in a British library. Curiously, the authorities who first put together the St. Bride collection omitted to acquire the vital sets of photographic periodicals which contain most of the earlier literature of photo--mechanical printing. The Royal Photographic Society's library is a valuable resource of these items but, unfortunately, they moved from London to Bath a few years ago. In the event the Science Library proved to be the best source for photographic periodicals. We also, incidentally, examined many titles in antiquarian bookshops -- in particular Messrs. Edwards, (the late) Seligmann, Sims & Reed, Sotheran, Quaritch, and Eric Golding. They probably didn't know that they were helping us, but our thanks are none the less due to them for their trust and courtesy as we combed their shelves (often with wallets quite unable to meet the purchase price of interesting items). Others who generously helped in various ways include Robin Myers, John Collins, Elizabeth A. Mosimann, and John Ballinger. To them and to all others not individually mentioned we express our thanks. May our readers forgive our errors, notify us of our omissions, and look charitably on this first attempt to describe some of the bibliographical byways of printmaking and picture-printing history.

List of abbreviations

et al.	and others
approx.	approximately
appx.	appendix
aquat.	aquatint
ch.	chapter
chromo-lith.	chromo-lithograph(y)
col.	colour (-ed)
collo.	collotype
comp.	compiled (-er)
corr.	corrected
drypt.	drypoint
edn.	edition
Ed. ed.	Editor, edited
electro.	electrotype
emb.	embossed
eng.	engraving (-ed)
enl.	enlarged
etch.	etching (-ed)
facsim.	facsimile
h-tone proc. eng.	half-tone process engraving
heliogr.	heliograph (-gravure)
heliot.	heliotype
illus.	illustration (-ed)
incl.	including
intro.	introduction
line eng.	line engraving
lith.	lithograph(y)
mezzo.	mezzotint
N.S.	new series
no.	number
orig.	original
pp.	pages
photograv.	photogravure
photo-lith.	photo-lithograph(y)
pl.(s)	plate(s)
proc.	process
pub.	published
rel.	relief
repr.	reprinted
rev.	revised
ser.	series
soft-gd. etch.	soft-ground etching
steel eng.	steel engraving (-ed)
stereo.	stereotype
stipp. eng.	stipple engraving
suppl.	supplement
t.p. t-p.	title page title-page
transl.	translated
typogr.	typography (-graphic)
vol.	volume
woodc.	woodcut
wood eng.	wood engraving
zincogr.	zincograph(y)
zincot.	zincotype

Section A: Printmaking & picture printing in general

Aa Bibliographies

This is primarily a record of the work of earlier bibliographers in the field. All of them omit coverage of articles published in periodicals (an omission which the present work seeks to rectify). This section also highlights some useful library catalogues.

There are relatively few bibliographies in all and they vary greatly in scale and treatment. Most have the interests of print collectors as their chief concern and only list the most accessible books on the major printmaking processes. Maberly provided the first such bibliography in his collector's manual of 1844, and in 1880 Hoe, the American printer, re-published it with a substantial supplementary list (A1). In 1897 Singer & Strang (A4) made the first serious effort to provide a comprehensive, if rather concise, list of literature on printmaking techniques. A decade and a half later Levis published his massive work (A6) covering the field in much greater bibliographical detail. It was essentially the work of a bibliophile, with emphasis on "externals" rather than content, and a large part of its text was concerned with the literature of print collecting. Ludman, Mason & Sirefman (A16) is a recent addition to the fold but again addresses itself to the print collector and connoisseur rather than the printing historian. The latter is best served by Bigmore & Wyman (A2) for literature down to the early 1880's.

Library catalogues, if they record the content of a worthwhile collection, have considerable bibliographical value. When they also provide a subject, as well as author guide, they are particularly useful. Their main function, of course, is to indicate the whereabouts of any particular title and are included here for that reason also. The most important collection of art literature in Britain is at the Victoria & Albert Museum (A13) and almost all the earlier, and much of the later, literature on printmaking can be found there. But the literature of picture printing, as distinct from creative printmaking, is best provided by the St. Bride Printing Library (A8). The Patent Office lists (A5 A7) also contain much of the technical literature on graphic arts and, unlike the St. Bride catalogue, they have the additional merit of a subject arrangement. The American counterparts of these catalogues are, for printmaking, the New York Public Library (A14) and, for printing history, The Newberry Library (A11) and the American Type Founders' Company (A15). All contain a wealth of British as well as American literature and provide subject as well as author entries. Valuable printing-history libraries in Europe include the Bersenverein der Deutscher Buchhändler (A3) and the V.B.B.B. in Amsterdam (A9). Their classified catalogues, apart from containing a representative proportion of English works, also provide an interesting picture of European technical literature throughout our period of interest.

For bibliographies dealing with individual graphic reproduction media see sections Ba, Ca, Da, & Ea <u>infra</u>.

A1 **Maberly, J.** 1880. The print collector. Ed. with notes,... & a bibliography of engraving by Robert Hoe Jr. New York. viii+350pp. 1st edn., London, 1844.
Maberly's bibliography is on pp.168-198 and Hoe's large supplementary list of ca. 475 titles on pp.311-340.

A2 **Bigmore, E.C. & C.W.H. Wyman.** 1880-86. A bibliography of printing. London. 3 vols. Repr. New York, 1945; London, 1969; & London & New Castle, Del., 1978.
Alphabetically arranged author list, noteworthy for its often lengthy and scholarly annotation. First appeared in the pages of the "Printing Times".

A3 **Borsenverein der Deutscher Buchhändler.** 1885. Katalog der Bibliothek. Leipzig. xx+1406pp.
Classified catalogue with a predominantly German content. Provides a good indication of the range of European literature available to the British printing trade. A number of important works published in England were translated from original German texts which can be found here.

A4 **Singer, H.W. & W. Strang.** 1897. Bibliography. In: Etching, engraving & other methods of printing pictures. pp.188-221. London.
Chronologically arranged short-title list with author index. Despite its brevity it is surprisingly comprehensive and still of use.

A5 **Patent Office.** 1904. Subject list of works on the fine & graphic arts (including photography) & art industries in the library of the Patent Office. London. 374pp. (Patent Office Library Series no.2; Bibliographical series no.1.)
As might be expected, the library contains much of the literature relating to technical and experimental aspects of printing and printmaking.

A6 **Levis, H.C.** 1912. A descriptive bibliography of the most important books in the English language relating to the art & history of engraving & the collecting of prints. London. xix+571pp.
----- 1913. ----- Supplement and index. London. 141pp. Both repr. as 1 vol. London, 1974.
The title accurately describes the content of this hefty work. It is a classified descriptive catalogue of books on artistic branches of printmaking incl. the techniques of intaglio, relief and lithographic printmaking. Coverage of the ancillary literature of print collecting, connoisseurship, individual monographs on printmakers, and all kinds of print catalogues, is thorough but outside our present interest. As a bibliophilic compilation it usefully incl. illus. of the t.p.'s of most early works and lengthy t-p. transcriptions. It is, however, this largely "external" emphasis that limits its value to the historian. Selected works are provided with transcribed contents lists but many others are left unexplained. The chapter on "Processes" incl. a rather poor selection of literature that clearly held no interest for the author. Nevertheless, it is a fundamental work and, happily, the reprint is much less weighty than the original edn!

A7 **Patent Office.** 1914. Subject list of works on the fine & graphic arts (excluding photo-mechanical printing & photography) in the library of the Patent Office. London. iv+224pp. (Patent Office Subject List, N.S. BM-BZ.)
An expansion of part of their earlier list (A5).

A8 **St. Bride Foundation.** 1919. Catalogue of the technical reference library of works on printing & the allied arts. London. xvi+999pp.
Compiled by R.A. Peddie, this is a short-title, unannotated, list of the contents of the most significant library in our field. Much additional material has since been added to their collection but is only accessible by using their internal card catalogues.

A9 **Vereeniging ter Bevordering van de Belangen des Boekhandels te Amsterdam.** 1920+. Catalogus der bibliotheek. The Hague. (Vol. 8 appeared in 1979.)
Classified subject catalogue of a vast international collection of literature with very broad book-trade and printing-history coverage. Contains a good representative collection on the graphic arts. Many articles in periodicals are given entries. Unfortunately, the preliminaries, contents lists, linking text, and subject headings are all in Dutch. Non-cumulative author indexes have been incl. from time to time. (Vols. 4 & 8 are entirely devoted to booksellers' catalogues.)

A10 **Manchester Public Libraries.** 1961-63. Reference library subject catalogue: Section 655 Printing. Ed. by G.E. Haslam. Manchester. 2 vols.
The graphic arts are not very well represented.

A11 **Newberry Library**, Chicago. 1962. Dictionary catalogue of the history of printing from the John M. Wing Foundation in the Newberry Library. Boston, Mass. 6 vols.
----- 1970. ----- Supplement. Boston. 3 vols.
----- 1981. ----- Second supplement. Boston. 4 vols.
Photo-facsimile of catalogue cards from a major world collection covering all aspects of printing. The coverage of graphic processes is good but far less impressive than for letterpress printing.

A12 **Watson, G.** Ed. 1969. Book production & distribution. In: The new Cambridge bibliography of English literature. Vol.3: 1800-1900. pp.25-90. Cambridge.
----- 1971. ----- Vol.3: 1660-1800. pp.249-312.
Very concise but remarkably thorough lists of the literature, largely based on the collection of the St. Bride Printing Library.

A13 **Victoria & Albert Museum**, National Art Library. 1972. National Art Library catalogue. Boston, Mass. 10 vols.
Photo-facsimile of some 300,000 catalogue cards. Author catalogue with exceptionally good coverage of graphic arts literature. The last vol. is a separate author list of pre-1890 titles not included in vols. 1-9. Incorporates the bulk of titles first published in:
South Kensington Museum. 1870-77. Universal catalogue of books on art. London. 2 vols. xvi+2188pp.; Supplementary volume. London. 655pp. Both repr. New York, n.d. (Burt Franklin Bibliography & Reference Series no. 47.)
Although this was essentially a catalogue of the National Art Library it also includes entries for additional relevant titles in other collections.)

A14 **New York Public Library**, Prints Division. 1975. Dictionary catalogue of the Print Division. Boston, Mass. 5 vols.
Photo-facsimile of some 83,000 catalogue cards. A well catalogued record of this significant collection with international coverage. Incl. many cataloguings for articles in periodicals. Supersedes an earlier work covering pre-1900 literature:
Weitenkampf, F. 1915. List of works in the New York Public Library relating to prints. Bulletin, New York Public Library 19: 847-935, 959-1002. Also pub. Separately: New York, 1916. iii+162pp. & suppl. 1917. 8pp.

A15 **Columbia University Libraries**, New York. 1980. The history of printing from its beginnings to 1930. The subject catalogue of the American Type Founders' Company Library in the Columbia University Library. With an introduction by K.A. Lohf. Millwood, N.Y. 4 vols.
Photo-facsimile of catalogue cards from another major world collection. Contains substantial holdings under such headings as: Color printing, Electrotyping, Engraving, Lithography, Photo engraving, Process engraving, and wood engraving. Of special value to the printing historian on account of its rich collections of technical and trade literature. It records many articles in periodical literature.

A16 **Ludman, J., L. Mason & C. Sirefman.** 1982. Fine print references: A selected bibliography of print-related literature. Millwood, N.Y.
A wide-ranging, classified bibliography much concerned with print collecting and connoisseurship but also incl. literature on the history and techniques of printmaking. Some entries are misplaced, like the inclusion of mezzotint under "Relief Processes", suggesting some unfamiliarity with technical details of printmaking.

Ab Printmaking & picture-printing techniques

Works which generally include all three of the major printmaking media, intaglio, relief, and planographic. Obviously those published before the 19th century do not mention lithography which was a late arrival on the scene.

It is only with the growth of the large encyclopaedias that we get the first general coverage of all aspects of printmaking. A special effort is made to record these because they have been almost total neglected by earlier bibliographers, despite their interest for the printmaking historian. Some were extremely good and contained articles contributed by acknowledged authorities in the field who generally attempted to describe the latest technical developments. "Books of Trades" and "Artists' Assistants" also included sections on printmaking but they were usually rather poor and repetitive. We have passed over most of these older works until the 1820's when "The Mechanic's Library" published Partington's excellent and much-quoted text (A26).

It was not until 1841 that Fielding provided the first comprehensive textbook appeared in which he gave serious treatment to all the known printmaking processes (A28). It is particularly valuable in that it includes actual examples of all the processes described, with the exception of photography. Hansard (A25) and Savage (31) have fairly concise descriptions of printmaking and picture printing in the context of general printing craft. However, the encyclopaedias continued to provide better coverage of the whole field until that milestone of printmaking literature, Stannard's "Art Exemplar", was published in ca. 1860 (A34). Although extremely rare (only 10 copies were produced) it has to be regarded as the most significant general work on printmaking within our period on account of the authority of its author, its breadth of coverage and the range of specimens which it provides.

By 1860 most of the traditional techniques had developed to their fullest efficiency as hand-processes and a great variety of alternative experimental methods, with chemical or mechanical bases, had been tried and sometimes adopted by the trade. Photography was beginning to be applied to photo-gravure, photo-lithography, and photo-relief work and within a few years the whole field was to be sharply divided between artist-printmakers and printing technicians. The former directed their efforts towards preserving creative printmaking as a fine art, the latter at cheapening and accelerating the mass--production of commercial picture printing.

The creative printmaker was served by Hamerton's works (A42 A47) and by Singer & Strang (A52). Hamerton's "Graphic Arts", in particular, related printmaking to creative drawing and painting, providing fine examples of some printmaking processes and excellent facsimiles of others. Singer & Strang produced a text-book in the same mould as Fielding's of half a century earlier and, like his, theirs was illustrated with a range of specially prepared examples of each process.

The traditional processes of printmaking and the technical developments in picture printing were given equal treatment by Stannard (A34) whose range of coverage is unrivalled in any other single book, for he attempted to include every known process with examples. The interests of the practical printer were also admirably served by the Society of Arts, always well to the fore in reviewing and discussing technical developments. The lectures given by Davenport (A35 A38) and Bolas (A41) are full of interest for the printing historian. Following Stannard's work the first book which treated printmaking from the points of view of both the picture printer and the publisher was Hodson's in 1884 (A43). It was liberally illustrated with examples of traditionally crafted and photo-mechanically manufactured illustrations. In 1892 Harland wrote some essays on picture printing for an audience of practical printers (A44 A48) which described some of these processes as "factory" operations, thus demonstrating the growing distance between the manufacturing and the artistic sides of printmaking.

In 1895, at Stuttgart, Goebel produced a substantial lavishly illustrated tome on the graphic arts which contains spectacular examples of all the processes then used in Germany (A50). It was also published in London under the imprint of the same firm who published the widely read "Stationer & Fancy Trades' Register", and in its pages they printed an English translation of Goebel's German text. Alongside the volume of illustrations this provided English printers with an impressive end-of-century survey of the state of graphic arts on the Continent from whence German and Austrian picture printers were making successful inroads into many portions of the British market.

Alongside these treatises the "Encyclopaedia Britannica" continued to provide its valuable coverage of printmaking processes right down to the end of the century.

For literature on photo-mechanical processes see section Eb.

A17 Anon. 1771. Encyclopaedia Britannica: Or, a dictionary of arts & sciences. Edinburgh. 3 vols.
Brief articles on: Engraving, Etching, Mezzotinto & Printing (incl. copper--plate).

A18 ----- 1778-83. Encyclopaedia Britannica: [etc.] 2nd edn. Edinburgh. 10 vols.
Articles: Engraving, pp.2803-2805; Etching, pp.2838-2840; Mezzotinto, p.4989; Cutting in wood, p.2354; Printing (incl. copper-plate), pp.6473-6486 & 1 pl. Generally good articles.

A19 ----- 1797. Encyclopaedia Britannica: [etc.] 3rd edn. Edinburgh. 18 vols.
Articles: Engraving, vol. 6: 667-672; Etching, vol. 6: 740-743; Aquatinta, vol. 2: 146; Mezzotinto, vol. 11: 687-689; Cutting in wood, vol. 5: 625-626; Printing (incl. copper-plate), vol. 15: 512-526 & 1 pl. Generally good articles.

A20 **Rees, A.** 1802-19. The cyclopaedia: Or, universal dictionary of arts, sciences, & literature. By A. Rees, with the assistance of eminent professional gentlemen. London. 45 vols. (Unpaged.)
Articles: Aquatinta, Copper (incl. copper plates for engraving), Engraving, Etching, Mezzotinto, Printing (incl. copper-plate), & Wood engraving. Generally informative articles.

A21 **Anon.** 1810. Encyclopaedia Britannica: Or, a dictionary of arts, sciences, & miscellaneous literature. 4th edn. Edinburgh. 20 vols. Repr. as: 5th edn., 1815; 6th edn., 1823.
Articles: Engraving, vol. 8: 130-141; Etching, vol. 8: 332-334; Aquatinta, vol. 2: 487-488; Mezzotinto, vol. 13: 787-789; Wood engraving, vol. 20: 736-738; Printing (incl. copper-plate), vol. 17: 361-379 & 1 pl. Good articles.

A22 **Brewster, D.** 1808-30. The Edinburgh encyclopaedia. Conducted by D. Brewster. Edinburgh. 18 vols.
Articles: Engraving, vol. 9: 41-55; Etching, vol. 9: 211-214; Aquatinta, vol. 2: 269-270; Mezzotinto, vol. 14: 196-197; Lithography, vol. 13: 44-47; Printing, vol. 17: 158-164; Printing press (incl. copper-plate), vol. 17: 164-170 & 1 pl; Printing machinery, vol. 17: 170-174 & 1 pl.

A23 **Wilkes, J.** 1810-29. Encyclopaedia Londinensis. Compiled by J. Wilkes. London. 24 vols.
Articles: Engraving, vol. 6: 809-814; Aquatinta, vol. 1: 840; Printing (incl. copper-plate & lithographic), vol. 21: 403-417.

A24 **Anon.** 1824. Supplement to the 4th, 5th, & 6th edns. of Encyclopaedia Britannica. Edited by E. Napier. Edinburgh. 6 vols.
Articles: Steel, engraving upon, vol.6: 547-548; Lithography, vol. 5: 278-286 & 1 pl; Printing (mainly on improvements in presses and stereotype), vol. 6: 369-384 & 4 pls; Pantograph, vol. 6: 109-110, illus.

A25 **Hansard, T.C.** 1825. Typographia: An historical sketch of the origin & progress of the art of printing; with practical directions for conducting every department in an office. With a description of stereotype & lithography. London. xvi+939+26pp. Repr. London, 1966.
Pt. II deals with practice and incl. chapters on copper-plate, lithographic and decorative printing.

A26 **Partington, C.F.** ca. 1825. The engraver's complete guide, comprising the theory & practice of engraving, with its modern improvements, in steel plates, lithography, etc. London. 52pp. (Forms part of: The Mechanics library, or book of trades, pp.97-144.)
An excellent, though concise, manual which was apparently widely used.

A27 **Harris, W. et al.** 1828-31. Oxford encyclopaedia: Or, dictionary of arts, sciences, & general literature. By W. Harris, J.A. Stewart, C. Butler, & J.H. Hinton, assisted by other literary gentlemen. Oxford. 7 vols.
Articles: Engraving, vol. 3: 244-247; Printing (incl. copper-plate), vol. 5: 747-755.

A28 **Fielding, T.H.** 1841. The art of engraving, with the various modes of operation under the following different divisions: Etching, soft-ground etching, line engraving, chalk & stipple, aquatinting, mezzotint, lithography, wood engraving, medallic engraving, electrography & photography. London. vii+109pp. & 10 pls. 2nd edn. 1844. Repr., (but without any of the pls.,) in: Maberly, J. 1880. The print collector. Ed. ... by R. Hoe Jr. pp.201-257. New York, 1880.
The pls are actual examples of etch., soft-gd etch., line eng., aquat. eng. (with 8 graded bitings), aquat. gd. (8 kinds), mezzo. (in 2 states), stipple or chalk, lith. (2 printings), a drawing on zinc, and a wood eng. in the text. Also a pl. illus. printmaking tools.

A29 **Anon.** 1842. Encyclopaedia Britannica. 7th edn. Edinburgh. 21 vols. Articles: Engraving (copper & steel), vol. 9: 44-55; Etching, vol. 9: 372-374; Aquatinta engraving, vol. 3: 315-317; Mezzotinto, vol. 15: 2-4; Wood engraving, vol. 21: 916-918; Lithography, vol. 13: 380-386; Printing (incl. stereotype, printing in colours, & copper-plate), vol. 18: 537-573 & 3 pls.
By this edn. the articles are growing in size and value. They were largely reprinted in the following item (A30).

A30 **Hansard, T.C.** 1841. Treatises on printing & typefounding. From the 7th. edn. of the Encyclopaedia Britannica. Edinburgh. vii+235pp. & 3 pls.

A31 **Savage, W.** 1841. A dictionary of the art of printing. London. viii+815pp. Repr. London, 1966.
Concise articles, but written with the authority of a master of the craft of picture printing.

A32 **Smedley, E. et al.** 1817-45. Encyclopaedia Metropolitana. Ed. by E. Smedley, Hugh J. Rose & Henry J. Rose. London.
Vol. 5. 1845. Mixed sciences, vol. 3. Article: Engraving, by J. Lindsay, pp.780-851. A substantial treatise which deals with all graphic processes from both historical and practical points of view. Incl. a pl. of eng. tools and a Taylor & Martineau lith. press. Another pl. has specimens of soft-gd etch., chalk eng., mezzo., aquat., line eng. - etched, and line eng. - finished. This vol. of the Encyclopaedia was re-pub. in 1848 as: The encyclopaedia of the fine arts: Comprising ... engraving. London. Orig. pagination retained.
Vol. 8. 1845. Mixed sciences, vol. 6. Article: Manufactures, by P. Barlow. pp.85-828. Incl. a section on printing dealing with letterpress, copper-plate, and lithographic printing and presses. pp.770-787.

A33 **Anon.** 1853-60. Encyclopaedia Britannica. 8th edn. Edinburgh. 21 vols.
Articles: Engraving (copper & steel), vol. 8: 799-813; Aquatinta engraving, vol. 3: 331-333; Mezzotinto, vol. 14: 733-734; Wood engraving, vol. 21: 902-904; Lithography, vol. 13: 510-514; Photo-lithography, vol. 17: 554-555; Photography, vol. 17: 544-554; Printing (incl. stereotype, nature printing, printing in colours, bank note printing, etc.), vol. 18: 520-563.
Modern technical developments are reported alongside traditional methods and photography is now incl. for the first time.

A34 **Stannard, W.J.** [Later called himself Harry Sandars.] ca. 1860. The art-exemplar: A guide to distinguish one species of print from another, with pictorial examples & written descriptions of every known style of illustration whether executed on gold, silver, brass, iron, tin, stone, wood, leather, steel, zinc, lead, pewter, glass, type metal, ivory, paper, plaister, antimony, fusible metal, etc., including all those under the following heterogeneous heads, viz. [followed by a 4 col. list of 156 technical terms & patent names]. London. viii+xii+216+8pp. & many examples of print processes.
Only 10 copies were produced, 4 on large paper and 6 small and, since all were illustrated with actual specimens, each copy is probably different. As the work is of such rarity a note of the contents is appropriate: Line engraving; Spiral style, Steel engraving, etc.; Etching; Soft etching & etching on glass & ivory; Stipple, dot & chalk engraving; Mezzotinto; Aqua-tinta; Machine-ruling, concentric, & eccentric chuck, rose engine & geometrical engraving; Siderographia, or bank note engraving; Anaglyptography, & Bates's & Stokes's patents; Phytoglyphy, or nature self-printing; Baxter process -- Baxterotype; Galvanography; Photography, etc.; Photogalvanography; Steel & copper-plate printing; Wood engraving; Typography, or letter-press printing; English typography & book work; Ancient books, book printing, etc.; Chiaro-oscuro & block colour printing; Chromotype & surface colour printing; Compound plate printing; Stereotypography -- polytypage, logotype, omotype, typometry, etc.; Glyphography, electrotint, acrography, Durertype, etc.; The "Letter-Press" etc.; Lithography (commercial lithography, fac-similes, writing, transferography, typolithography, transfers from copper or steel plates, pen & ink work on stone, engraving or etching on stone -- machinagraphy, etc, wood-cut style, chalk style, tinted lithographs, rubbing style, lithotint, stump drawing, lithozôgraphia, chromolithography or color-printing, zincography etc., anastatic printing, printing from stone zinc etc., lithographic stones); Sundries (polaplasiasmos, omnigraphy -- Becker's patent, cast engravings, paleiconography -- Tissierography and other alto-relievos for letter-press printing, papyrography, metallography etc.)
For a description of his own copy see Levis (A6), pp.527-529, where a full title-page transcription is given. For a comment on the background and importance of this work see Harris (A265), (first article) pp.41-46.

A35 **Davenport, S.T.** 1865. Engraving & other reproductive art processes. Journal, Society of Arts 13: 131-140. Also pub. in: Typographic Advertiser 3: 79, 86, 103, 110, 122, 1865; 4: 16, 24, 32, 1865; & Photographic News 9: 43-44, 55-56, 66-68, 79-80, 91-92, 103-104, 166, 177-178, 200-201, 1865.
General survey of all processes with emphasis on techniques.

A36 **Marples, D.** 1866. On picture printing. Proceedings, Literary & Philosophical Society of Liverpool 19: 80-96.
----- 1868. ----- Chromo-lithography. Ibid. 22: 193-224, & 1 pl., a chromo-lith. with 9 col. separations.
A general survey by a leading provincial decorative printer.

A37 **Knight, C.** 1866-68. English cyclopaedia. Conducted by C. Knight. 4th. div. Arts & sciences. London. 8 vols.
Articles: Engraving, vol. 3: 882-892; Aquatinta engraving, vol. 1: 453-455; Mezzotinto, vol. 5: 617-619; Electro-metallurgy (incl. electrotype, galvanic etching & engraving), vol. 3: 818-823; Bank note manufacture, vol.

1: 860-863; Lithography, vol. 5: 302-305; Printing (incl. nature printing & electro-printing), vol. 6: 744-767. [N.B. Reference is to columns, not pages.]
A very useful series of articles with emphasis on up-to-date technical developments.

A38 **Davenport, S.T.** 1869. On prints & their production. Journal, Society of Arts 18: 62-71, also letter from S.T.D. p.99. Also pub. in: Photographic News 14: 20-21, 32--33, 43-44, 68, 79-80, 93, 128-129, 140, 176-177, 1870.
An updated account of technical progress in picture printing incl. developments since his earlier lectures (A35).

A39 ----- 1876. Engraving. In: Bevan, G.P., Ed. British manufacturing industries. pp.75-124. London. 2nd. edn., 1877; 3rd edn., 18??; 4th edn., 1892.
Written for a popular readership.

A40 **Anon.** 1875-89. Encyclopaedia Britannica. 9th edn. Edinburgh. 24 vols.
Articles: Engraving, by P.G. Hamerton, vol. 8: 435-446; Lithography, by G. Reid, vol. 14: 697-701; Photography (incl. photo-mechanical processes), by W.de W. Abney, vol. 18: 821-840; Typography, by J.H. Hessels & J. Southward, vol. 23: 681-710.
Leading specialists contribute substantial essay reviews in their fields

A41 **Bolas, T.** 1880. Modern autographic printing processes. Journal, Society of Arts 28: 135-138.
Discusses various novel processes incl. Griggs's photo-lithography, Zuccato's electro-chemical process, Pumphrey's process, Hectograph process, Dallas's process, etc.

A42 **Hamerton, P.G.** 1882. The graphic arts: A treatise on the varieties of drawing, painting & engraving in comparison with each other & with nature. London. xvi+384pp. & 49 pls.
Ch. XXIV-XXVII describe: Wood engraving, Etching and dry point, Line-engraving, Aquatint and mezzotint, and Lithography, pp.302-378. The pls. incl. actual examples of wood engs. (5), drypt., soft-gd etch., stipp. engs. (2), line engs. (3, one in 2 states), aquat., mezzo., and lith. Other pls. are facsims. of different proc. of drawing and printmaking in heliogr., Goupil-grav., Dawson's typogr. etch., and Autotype, with outstanding results.

A43 **Hodson, J.S.** 1884. An historical & practical guide to art illustration in connection with books & periodicals & general decoration. With numerous specimens of the various methods. London. viii+224pp. & 24 pls.
Describes: Plate engraving, Wood engraving, Lithography (incl. chromo-printing), Engraving by chemical or mechanical processes (incl. zincography, *Duclos' processes, typographic etching, *Dawson's positive etching, relief aquatint, Shanks's patent engraving, *Graphotype), Photographic processes [for details of which see (E44)]. All except those starred are illustrated by actual specimens.

A44 **[Harland, J.W.]** 1887-88. Roundabout papers on lithography, printing & engraving. Printing Times & Lithographer N.S.13: 9-11, 27-28, 47-49, 81-83, 99-101, 138-140, 155-156, 174-176, 194-195, 216-217, 1887; Ibid. N.S.14: 4-6, 23-26, 44-45, 64-65, 85-86, 124-125, 143-144, 161-163, 183-184, 222-223, 1888.
Most of this material was repr. in (A48).

A45 **Koehler, S.R.** 1889. Modern processes of engraving: Some leading methods briefly explained. British & Colonial Printer 22: 331, 367, 383.
A "pocket encyclopaedia" of processes, incl. some recent novelties, viz.: Relief engraving, Wood engraving, Intaglio work, Etching, Mezzotint, Point work [i.e. drypoint], Aquatint, Other processes, Soft ground etching, Sand etching, Glass etching, Machine ruling, Galvanography, Hyalography, Stylography, Chemitypy, Ektypography, Glypnography, Mineralography, Nature printing, Wax process, Graphotype, Clay processes, Etching, Photo-mechanical processes, and Woodburytype.

A46 **O'Brien, M.B.** 1890. A manual for authors, printers, & publishers: Being a guide to all matters pertaining to or incidental to printing & publishing. Illustrated with specimens of chromo-lith., woodc., proc. blocks [zincot. & h-tone proc. eng.], Photophane [collo.], fine art illus., electro. & stereo. London. 130pp. & 6 pls.
Incl. a general survey of book illustration process.

A47 **Hamerton, P.G.** 1892. Drawing & engraving: A brief exposition of technical principles & practice. London. xxii+172pp. & 23 pls.
A repr. of articles from Encyclopaedia Britannica, 9th edn. (A40). The pls. incl. a litho., line engs. (5), etch., and mezzos. (2).

A48 **Harland, J.W.** 1892. The printing arts: An epitome of engraving, lithography & printing. London. viii+180pp.
Deals with the running of a lithographic printing works, wood engraving and cutting posters on soft wood etc., zincography, chalking on stone, etching, mezzotint and engraving on copper and steel, colour printing, American lithography, grained paper and its use, etc. All these operations are discussed from the standpoint of the practical printer. The book is unillustrated.

A49 **Vinycomb, J.** 1894. On the processes for the production of Ex-Libris (Book Plates). London. xii+96pp. & 18 pls.
Based on articles first pub. in the "Journal of the Ex-Libris Society". The pls. incl. examples of chromo-lith., line eng., eng. transferred to stone, transfer drawings from stone, liths. of pen & ink drawings, and line proc. (zincot.)

A50 **Goebel, T.** 1896-97. [Chapters from his work "Die graphischen Kunst der Gegenwart: Ein Führer durch das Buchgewerbe". Stuttgart & London, 1895.] Stationer & Fancy Trades' Register 1896 & 1897.
Includes: Lithography, 1896: 748-762, 845-858; Heliography & photogravure, 1897: 22-28; Collotypy, 1897: 157-160; Zincography, autotype, typogravure, 1897: 192-202; Typographical illustration, wood engraving, 1897: 254-264; Etching & copper and steel engraving, 1897: 302-308.

A51 **Pennell, J.** 1896. The illustration of books: A manual for the use of students. Notes for a course of lectures at the Slade School, University College. London. xii+166pp.
Also describes printmaking processes for the reproduction of artwork by both traditional and photo-mechanical methods.

A52 **Singer, H.W. & W. Strang.** 1897. Etching, engraving & other methods of printing pictures. London. xv+228pp. & 14 pls.
Includes: Relief processes, Intaglio processes (line engraving, etching, dry point, mezzotint, aquatint, chalk-style (crayon), stipple, hammered prints, soft-ground etching, monotype), Colour printing by relief and intaglio, Lithography, Photo-mechanical processes (zincos, half-tones, three--colour, collotype, heliogravure, photogravure). The pls. incl. a woodc., white-line woodc., line eng., etch., drypt., soft-gd. etch., mezzos. (2, one a sand-paper), chalk-style lith. (2), rel. zinc etch., h-tone proc. eng., collo., and photograv. It is interesting to note that this text-book, which is essentially written for artists, also includes a discussion of the new photo-mechanical processes.

A53 **Gerring, C.** 1898. Notes on book illustration. Nottingham. 22pp. & 12 pls. (Nottingham Sette of Odde Volumes, Opusculum 10.)
The pls. incl. 2 "old woodcuts", 3 "woodcuts" (actually wood-engs.), steel eng., electros. (2), zincogr., stereos. (2, of wood engs.), and a collo.
A superficial survey of methods.

A54 **Ward, W.H.** 1900. The printing arts: A description of the methods now in use, more particularly with regard to illustration. Paris. 16pp. h-tone illus.
Produced for the Exposition Universelle of 1900, this general review of the field places special emphasis on modern photo-mechanical processes which, by this date, had ousted most traditional methods for commercial picture printing.

A55 **Anon.** 1902. The new volumes of the Encyclopaedia Britannica constituting ... the 10th edn. Edinburgh & London. vols. 25-33.
Articles: Engraving (by various authors), vol. 28: 263-268; Illustration (incl. technical developments), by E.F. Strange, vol. 29: 406-412.

A56 **Kirkbride, J.** 1903. Engraving for illustration: Historical & practical notes. London. vii+72pp. & 6 pls.
The illustrations incl. electro. copies of wood engs. and 2 ink-photos.
Compared with Ward's little booklet of 1900 (A54) this gives the appearance of being far behind the times!

Ac **Colour printing & bronzing techniques**

Colour printing, as a special topic, scarcely appears in the literature before the 1870's. When it was mentioned it was usually treated as a branch of relief printing and seems to have depended for its success more on individual craftsmanship than on general printing skill. With the creation of new markets for the sale of attractive colour work in advertising, fancy stationery, and illustrated periodicals, coupled with the advent of power-driven machinery of increasing sophistication, new possibilities opened up. Printers began to experiment with colour work and to write about its theory and practical applications in printing. Watt was the first to produce a general manual on colour printing (A58). He was followed by Noble's (A61 A62) contributions which were much more advanced and were backed by his long experience with De la Rue, the playing-card printers. Ink manufacturers were naturally anxious to encourage the successful use of their products and Irvine's lecture (A64 A65) emphasises this concern. Just over a decade after its first appearance, Noble revised his colour printing manual in the form of another series of periodical articles (A69).

Despite the widespread use of bronzing in association with colour printing literature about it is sparse. A few articles in trade periodicals are included but, so far as we know, no book ever appeared on the subject.

For literature on general photo-mechanical colour printing see section Eh.

A57 **Watt, P.B.** 1870. Hints on colours. Lithographer 1: 2-3, 26-27, 106-107.

A58 ----- 1872. A few hints on colour & printing in colours. London. 32pp.

A59 ----- 1873. A few remarks on printing in gold. Lithographer 4: 43-44.

A60 ----- 1877. Bronze work. Printers' Register 16: 31-32.

A61 **Noble, F.** 1878-80. Colour printing. Printers' Register 17: 137-140, 164-165, 178-180, 199-201, 213-215, 1878; 18: 8-10, 28-30, 47-50, 66-68, 87-89, 106-107, 128-129, 144-145, 165-167, 182-183, 202-204, 221-222, 1878/79; 19: 6-7, 27-28, 46-48, 65-67, 87-88, 107-108, 128-129, 147-148, 166-167, 207-209, 226-228, 1879/80.
These unillustrated articles were repr. without alteration in the following book (A62).

A62 ----- 1881. The principles & practice of colour printing stated & explained. London. vi+174pp. & 50 pls.
Deals with varnishes, driers, the various coloured inks, gold and silver leaf and dusted colours, enamelled papers, preparation of colour blocks, machine colour printing, laws and harmonies of colours, etc. The pls. show the same motif printed in 50 separate colours. The book concludes with a valuable account of the printing of the "Graphic" coloured suppl. for Christmas 1879 which was printed by Hodson's relief aquatint method.

A63 **Anon.** 1881. Practical wrinkles in bronze printing. London, Provincial & Colonial Press News 1881 (Dec.): 23-24.

A64 **Irvine, R.** 1891. The chemistry of colour printing: A lecture. British Printer 4 (21): 7-11.
Deals with the theory of colours and the chemical interactions of different coloured inks.

A65 ----- [1891.] The chemistry of colour printing: A lecture. Leicester. 16pp. Also repr. in: Fleming, A.B. & Co. n.d. Specimen book of fine colours for letterpress and lithographic printers. pp.1-18. Edinburgh. Other edns. of (A64).

A66 **Anon.** 1892. Bronzing & dusting - old & new methods. British Lithographer 1 (3): 18-20.

A67 **Francis, H.** 1892-93. Art printing. Printing Times & Lithographer N.S.1: 36, 90, 153, 283-284, 1892; N.S.2: 23-24, 71-72, 121-122, 208-209, 1893.

A68 **Waldron, A.** 1892-94. Guide to printing in colours. [From the German of...] Printing Times & Lithographer N.S.1: 171-173, 227-229, 281-283, 339, 1892; N.S.2: 29-30, 76-77, 125-126, 146-147, 214-215, 259-260, 297-298, 340-341, 381-382, 415-416, 1893; N.S. 3: 3-4, 1894.

A69 **Noble, F.** 1892-95. Colour printing. Printers' Register 32: 126-127, 149-151, 169-171, 189-190, 209-210, 229-231, 1892/93; 33: 7, 27, 47, 67-69, 87, 107, 129, 147, 167, 187, 207, 227, 235, 1893/94; 34: 7-9, 27, 47-49, 69, 89-91, 109, 133, 149-150, 169, 189, 209-210, 229, 1894/95; 35: 7, 27-28, 1895. Also pub. in: Southward, J. Practical printing. 5th edn. ed. by A. Powell. Vol. 2, pp.1-199. London, 1900.
A revised version of his earlier book (A61 A62). [N.B. We were unable to locate a perfect copy of vols. 33 & 34 of the Printers' Register. As a result only fragments of the text were examined and the pagination given for articles in those vols., based on their indexes, probably only indicates the opening page of each article.]

A70 **Seymour, A.** 1905. Modern printing inks & colour printing. Modern Lithographer 1: 15-16, 37-38, 55-56, 78-79, 103-104, 135-136, 173-174, 195-196.

Ad **Special colour printing techniques: Baxter process. Stenochromy.**

Baxter's process, which combined an intaglio "key" and relief colour blocks, attracted great attention in the 19th century. However, the informative literature about the process dates from many years later. Baxter spent much time defending his right to hold the patent and to grant licences but never published any description of his process. The best practical accounts are by Seeley (A74 A75) who was formerly manager of Kronheim & Co., the successors to J.M. Kronheim, one of Baxter's most successful licencees. Baxter's work has been described as more of a personality than a process since he did no more than combine two existing methods and apply exacting standards of personal craftsmanship.

Seeley's first account of the Baxter process was addressed to a gathering of printers, rather in the nature of a look back at the "good old days". However, it was of more interest to the fast growing band of Baxter collectors and, significantly, his later expended account was published in their Society's journal. At any rate, no printer seems to have been induced to try to revive it!

Meyerstein's Stenochromy was utterly different and impossible to place within the usual categories of printmaking media. It involved making a mosaic design, map, or picture, in special coloured "inks" which solidified into a block. Printing was achieved by pressing a sheet of paper, moistened with a solvent, against the face of the block. This caused the surface film to dissolve and a coloured image was taken up by the paper. The process was something of an eccentricity and, apart from some samples mentioned below, doesn't seem to have found any practical application for book illustration or pictorial stationery (A76-A79).

Baxter process.

A71 **Baxter, G.** 1835. [Baxter's patent specification.] In: Clarke, H.G. & J.H. Rylatt. 1936. The centenary Baxter book. Leamington Spa. vii+176pp. Reprints the patent and the patent renewal. Also describes the prints which Baxter submitted in support of his application. The original letters patent are reproduced.

A72 **Carpmael, Mr.** 1836. [Preface describing Baxter's] Picture printing. In: The pictorial album, or cabinet of paintings, for the year 1837. London. xvi+71pp. & 10 Baxter proc. pls.
A brief, very guarded, account with little useful information.

A73 **Baxter, G.** 1849. Scientific adjudication: Baxter's extension before the Judicial Committee of the Privy Council... 21st June 1849. London Journal of Arts & Sciences, conjoined ser. 34: 434-438.

A74 **Seeley, F.W.** 1908. Baxter colour prints: How they were produced. A lecture & discussion at the Printers' Managers & Overseers' Association. British & Colonial Printer 62: 161-165.

A75 ----- 1924-25. The production of a Baxter colour print. Baxter Times 2: 109-110, 131, 135, 169-171, 205-207, 236-239, 271-274, 304-307.
A practical printer's detailed, well illustrated, account which unravelled all the "mysteries" of the process for his admiring audience of Baxter collectors.

Stenochromy

A76 **Meyerstein, E.** 1876. Stenochromy: A new process for printing a number of colours at the same time. Journal, Society of Arts 25: 68-74 & 1 pl.
The pl. is a pictorial specimen.

A77 **Anon.** 1877. Stenochromy. Printing Times & Lithographer N.S.3: 4-6.

A78 ----- 1877. The Stenochromic international colour scale. Printing Times & Lithographer N.S.3: 191-192 & 1 pl.
The pl. is an example of the 42 colour scales described.

A79 ----- 1877. Stenochromy. Printers' Register 16: 124-125.

Ae Nature printing in general

This group of titles includes literature about printing both from the surfaces of natural objects (a form of relief printing) and also from intaglio plates in which the sunken image was derived from the natural object. The latter version was that used by Henry Bradbury who produced the best-known examples of this genre of Victorian printing. He was involved in a heated dispute with Auer, head of the Imperial Printing Office in Vienna, over their respective claims to the title of "inventor" of nature printing, and both published detailed accounts of his version of nature printing (A86 A88 A89). Most other forms described in the literature were experimental in nature and did not produce results of any significance to the development of printmaking technique. Indeed, no examples of some kinds seem to have survived at all.

A curious form of nature "printing" was that of making prints from Butterfly wings. The wing was laid onto a gummed surface and the coloured wing scales remained adhering to the paper when the wing was lifted off. A fresh insect was required for each "print". This process was used for one commercially published American book at the turn of the century* but no British counterpart is known. A couple of references are included here for curiosity's sake (A95 A98). Examples of this proces can sometimes be found on fancy pictures and cards in old scrap books.

(* Denton, S.F. 1897-1900. As nature shows them: Moths & butterflies of the United States east of the Rocky Mountains. Boston. 2 vols., 107 nature prints on 56 pls. "Direct transfers from the insects themselves".)

A80 **Martin, B.** 1772. Typographia naturalis: Or, the art of printing, or taking impressions from natural subjects, as leaves, shells, fossils, etc. by means of Isinglass. London. 8pp.
Concerns the taking of imprints of natural objects for decorative purposes rather than the making of nature prints in the present sense.

A81 **Morison, D.** ca. 1839. The ample page of knowledge rich with the spoils of time. London.
Not seen. Describes his "orphine" process.

A82 ----- 1841. Improvements in printing. Inventors' Advocate 2: 415.
The patent specification for the orphine process.

A83 **Anon.** 1844. Ophinine [sic] process of printing. Magazine of Science 5: 231-232.
Morison's orphine process.

A84 **Branson, F.** 1851. On a method of engraving plates from natural objects. Transactions, Society of Arts 57: 96.

A85 **Aitken, W.C.** 1854. Ancient & modern metal working & ornamentation; with some allusion to the newly discovered art of nature printing. Journal, Society of Arts 2: 227-235.
The short suppl. lays claim to priority in the invention of nature printing from an indented plate.

A86 **Auer, A.** 1854. The discovery of the natural printing process: An invention for creating by means of the original itself, in a swift & simple manner, plates for printing copies of plants, materials, etc. without the aid of drawing or engraving. London. 75pp. & 19 pls.
Text in English, German, Italian, and French. A useful account of the Vienna method of nature printing which Auer claimed had been plagiarised by Bradbury and patented by him in England as his own invention. The pls. are specimens of nature printing.

A87 **Abate, F.** 1854. Method of representing objects by printing direct from the objects themselves. Journal, Society of Arts 2: 539-540.
The method was recommended for various applications besides illustration, such as wallpaper. The author developed this idea the following year:
----- 1855. Direct printing from wood, in an endless way, applied to the decorative arts. Ibid. 3: 544-545.

A88 **Bradbury, H.** 1855. Lecture on nature printing at the Royal Institution, May 11th, 1855. Proceedings, Royal Institution of Great Britain 1854/58: 106-118.
A detailed account of the development of nature printing, and Bradbury's part in it, delivered as a rejoinder to Auer's claim to its invention.

A89. ----- 1856. Nature printing: Its origin and objects. London. 28pp.
A new large-paper edn. of the above lecture.

A90 **Dresser, C.** 1857. A new system of nature printing. Journal, Society of Arts 5: 285-291; also letters from J. Leighton, the author & H. Bradbury, pp.304, 315.

A91 **Bradbury, H.** 1860. Autotypography: Or, the art of nature printing. London. 68pp.
Not seen. The British Library copy is lost and no other could be located.

A92 **Anon.** 1862. Nature printing. Typographic Advertiser 1: 46.
Actally about Bradbury's use of Wood's Stereotype Planing Machine to obtain the mirror finish on stereotype plates required for his nature printing process.

A93 **Stirling, Mrs.** 1863. On an easy & effective style of nature printing. Edinburgh New Philosophical Journal N.S.18: 164-165.

A94 **Dean, W.** 1869. On xylography, or printing & graining from the natural surfaces of woods. Journal, Society of Arts 17: 154-159; also letters from J.R. Jackson & the author, pp.185, 203.

A95 **C., A.M.** 1880. A guide to nature-printing butterflies & moths. By "A.M.C." London. 31pp. & 1 pl.
Describes: The old French process; The gum process; Wax process; Rice water process; White of egg process; Varnish process; and The collodio--gelatine process. Also incl. a list of butterflies and moths which have been printed successfully either on paper or gelatine. Pl. shows 3 examples.

A96 **Anon.** 1905. The physiotype process & its applicability to lithography. Modern Lithographer 1: 101-102, & specimen.
The invention of F. Sheridan.

A97 ----- 1905. Physiotype: A new printing process. Modern Lithographer, 1: 297-300.

A98 **Woodhouse, L.G.O.** 1935. Notes on a special method of making butterfly pictures. Transactions, Royal Entomological Society of London 1935: 5-9.

Af Electrotype preparation & multiplication of printing surfaces

The electrotype process is given detailed treatment in the general section of this work because it was used with equal facility for preparing and reproducing intaglio or relief printing surfaces. Electrotype was also widely used for reproducing many objects outside the realm of printing and some of the literature reflects this. We have given a selection of what we consider to be the most significant literature useful to the contemporary printer. This section also includes works which describe a number of novel applications of the electrotype principal to experimental or practical graphic reproduction processes, both intaglio and relief.

It was in 1839 that Spencer's successful experiments (A99 A100) were published together with the almost simultaneous announcements of Jordan in London (A101) and Jacobi in St. Petersburg (A102 A103). Almost immediately there was a great surge of books and articles which continued for the next dozen years or so, of which Smee's 1841 text book (A113) and its two enlarged editions (A123 A127) were probably the high water mark. Walker's little manuals (A116) must have been of wide practical utility, if the extraordinary number of editions is any measure.

By the 1880's new sources of electricity began to replace the battery, power--driven printing machinery was introduced for mass producing illustrated books and periodicals, and electrotyping grew to be almost a separate industry. Stereotype multiplication of wood blocks for the press was almost entirely superseded and it became standard practice to use electrotypes rather than original blocks for edition printing. They were greatly preferred to stereotypes for the reproduction of wood blocks because the latter could distort upon cooling. In everyday printer's vocabulary "an electro" came to mean a relief illustration or ornamental block. Some large firms, such as Cassell, ran impressive electrotype departments producing thousands of electros from wood-engraved "stock blocks" which were widely marketed throughout the printing trade. In charge of Cassell's printing department was Fredk. Wilson whose electrotype manual (A133) was to appear in several editions before the end of the century, proving to be a standard printer's text-book.

Descriptions of electrotype can also be found in the general works by Knight (A37) and O'Brien (A46) as well as in many standard printers' manuals such as J. Southward's "Practical Printing", London, 1882; (5th edn., 1900).

Although electrotype methods were a highly important element in 19th century graphic reproduction processes the subject is frequently passed over by historians of printmaking and picture printing. For our part we give fuller annotation than usual to items in this section in order to emphasize the extent to which this subject was discussed and used from the 1840's onwards.

For literature on stereotype methods for multiplying printing surfaces see section Cc.

A99 **Spencer, T.** 1839. An account of some experiments made for the purpose of ascertaining how far voltaic electricity may be usefully applied for the purpose of working in metal. Being a paper read at a meeting of the Liverpool Polytechnic Society... 12th September, 1839. Liverpool. 26pp. & 1 table.
The first application of electro-metallurgy to printing techniques. The text of the original paper is accompanied by an introduction and extensive addenda. Spencer's experiments explained how to, A: Engrave in relief on a plate of copper; B: Deposit a voltaic copper plate, having the lines in relief; C: Obtain a fac-simile of a medal (reverse or obverse), or of a bronze cast; D: Obtain a voltaic impression from plaster or clay; E: Multiply the number of already engraved copper plates. There is an illus. of the apparatus "produced [in relief] by the Electro-Chemical Process described... and is the first result of that process appearing in print". The table of the metals used in his experiments is "printed from a solid plate of copper, deposited by the action of voltaic electricity. By Thomas Spencer". Spencer's work was fully reported in the technical periodicals of his day.

A100 **Spencer, T.** 1839. Experiments upon forming copper plates for printing, medals, & other metallic designs, by galvanism. Mechanics' Magazine 32: 54-61.
An early report of the preceding lecture (A99).

A101 **Jordan, C.J.** 1839. Engraving by galvanism. Mechanics' Magazine 31: 163-164.
A brief account of Jordan's experiments and his method of intaglio galvanic etching. For an account of his claim to priority for this invention, over Spencer and others, see Dircks (A255).

A102 **Jacobi, M.H.** 1839. Engraving by voltaic action; in a letter to Mr. Faraday. Magazine of Science 1: 199.
This St. Petersburg professor (sometimes spelt Jakoby) briefly reported his work on electrotype, or galvanoplasty, as it was termed on the Continent.

A103 ----- 1839. On the method of producing copies of engraved copper plates by voltaic action, etc. London & Edinburgh Philosophical Magazine 15: 161-165. Also pub. in: Proceedings, London Electrical Society 1837/40: 175.
Jacobi's work on the electrotype copying of engravings (simultaneous with Spencer's and Jordan's) was just one facet of his research on galvanism which he described in over 55 papers in European scientific periodicals.

A104 **[Smee, A.]** 1840. Electrotype. London Journal of Arts & Sciences, conjoined ser. 16: 101-103, & pl.7.
The pl. is an electro. copy of an intaglio eng.

A105 ----- 1840. On the production of electrotypes. Philosophical Magazine 16: 530-532, & 1 pl. Also pub. in: Memoir of the late Alfred Smee, by his Daughter. pp.172-174. London, 1878.
The pl. shows an example of electro. eng.

A106 **Spencer, T.** 1840. On further improvements in the voltaic process of multiplying works of art in metal. Mechanics' Magazine 33: 128-129.
A method of silvering non-metallic surfaces to render them electrically conductive.

A107 **Bachhoffner, G.H.** 1840. The working of metals by voltaic electricity. Polytechnic Journal 3: 241-252, & 3 pls.
Mentions the use of pure plumbago for coating wax moulds, for which "we are indebted to Mr. Murray of Regent Street" (see A117). Based on lectures and demonstrations at the Polytechnic Institution, Regent Street. The pls. are a machine eng. intaglio design and an electro. facsim. of it.

A108 **Spencer, T.** 1840. Instructions for the multiplication of works of art in metal, by voltaic electricity. With an introductory chapter on electro--chemical decompositions by feeble currents. Glasgow. viii+62pp.
The 2nd edn. of his 1839 paper (A100) with an introductory chapter and a great deal of supplementary material. Describes his five basic processes, the simple and compound forms of the apparatus, and the galvanic battery.

A109 **Anon.** 1840. Electrotype. Compositors' Chronicle 1840: 29; Also a letter by Spencer, Ibid. 1841: 80.
On recent advances by Spencer and Murray.

A110 **Anon.** 1840. The electro-type; or, engraving by voltaic electricity. Magazine of Science 1: 393-394, 405-407, 411-412.
Chiefly abstracted from Spencer's paper and suppl. by a letter from W. Sturgeon.

A111 **Barclay, G.** 1841. The first steps in electrotype. London. 34pp. & 1 pl. 2nd edn., 1841.
Includes: General principles -- batteries, solutions, methods for seal impressions, plaster casts, coins & medals, wood engravings, engraved copper plates, fruit, leaves, vegetables, gilding or silvering. The pl. shows the "simple" and "battery" processes.

A112 **Savage, W.** 1841. Galvanism. In: A dictionary of the art of printing. pp.249-261. London. Repr. London, 1966.

A113 **Smee, A.** 1841. Elements of electro-metallurgy: Or, the art of working in metals by the galvanic fluid. London. xxviii+163pp.
The first appearance of a key work on this subject. The author was inventor of the improved battery which was the mainstay of electrotyping until replaced by the dynamo in the late 1870's. Deals with all aspects of electro-metallurgy and includes an introductory history. Bk. 5: On the electrotype; Bk. 6: On galvanic etching [both intaglio & relief]. Extracts from Bks. 5 & 6 were also pub. in: Polytechnic Journal 6: 363-368, 1842 & 7: 361-368, 1842.

A114 **Palmer, E.** 1841. Electrotype illustrations: Intended as an accompaniment to Smee's Elements of Electro-metallurgy, ... more particularly as illustrative of its application to the various styles of engraving, etc. London.
Not seen.

A115 **Spencer, T. & J. Wilson.** 1841. Certain improvements in the process of engraving on metals by means of voltaic electricity. Mechanics' Magazine 34: 333.
Abstract of their patent specification.

A116 **Walker, C.V.** 1841. Electrotype manipulation. Part 1: Being the theory, & plain instructions in the art of working in metals, etc. London. 10th edn., 1842; 22nd edn., 1849; 29th edn., 1859.
----- 1841. ----- Part 2: Containing the theory & plain instructions in the arts of electro-plating, electro-gilding, & electro-etching, etc. London. 5th edn., 1842; 13th edn., 1850; 19th edn., 1855.
These two little manuals (together running to about 50 pages) are generally found bound together. Each comprises a series of numbered paragraphs (about 260 in all) of ideas, instructions, notes, and "wrinkles" on various procedures and the content relating to printing is comparatively small. Each part went through numerous edns. and a few more paragraphs were apparently added each time. It must have been a widely used work but, despite the multiplicity of editions, is unusually scarce and we could only trace a handful of copies, let alone see them.

A117 **Murray, R.** 1841. Application of plumbago to non-conducting substances for the production of voltatypes. Transactions, Society of Arts 53 (2): 10-18.
The discovery of a process which was basic to electrotype manipulations throughout the century. It completely eclipsed Spencer's idea of silvering (A106).

A118 **Palmer, E.** 1842. Improvements in producing printing surfaces, & in printing china, pottery ware, music, maps, & portraits. Repertory of Patent Inventions N.S.17: 101-108. Abridged version pub. in: London Journal of Arts & Sciences, conjoined ser. 20: 172-176, 1842.

A119 **Sampson, T.** 1842. Electrotint: Or, the art of making paintings in such a manner that copper-plates and "blocks" can be taken from them by means of voltaic electricity. London. v+26+12pp. & 3 pls.
Pt. 1: Electrotint painting in intaglio; Pt. 2: "Surface" electrotint painting. The 3 pls. show the necessary tools and examples of both forms of the process. This simply involved making a freehand drawing with a thick "paint" on a plate and electrotyping this to create a printing surface. For the intaglio method the "highs" of the impasto formed the recesses of the plate; for the relief method it was the spaces between the impasto ridges that formed the "surface" image on the block. Much of the text describes methods of producing textures and creating "effects".

A120 **Sampson, T.** 1842. Electrotint painting. Polytechnic Journal 6: 207-210.

A121 **Anon.** 1842. Process of electrotint. Art Union 4: 83.

A122 ----- 1843. The electrotype. Art Union 5: 109-111.
An early description of the process in the leading art periodical.

A123 **Smee, A.** 1843. Elements of electro-metallurgy: [etc.] 2nd edn. London. xxx+338pp.
A considerable enlargement of the 1st edn. (A113). Bk. 5: On the electrotype; gives detailed information on the multiplication of type, copper and steel engravings, woodcuts [illustrated with glyphographic text illus.], and Daguerreotype; Bk. 6: On galvanic etching; Appx. 1: On electro-metallurgical patents. The t.p. is an electro. rel. copy of an anaglyptographic design printed in gold. Extracts from Bks. 5 & 6 pub. in: Polytechnic Journal 8: 104-110, 1843.

A124 **Palmer, V.** [184?] Electrotype: Being a description of the art of working in metal by voltaic electricity, with illustrations. To which is added a brief description of the calotype, daguerreotype, or photographic processes. London. 8th edn., 1845. 46pp.
Only the 8th edn could be traced. Describes: Batteries, electro-metallurgical methods, how to prepare the surface of copper-plates and medals for electrotyping, etc. The author was described as "Electrotypist to the Polytechnic Institution, The Art Union of London," etc. For a specimen of his electrotyped engraving for the latter see (A254).

A125 **Croucher, J.H.** 1847. A popular guide to the electrotype: Containing concise & simple instructions in the various processes of electro-metallurgy, with the art of moulding in plaster, wax, fusible metal, etc. Part 1. London. 54pp. & 1 pl.
Describes: Batteries, electrotype manipulation, electro-metallurgic apparatus, multiplying engraved plates, etching by galvanism, & glyphography. The pl. is a "Specimen of Palmer's Patent Glyphography".

A126 **Hunt, R.** 1848. On the applications of science to the fine & useful arts: The electrotype. Art Union 10: 101-103.

A127 **Smee, A.** 1851. Elements of electro-metallurgy: [etc.] 3rd edn. rev., corr. & enl. London. xxxi+364pp.
Expanded treatment of all the sections described for the 1843 edn. (A123), again illus. with eletrotyped wood engs. & glyphographs, but without the decorative t.p.

A128 ----- 1854. On the new Bank of England note, & the substitution of surface printing from electrotypes for copper-plate printing. Journal, Society of Arts 3: 81-89. Repr. in: Memoir of the late Alfred Smee, by his Daughter. pp.299-316. London, 1878.

A129 **Grubb, T.** 1855. An examination of Mr. Alfred Smee's paper "On the substitution of surface printing, for copper-plate, in the production of bank notes". Journal, Society of Arts 3: 238-241, 545-547.

A130 **"Phosphorus".** 1863-64. Pages of thought & practice, etc. Subject 1: Electro-metallurgy as applied to printing. Typographic Advertiser 2: 30, 37, 42, 50-51, 62-63, 86-87, 94-95, 100-101, 112-113, 1863/64; 3: 14-15, 34, 1864.
General description of electrotype methods then in use.

A131 **Urquhart, F.W.** 1881. Electrotyping: A practical manual, forming a new & systematic guide to the reproduction & multiplication of printing surfaces & works of art by the electro-deposition of metals. London. x+226pp.
Much information on electro-metallurgy, sources of electricity (incl. the newly introduced dynamo machine), moulding apparatus & materials, preparation of the work, the depositing process, hard facings for electrotype, etc.

A132 **Wilson, F.J.F.** 1881. Electrotyping for printers. Printing Times & Lithographer N.S.7: 7-10, 32-34, 66-68, 89-90, 112-114, 140-141, 177-178, 198-199, 226-228, 249-251, 276-279, 303-305.
First appearance of the electrotyping section of the following item.

A133 ----- [1882.] Stereotyping & electrotyping... with instructions for depositing copper by the battery or by the dynamo machine, also hints on steel & brass facing, etc. London. xv+195pp. Other edns., down to 6th. edn., 1898.
Electrotyping occupies pp.95-195, incl. historical, theoretical & practical details, dynamo-electro machines, etching for copperplate printing, steel & iron facing, brass facing, materials used in electrotyping, etc.

A134 **[Whetton, H.]** 1901. Practical notes on stereotyping & electrotyping from "The British Printer". Compiled by the Editor. London. vii+140pp.
A useful end-of-century survey of progress in the field.

Ag **Printmakers' & printers' equipment, materials, etc.**

Most of the general works on printing machinery were inclined to be wholly concerned with letterpress equipment. Only incidentally does one find mention of application to graphic work as, for example, in Wilson (A138 A139) and Wilson & Grey (A147). Nevertheless, the mechanical improvement of letterpress machines is important in this context because a number of the same developments were later applied to power-driven lithographic, collotype, and even plate-printing machines. Clowes (A144) provides an engineer's review of printing machinery, whilst the text-books of Wilson (A138 A139), Southward (A142 A146), and Wilson & Grey (A147) looked at mechanical details from the standpoint of practical operation.

Jacobi's handbook (A145 A148) contained a wealth of information on all sorts of materials and recipes of use to printmakers and printers, following in the tradition of Savage's Dictionary (A31) published 46 years earlier.

Bronzing and varnishing were both finishing operations that were applied to all media of picture printing. With the tremendous growth in the quantity and variety of fancy stationery being produced towards the end of the century, both these operations became mechanised; a list of relevant articles is appended here (A152-A157).

For literature on specialised printing machinery see sections Bh Ch Df & Ek <u>infra</u>.

A135 **Anon.** 1843. The printing press. Magazine of Science 4: 387-389, 396-398, 404-405.
Detailed account of construction of the wooden press, and a review of modern developments by Stanhope, Ruthven, Clymer, Cope, and Sherwin & Cope.

A136 ----- 1843. The printing machine. Magazine of Science 4: 321-323.
Brief account of the machines of Koenig, Cowper, and Applegath & Cowper.

A137 **Lardner, D.** Ed. 1859. The printing press. Lardner's Museum of Science 11: 1-32.

A138 **[Wilson, F.J.F.]** 1877-79. Practical papers on printing machines & machine printing. Printing Times & Lithographer N.S.3: 1-4, 30-33, 45-47, 73-75, 94-96, 168-169, 207-209, 229-231, 1877; N.S.4: 1-4, 26, 42-46, 66-67, 113, 129-131, 188-189, 210, 254-255, 1878; N.S.5: 8-10, 26-27, 47-50, 141-142, 166-168, 213-215, 239-241, 261-262, 1879.
These articles were repr. in the following book (A139).

A139 **Wilson, F.J.F.** 1879. Typographic printing machines & machine printing. A practical guide to the selection of bookwork, two-colour, jobbing, & rotary machines, with remarks upon their construction, capabilities, & peculiarities, & instructions in making-ready, the preparation of engravings, etc. London. xvi+202pp. 2nd. edn., 1882. xvi+208pp.; 3rd. edn., ca. 1885. xvi+214pp.
A widely used, well-illustrated text-book for printers & machine minders which was twice revised before being replaced by Wilson & Grey (A147).

A140 **[Wyman, C.W.H.]** 1882-83. Glossary of technical terms used in connexion with printing machinery. Printing Times & Lithographer N.S.8: 8-10, 35-36, 65-66, 89-91, 116-117, 141-143, 167-169, 196-197, 244-245, 269-270, 1882; N.S.9: 69-70, 96-97, 145-146, 208-209, 233-235, 258-260, 278-279, 303-304, 1883.
These articles were repr. in the following book (A141).

A141 ----- 1882. A glossary of technical terms used in connexion with printing machinery. London. 80pp.

A142 [Southward, J.] 1886. Principles & progress of printing machinery. Printing Times & Lithographer N.S.12: 42-43, 61-63, 81-82, 100-102, 120-121, 139-140, 158-159, 175-176, 193-194, 212.
These articles were repr. in book form, see (A146).

A143 **Clowes, E.A.** 1887. Printing machinery. 47pp. & 2 pls.
A paper read to the Institution of Civil Engineers. Well illustrated account of the engineering design of modern machinery.

A144 ----- 1887-88. Printing machinery. British & Colonial Printer 19: 1-2, 33, 65-66, 97-98, 177-178, 257-258, 337-338, 401, 1887; 20: 33, 177, 257-258, 305-306.
Repr. of the preceding item (A143).

A145 **Jacobi, C.T.** 1887. The printers' handbook of trade recipes, hints & suggestions relating to letterpress & lithographic printing, etc. London. vi+197pp.
Incl. numerous notes on equipment and materials.

A146 **Southward, J.** 1888. The principles & progress of printing machinery. With an account of modern printing machines by F.J.F. Wilson. London. 156pp.
Incl. much of the material from the articles in (A142).

A147 **Wilson, F.J.F. & D. Grey.** 1888. A practical treatise upon modern printing machinery & letterpress printing. London. vii+455pp.
The major text-book on the subject, very well illustrated. Includes illustrative examples of make-ready techniques used in the successful printing of relief illustrations.

A148 **Jacobi, C.T.** 1891. The printers' handbook of trade recipes, etc. 2nd. edn., enl. & classified. London. xiii+360pp.
Re-organised version of (A145). Incl.: Machine & press work; Inks, varnishes, etc.; Stereotyping & electrotyping; Lithography; Engraving & process work.

A149 **Fisher, C.H.** 1893. Platen machines & their construction. British Printer 6: 75-84.

A150 **Jackson, T.** 1893. The cylinder machine & its work. British Printer 6: 151-156.

A151 **Powrie, W.** 1899. Machinery for book & general printing. London. 24pp. & 17 pls. Also pub. in: Printing Times & Lithographer N.S.8: 22-24, 40-41, 59-60, 1899.
A paper read to the Institution of Mechanical Engineers. A well illustrated end-of-century survey of machinery developments incl. hand, single-cylinder, fine-art, two-revolution, two-colour, prefecting, & platen machines.

Bronzing & varnishing machinery.

A152 **Anon.** 1878. Leeming, Ray, & Lynde's patent bronzing machine. Printing Times & Lithographer N.S.4: 208-209.

A153 **Anon.** 1885. Rawcliffe's patent varnishing machine. Printing Times & Lithographer N.S.11: 175.

A154 ----- 1885. A new patent bronzing machine. Printing Times & Lithographer N.S.11: 232; see also advert. & illus. on p.249. Also reported in: British & Colonial Printer 15: 373, 1885; & World's Printers ... Effective Advertiser 1886 (Mar.): 53.
Apropos Silverlock's machine.

A155 ----- 1888. Silverlock's bronzing machine. Printing Times & Lithographer N.S.14: 88-89. Also reported in: British & Colonial Printer 20: 355, 1888; & World's Printers' ... Effective Advertiser 1889 (Jan.): 11.
An improved version of the 1885 model.

A156 ----- 1891. Silverlock's bronzing & dusting machine. British & Colonial Printer 28: 138.
Further improvements in this widely used machine.

A157 ----- 1893. Newsum's patent bronzing & dusting machine. Printing Times & Lithographer N.S.2: 440.

Ah Printmakers' & printers' equipment, etc.: Trade catalogues

The trade catalogues of machinery manufacturers and dealers are a neglected section of the literature on picture printing. Unfortunately, they are now extremely scarce and only a few major libraries have representative collections -- the St. Bride Printing Library being our principal source for these. A selection of catalogues is listed here, most of which we have examined.

There are two particular problems relating to these items. Firstly, the contents of each may vary from issue to issue as new products were included and old ones were dropped. Secondly, manufacturers were seemingly reluctant to state the dates of publication and they are very difficult to ascertain. We have therefore omitted statements of pagination and have been unable to provide more than tentative dates of publication.

Most are illustrated, to a greater or lesser extent, and thus provide a valuable record of the printmaker's and printer's secret armoury including such gadgets as ruling machines, pantographs, shading apparatus, air brushes, mechanical litho stipplers, reducing or enlarging apparatus, and the like. The more familiar tools and equipment are also admirably illustrated through the various stages of their evolution. We have not been able to find any dating from before about 1860.

The British market was successfully exploited by some leading overseas manufacturers and some of our printers found their products generally more advanced than their native counterparts. We have included a small number of overseas catalogues in order to indicate starting points for further research.

A158 **Harrild & Sons.** [ca. 1860.] List of prices of printing machines, presses, steam engines, & every other article connected with the various branches of the printing business, etc. London.

A159 **Hopkinson & Cope.** 1862. Printing presses & machines. London.

A160 **Middleton, T.** 1862. Middleton's illustrated catalogue of printing machines. London.

A161 **Salmon, J.** [ca. 1862.] List of patent machinery for bookbinders, printers & stationers. Manchester.

A162 **Hughes & Kimber.** [1865?] List of machines & materials for the use of printers, stationers, bookbinders, etc. London.

A163 **Hoe, R. & Co.** 1866. Printing machines, power presses, etc. New York.

A164 **Hughes & Kimber.** [1866.] Catalogue of materials for engravers, lithographers, etc. London.

A165 **Harrild & Sons.** [1868.] Illustrated catalogue of superior machinery & materials for letterpress, lithographic, & copperplate printers, bookbinders & stationers. London.

A166 **Dryden & Co.** [ca. 1870.] Illustrated catalogue of steam printing machinery. London.

A167 **Hopkinson & Cope.** 1872. Lithographic department. Revised illustrated list of lithographic printing presses & machines, litho-stone grinding machines, materials, ink, etc. London.

A168 **Powell, J.M.** 1876. An illustrated price list of machinery & material used by printers, lithographers, etc. London.

A169 **Harrild & Sons.** 1877. New & revised illustrated catalogue of superior machinery & materials for letterpress, lithographic, & copperplate printers, etc. London.

A170 **Hughes & Kimber.** [ca. 1880.] Catalogue of machinery & materials for letterpress, lithographic & copperplate printers, also for engravers, bookbinders & stationers. London.

A171 **Hoe, R. & Co.** 1881. Catalogue of printing presses & printers' materials, lithographic presses, stereotyping & electrotyping machinery, etc. New York.

A172 **Ullmer, F.** 1884. Illustrated list of machinery & materials for printers, lithographers, etc. London.

A173 **Alauzet & Cie.** [ca. 1885.] Presses typographiques et lithographiques. Paris.

A174 **Harrild & Sons.** [ca. 1885.] Illustrated catalogue of printing, lithographic & binding machinery & materials. London.

A175 **Hughes & Kimber.** [ca. 1885.] Catalogue of machinery & materials for lithographers & copper-plate printers. London.

A176 ----- [ca. 1887.] Catalogue of machinery & materials for engravers, copper-plate printers, die sinkers & stampers. London.

A177 **Harrild & Sons.** [1889.] Illustrated catalogue of printing, lithographic & binding machinery & materials. London.

A178 **Pallister, G.** [ca. 1890.] Illustrated catalogue of new machinery & materials used by printers, lithographers, bookbinders, etc. Leeds.

A179 **Furnival & Co.** [ca. 1892.] [Catalogue of printing machinery, etc. Reddish.]

A180 **Harrild & Sons.** [1892?] Complete illustrated catalogue of printers', bookbinders' & stationers' machinery & materials. London.

A181 **Klimsch & Co.** 1892. "Export." [Illustrated price list of machinery & tools for engravers & lithographers.] Frankfort on the Main.
Includes ruling machines, engraving needles, lithographers' ruling pens, etc., etc.

A182 **Sauvée, A. & Co.** 1894. Catalogue of Marinoni printing machinery. London.

A183 **Hoe, R. & Co.** 1897. Catalogue of printing materials. New York.

A184 ----- [1898.] Catalogue of machinery & materials for electrotyping, stereotyping & photo-engraving. New York.

A185 **Hughes & Kimber.** [ca. 1899.] Catalogue of machinery & materials for engravers, copper-plate printers, die sinkers & stampers. London.

A186 **Charlesworth, S. & Co.** [ca. 1900.] Litho. & letterpress printing machines; litho. & copperplate presses. Oldham.

A187 **Greig, J. & Sons.** [ca. 1900.] Complete catalogue of machines, presses, appliances, etc., for the paper, printing, lithographic, bookbinding, stationery, boxmaking & allied trades. Edinburgh.

A188 **Hewitt, T.H.** 1900. Illustrated catalogue of printers', lithographers' & bookbinders' machinery & materials. London.

A189 **Lockett, W.H. & Co.** 1900. Illustrated & priced catalogue of machinery, material & appliances for printers. London.

Ai Printing inks

Although ink is basic to any printing process the literature about it -- its preparation and use -- is surprisingly small.

The most interesting aspect of the subject is that relating to the preparation of coloured inks for various printing processes. Savage (A190) gives a detailed account of his methods for which Copaiba Balsam was used. Richmond (A194) contributed a detailed text-book on the many sorts of coloured ink that were employed in the mature years of machine-printed chromo-lithography. Little known, but without equal, is Waterhouse's authoritative catalogue of ink ingredients (A196). Mitchell & Hepworth's text-book (A198) includes a very useful catalogue of English ink patents. Some of the general accounts of printing in section Ab also include details on ink.

A190 **Savage, W.** 1832. On the preparation of printing inks, both black & coloured. London. 185pp.

A191 **Anon.** 1845. Printing ink for fine work. Art Union 7: 171. Report on improved inks for block printing by Parsons & Fletcher.

A192 **Underwood, J.** 1857. On the history & chemistry of writing, printing, & copying inks, & a new plan of taking manifold copies of both written & printed documents, maps, charts, plans & drawings. Journal, Society of Arts 6: 67-74.
Repr. in the following book.

A193 ----- [1858.] The history & chemistry of writing, printing & copying inks. London. 28pp.

A194 **Richmond, W.D.** [1885.] Colour & colour printing: As applied to lithography. Containing an introduction to the study of colour, an account of the general & special qualities of pigments employed, their manufacture into printing inks, & the principles involved in their application. London. x+169pp.

A195 **Zander, C.G.** 1896. Half-tone & photochromic printing inks. Penrose Annual 2: 63-67.

A196 **Waterhouse, J.** 1898. Notes on the principal oils, fats & resins used in printing & photo-process work. Penrose Annual 4: 110-121.

A197 **Andés, L.E.** 1903. Oil colours & printers' inks. Translated from the German. London. xi+212pp.

A198 **Mitchell, C.A. & T.C. Hepworth.** 1904. Inks: Their composition & manufacture, including methods of examination & a full list of English patents. London. xiv+251pp.

A199 **Seymour, A.** 1905. Modern printing inks & colour printing. Modern Lithographer 1: 15-16, 37-38, 55-56, 78-79, 103-104, 135-136, 173-174, 195-196.

Aj Printing inks: Trade catalogues.

The chief interest that attaches to these catalogues is the range of samples that the manufacturers frequently provided. These demonstrated both the range of colours available and the specialised kinds of ink made for different applications and processes. Typical ornamental and pictorial work was often used for their demonstration and colour printed work was sometimes provided with colour separations. As with machinery catalogues these are scarce and only available in a few specialised libraries. We list a selection below but have only seen about 50% of them.

A200 **Shackell & Edwards.** [1853.] Specimen of printing inks. London.

A201 **Fleming, A.B. & Co. Ltd.** [1874.] Specimens of printing ink. [Leith.]

A202 **Winstone, B.** [ca. 1875.] Specimens of printers' ink. London.

A203 **Horle, F.** [1883.] Catalogue of fine colours, litho. & letterpress inks. London.

A204 **Fleming, A.B. & Co. Ltd.** [ca. 1890.] Specimens of printing inks. [Edinburgh.]

A205 **Coates Bros. & Co.** [ca. 1890.] Printing inks. London.

A206 **Richardson Printing Ink Co. Ltd.** [ca. 1890.] Specimens of printing inks. Gateshead.

A207 **London & Provincial Printing Ink Co.** [ca. 1890.] Specimens of printing inks. London.

A208 **Mander Bros.** 1891. Price list [& specimens] of printing inks. London.

A209 **Culross & Co. Ltd.** 1892. Specimens of ink.

A210 **Stanbury, G. & Sons.** 1893. Specimens of coloured printing inks. London.

A211 **Fleming, A.B. & Co. Ltd.** [ca. 1896.] Specimens of printing inks. Edinburgh.

A212 **Kidd, J. & Co.** [ca. 1897.] Printing ink specimens. London.

A213 **Mander Bros.** [1897.] Price list [& specimens] of printing inks. Wolverhampton.

A214 **Slater & Palmer.** [1897.] Specimens of printing inks. London.

A215 **Ault & Wiborg Co.** 1899. A few of our regular shades of ink for half-tone work. London.

A216 **Sparks, H. & Co.** [ca. 1900.] Sample book of lithographic & letterpress inks. London.

A217 **Mason & Mason Ltd.** [ca. 1900.] Price list of specimens of inks. London.

A218 **Fleming, A.B. & Co. Ltd.** [ca. 1900.] Specimens of high-class chromo-litho & poster printing inks. Edinburgh.

A219 **Ault & Wiborg Co.** [1900.] Specimens of lithographic ink. London.

A220 **Shackell, Edwards & Co. Ltd.** 1900. Specimens of black & coloured printing inks. London.

A221 **Mander Bros.** 1901. Examples of half-tone printing with inks made by Mander Bros. Wolverhampton.

A222 **Fleming, A.B. & Co.** [1902.] Specimens of coloured inks. Edinburgh.

Ak Printing papers

The literature on papermaking is so extensive that it would be inappropriate to list it here. Nevertheless, paper is of fundamental importance to the printmaker and picture printer both as the support for the ink which constitutes the "print" and for the way its colour and texture can influence the look of the print. Furthermore, different graphic reproduction processes sometimes demanded different kinds of paper; e.g. special plate paper for engravings, waterleaf for lithography, and coated paper for photo half-tones.

We have listed only a small selection of works and have chosen those which include samples of the variety of papers available in their day. When examining prints or book illustrations it may be useful to be able to turn to named samples to assist in determining the kind of paper in hand. Herring (A223) and Ruse & Straker (A224) provide mid-century selections while Spalding & Hodge demonstrates the end-of-century range provided by a leading manufacturer. This firm produced a number of sample books, as did several others, and this title is merely included as a typical example.

Although compiled half a century after our period, Labarre's Dictionary (A226) is undoubtedly the best survey of the history and varieties of papers that were in use in England during the 18th. and 19th. centuries.

For a comprehensive bibliography of the literature of papermaking see Hunter (A331) and for a concise list see the introduction to Labarre.

A223 **Herring, R.** 1860. A practical guide to the varieties & relative values of paper, illustrated with samples of nearly every description & specially adapted to the use of merchants, shippers & the trade. London. [iv]+36pp., 2 pls. & samples.

A224 **Ruse, G. & C. Straker.** 1860. Printing & its accessories: ... together with 156 samples of English & foreign papers, & tabular indexes, showing their comparative mill numbers, weights, etc. London. xv+319pp. & 113+43 samples.

A225 **Spalding & Hodge Ltd.** 1902. A sample book of printing & plate papers designed for the use of publishers. London.

A226 **Labarre, E.J.** 1952. Dictionary & encyclopaedia of paper & paper making. 2nd edn., rev. & enl. London. 1952. xxiv+488pp.
See also: Supplement. By E.G. Loeber. Amsterdam, 1967. x+104pp.

Al Colouring & finishing of prints & photographs

The hand-colouring of prints and book illustrations in the later 18th and the 19th centuries was such a widespread and highly-developed skill that it is surprising to find so little literature describing the process. There was, however, no shortage of literature on water-colour painting in general including a number which provided samples of primary and mixed tints.

The finishing of prints cannot be said to be a "printmaking" process but it was nevertheless a significant part of graphic reproduction in that a number of prints, and certainly a great many book illustrations, were specifically prepared with hand-colouring in mind. Hand-colouring could, of course, be added at any time and innumerable prints from that period are being "coloured--up" for sale today, including many steel engravings that were never intended to be so. It is therefore of interest to know something about the style and techniques of colouring as well as the range of pigments available at the time in order to be able to pass an informed judgement on the authenticity of any print colouring.

The works of Fielding are of special interest (A232 A233) for their samples of water-colour tints from the first half of the century while Winsor & Newton (A239) include an impressive range of their end-of-century products. In contrast to the paucity of works on print colouring there is quite a wealth of literature on the colouring of photographs. Apparently this was a much more widespread amateur occupation than one might have guessed. Colouring a photo was not so far removed from colouring a tonal print, and the instruction these authors provide on how to produce detailed "effects" is instructive in general terms which induced us to include a selection here.

"Transparencies" were a short-lived fad at the turn of the 18th century and are graphically described by Orme (A230). They were produced by rendering parts of the image translucent so that, when illuminated from behind, a dramatically heightened effect was created by the "lights" showing through the colouring. In earlier years coloured prints intended for framing were only occasionally varnished. But towards the end of the 19th century varnishing formed a regular part of the manufacture of chromo-lithographs and "oleographs". It is described in some printers' manuals and in an 1892 article (A240). The hot-pressing of prints was often performed by plate printers to produce a sleeker finish, to lessen the strength of the plate mark, or to minimise the cockling that could result from hand-colouring. However, the only literature reference that has come to our notice is an 1863 article in a typographic magazine (A236). In contrast, the later years of chromo-lithography saw the production of prints with a deliberately embossed finish which simulated the impasto of oil painting. Embossing of ornamental and pictorial work also formed a significant part of the stationery trade and was a requisite part of die stamping. The production of "oleographs" is described by Anon. (D103) while Herrick's textbook (A236) provides a general account of all aspects of embossing for printers.

A227 **Edwards, G.** 1743-51. Method of colouring engravings. In: A natural history of birds. Vol. 1: xvii-xviii & vol. 4: 230-235. London.

A228 ----- 1770. An idea of drawing & painting in water colours. In: Essays upon natural history. pp.141-157. London.

A229 **Clark, J.H.** 1807. A practical essay on the art of colouring & painting landscapes in water colours. Accompanied by ten engravings. London. 27pp. & 10pls.
Includes : Essay on the art of colouring. pp.9-25.

A230 **Orme, E.** 1807. An essay on transparent prints & on transparencies in general. London. [iii]+64pp. & 15 pls.

A231 **Hassell, J.** [1818.] Aqua pictura: Illustrated by a series of original specimens from the works of Messrs Payne, Munn, Francia [& 16 others] exhibiting the works of the most approved modern water coloured draughtsmen, with their style of touch, engraved & finished in progressive examples. 2nd. edn. London. 3pp. & 72 pls.
Actually a series of 18 pls., each in 4 states which terminate in a fully-coloured example.

A232 **Fielding, T.H.A.** 1830. Index of colours & mixed tints for the use of beginners in landscape & figure painting. London. 40pp. & 18 pls.
The pls. are a series of samples of mixed water-colour tints.

A233 ----- 1842. On the theory of painting: To which is added an index of mixed tints, & an introduction to painting in water colours, with precepts. 3rd edn. much enl. London. xi+146pp. & 15 pls. 4th edn., 1846; 5th edn., 1854.
6 of the pls. display mixed tints.

A234 **"Artist-Photographer".** 1859. The principles & practice of harmonious colouring in oil, water, & photographic colours, especially as applied to photographs on paper, glass, & silver-plate. London. xi+98pp. 6th. edn., 1867. xii+120pp.

A235 **Anon.** 1859. How to colour a photograph: Or, lessons on the harmony & contrast of colours, principally in their application to photography. London. vii+64pp.
Repr. from notes in the Photographic News. Deals with colouring in oil & water-colours on albumenised paper.

A236 ----- 1863. Hotpressing. Typographic Advertiser 1: 75.

A237 **Rees, D.** [1868.] The art of photographic colouring, in easy progressive lessons, illustrated with coloured photographic portraits, etc. London. 26pp. & 2 pls.

A238 **Wake, J.** 1878. Manual of photographic colouring, forming a handy-book on the art of painting on the photographic image. London. iii+62pp.

A239 **Taylor, J.S.** 1887. A descriptive handbook of modern water colours, illustrated with actual washes of the pigments on Whatman's drawing paper. London. v+71pp. & 3 pls.
Various later edns. Each has dozens of colours shown in small shaded samples, the number increasing in each edn.

A240 **Anon.** 1892. Varnishing by machinery. British Lithographer 1 (5): 23-24.

A241 **Herrick, T.P. Ed.** [ca, 1908.] Embossing, blocking & die stamping: A practical guide to these processes. 2nd. edn. London & Leicester. 76pp.
The 1st. "edition" appeared as a miscellany of articles in the British Printer. Describes several processes, hot & cold, and their working on platen, cylinder, & lithographic machines, together with blocking & die stamping in colours & metallic foil.

Am Patents relating to printing & allied subjects

Patent literature is a fertile source of information for the history of graphic reproduction processes but one that is often overlooked by historians. The Abridgements of Specifications published by the Patent Office provide accurate documentation on hundreds of new inventions, machines, gadgets, processes, & refinements, whether practicable, experimental, or just plain crankish. They are, however, only synopses and it may be necessary to consult the full patent specification for complete information. The Abridgements were first published in the 1850's as a complete retrospective record of all existing patents. Prior to their compilation the growing number and importance of patents had led to the foundation of several periodicals which were largely concerned with the publication of new patent specifications, often in full and with accompanying illustrations. It has not been possible for us to make a complete survey of the great quantity of patents published in this form but a considerable number have been researched and included in the relevant parts of this bibliography. The patent abridgements often included literature references to earlier periodical sources for each patent.

Following the Patent Law Amendment Act of 1852 the Patent Office was required to publish a printed specification for each one and the full reports in periodicals ceased to be necessary. Besides being held by the Patent Office, complete sets of printed specifications were deposited in selected major libraries. We have not attempted to list the multitude of these individually printed relevant specifications.

In addition to the individual printed specifications the Patent Office regularly added supplements to its first series of Abridgements and eventually published an illustrated series. Both series of Abridgements are much more accessible to the general reader than the individual specifications so we have listed all those that relate to our field.

The true nature of some inventions is not made entirely clear by the patent specification. The title may be uninformative, the description often deliberately formal, and crucial details sometimes evasively worded so as to "give away" as little information as possible. Fortunately, the Abridgements, which were chronologically presented, included helpful classified subject indexes; all have lists of patentees.

The arrival of photography, and its widespread practice by numberless enthusiasts, gave rise to an extraordinary range of experimentation and innovation and claims to priority in these were legion. The photographic periodicals, some of them weeklies, were filled with these controversies. Since a patent granted exclusive rights to its patentee it was important to publicise it in order to establish individual territorial rights in the fields of research activity and commercial exploitation. In their fast moving field the photographic journals seem to have found it necessary to continue the old tradition of reprinting the more important patent specifications in full. We have included a number of these in Section E. The general printing trade were apparently less excited by patent activity and their periodicals rarely did more than provided more than brief reports of new patents.

Useful information on patent literature is given in : National Reference Library of Science & Invention [later British Library, Science Reference Library]. Aids to readers, no.10: Literature in the British patents section (Holborn Division.) London, June 1973. 6pp.

General.

A242 **Patent Office.** 1854. Alphabetical index of patentees of inventions from March 2, 1617 (14 James I) to October 1, 1852 (16 Victoriae). London. Repr. with an introduction & corrected entries, London, 1969. xv+647pp.
----- 1854+. Alphabetical index of patentees & applicants (Name index of applicants) for patents of invention from 1st October 1852 to 31st December 1853. [Annual vols.] London.

Printing - letterpress, lithographic, intaglio.

A243 **Patent Office.** 1859. Abridgements of specifications relating to printing, including therein the production of copies on all kinds of materials (excepting felted & textile fabric), by means of types, stereotype, blocks, plates, stone, dies, stencil plates, paper writings, electrochemicals, & light. London. Repr. with a prefatory note by J. Harrison and a suppl. which appeared with the Abridgements ... Part II, London, 1878. London. xxi+631+311-369pp.
----- 1878. Abridgements of specifications relating to letterpress & similar printing (excluding electro-telegraphic & photographic printing). Part II. A.D. 1858-1866. 2nd edn. London. xiii+382pp.
Includes a suppl. to Part I., pp.311-369. This suppl. incl. with the repr. of Part I.
----- 1880. Abridgements of specifications relating to letterpress & similar printing, 1867-1876. London. xiii+586pp.

A244 ----- 1893+. Abridgements of specifications. [Illustrated series.] Class 100. Printing, letterpress & lithographic, 1855-1866. London.
Further issues in this series covered the years: 1867-1876, 1877-1883, 1884-1888, 1889-1892, 1893-1896, 1897-1900, 1901-1904, etc.
----- 1893+. Abridgements of specifications. [Illustrated series.] Class 101. Printing, other than letterpress or lithographic, 1855-1866.
Further issues covered the same years as Class 100.

Photography

A245 **Patent Office.** 1861. Abridgements of specifications relating to photography. Part I. 1839-1859. London. xx+165pp.
----- 1872. Abridgements ... Part II. 1860-1866. 2nd edn. London. xxiv+179pp.
----- 1878. Abridgements ... Part III. 1867-1876. London. vii+117pp.
----- 1885. Abridgements ... Part IIIa. 1877-1883. London. viii+136pp.

A246 ----- 1893+. Abridgements of specifications. [Illustrated series.] Class 98. Photography, 1855-1866. London.
Further issues in this series covered the years: 1867-1876, 1877-1883, 1884-1888, 1889-1892, 1893-1896, 1897-1900, 1901-1904, etc. Repr. of 8 lists, covering 1839-1900 (pub. 1839-1903). New York, 1979. 2 vols. (Sources of Modern Photography.)

Inks, colours, etc.

A247 **Patent Office.** 1871. Abridgements of specifications relating to paints, colours & varnishes. 1618-1866. London. xxiii+499pp.

A248 **Mitchell, C.A. & T.C. Hepworth.** 1904. List of English patents. In: Inks: Their composition & manufacture. pp.227-242. London.

An Miscellaneous literature

An assortment of literature on graphic processes which add supplementary comment or criticism to the previously listed technical works listed before and provide sidelights on the progress of the trade.

A249 **[Nicholson, W.]** 1797. Observations on the art of printing books & piece goods by the action of cylinders. Journal of Natural Philosophy, Chemistry & the Arts 1: 18-23.
General discussion of the advantages of printing, especially in colours, from cylinders onto paper or fabric.

A250 **Babbage, C.** 1833. Of copying. In: On the economy of machinery & manufactures. 3rd edn., enl. London, 1832. [The preface is dated Feb. 11th, 1833.]
Review of contemporary graphic reproduction processes under the following headings: Printing from cavities; Printing from surface; By casting; By moulding; By stamping; By punching; With elongation; With altered dimensions. Incl. mention of the pantograph and medal engraving (Anaglyptography), etc.

A251 **Parkes, Mrs M.** 1842. The electrotype as misapplied to engraving in the Art Union. London. 20pp. 2nd edn., with additions, 1842; 3rd edn., with additions, 1842. ??pp.
Only the 2nd edn. has been seen. A complaint against Moon, the print publisher, and his plan to associate with the Art Union in publishing prints from electrotypes of copper-plates too worn for conventional hand printing. Electrotype was thus seen as a threat to the livelihood of engravers, for by its means publishers could continue to make profit from their stocks of old coppers.

A252 **Anon.** 1843. Electrotyped plates. Art Union 5: 44, 89, & 247.

A253 ----- 1844. The electrotype. Art Union 6: 8-9.

A254 ----- 1847. "The Children in the Wood" -- the electrotype. Art Union 9: 62, & 1 pl.
A comment on the value of electrotype exemplified by an accompanying print made by Vaughan Palmer from an engraving by W. Greatbach. Also incl. statements by Dixon & Ross and McQueen, plate-printing firms, expressing their satisfaction with printing large editions from electrotypes.

A255 **Dircks, H.** 1852. Jordantype, otherwise called "Electrotype": Its early history, being a vindication of the claim of C.J. Jordan as the inventor of electro-metallurgy. London. 24pp.
Incl.: A preliminary statement of the case; Examination of the merits of Mr. Jordan's case; Parallel of Mr. Jordan's and Mr. Spencer's publications; Strictures on Mr. Spencer's dinner speech at Liverpool. Gives an interesting, if biassed, account of the early developments of electrotype by one of its joint discoverers.

A256 **Anon.** 1853. Illustrative art: Exhibition of chromo-printing. Journal, Society of Arts 2: 101-103.
Review of contemporary methods. Written to accompany an exhibition.

A257 **Smith, H.W-.** 1892. The position of the colour-printing trade. Printing Times & Lithographer N.S.1: 33-34.

A258 **Anon.** 1894. A new era in colour printing. British Printer 7: 20.
Apropos the introduction of photo-mechanical printing methods.

A259 Anon. 1895. The past, present, & future of colour printing. Artist 16: 58-61. Also pub. as: Colour printing, as it was, is, and will be. British Lithographer 4: 101-103, 1894-95.
A review of the declining state of colour-printing craft and the role of photo-chromo methods in restoring standards.

Historical

Ao General history of printmaking & picture printing

There are many histories of printmaking but relatively few which cover the whole spectrum of printmaking and picture printing processes. We give only a selection here.

Pye, well-known as an engraver in his day, provides a valuable insight into the organisation of the craft during his lifetime (A260). Southward's historical sketch (A261) has the advantage of being written by a practical printer but lacks adequate historical perspective. Later histories, in contrast, are generally the work of art historians, critics, and curators, rather than printmakers or printers. General printmaking histories can be found in the works by Whitman (A262), Gray (A263), and Godfrey (A270). Mayor's work, although styled a "social history", nevertheless includes much about the history of printmaking techniques (A267). Griffiths (A271) is the most up-to-date general survey and is accompanied by useful illustrations which include enlargements of the finer details of many processes.

Harris (A265) was unique in first paying attention to the extraordinary range of new processes, experimental as well as practicable, which were proposed or practised in the first half of the 19th century. Wakeman (A268) shows how several of these new processes were successfully introduced into commercial book illustration production and chronicled the arrival of the photo-mechanical revolution. Both are essentially technological histories and fill a long-felt need in the retrospective literature. The technology of map reproduction, which was essentially a large-scale graphic printing operation, is the particular concern of several historical essays edited by Woodworth (A269).

Berry & Poole (A264) provide a chronological framework within which all picture printing processes can be viewed in relation to advances in general printing. Wakeman's "leaf" histories (A266, A272 & A273) are latter-day equivalents of Stannard's Art Exemplar (A34) but written from a retrospective viewpoint.

A260 **Pye, J.** 1845. Patronage of British art, or historical sketch: Comprising an account of the rise & progress of art & artists in London from the beginning of the reign of George the Second. London. x+422pp. Repr., With an intro. by R.W. Lightbown. London, 1970.

A261 **Southward, J.** 1897. Progress of printing & the graphic arts during the Victorian era. London. 96pp.

A262 **Whitman, A.C.** 1912. Whitman's print-collector's handbook. 6th edn., rev. & enl. with additional chapters by M.C. Salaman. London. xxi+376pp. 1st edn., 1901.

A263 **Gray, B.** 1937. The English print. London. xv+225pp.

A264 **Berry, W.T. & H.E. Poole.** 1966. Annals of printing: A chronological encyclopaedia from the earliest time to 1950. London. xix+315pp.

A265 **Harris, E.M.** 1968-70. Experimental graphic processes in England, 1800-1859. I & II. Journal, Printing Historical Society 4: 33-86, 1968.
----- ----- III. Ibid. 5: 41-80, 1969.
----- ----- IV & V. Ibid. 6: 53-89, 1970.

Contents of the five parts; I: The classification of printing processes; II: Congreve's compound plate printing, siderography, medal engraving; III: Metal relief engraving, acrography, glyphography; IV: Nature printing, electrotint; V: Explanation of processes [alphabetically arranged under 69 headings]. Good bibliographic documentation and excellent illus. (some in col.), several showing enlarged details of different processes.

A266 **Wakeman, G.** 1970. XIX century illustration: Some methods used in English books. Loughborough. 7pp, & 15 fascicles. Limited to 75 copies. Each fascicle describes a separate graphic process and contains one or more contemporary examples of it. Incl.: Wood engraving, copper engraving, etching, aquatint, steel engraving, medal engraving, omnigraphy, anastatic printing, natural illustration, colour printing (relief & lithographic), chemitype, photography, lithography, autotype & Woodburytype, photo-mechanical printing (collotype, photogravure, Meisenbach half-tone).

A267 **Mayor, A.H.** 1971. Prints & people: A social history of printed pictures. New York. [495]pp.

A268 **Wakeman, G.** 1973. Victorian book illustration: The technical revolution. Newton Abbot. 182pp.

A268* ----- 1974. Plates to accompany Victorian book illustration. Loughborough. 44ff. & 20 specimens. Limited to 23 copies.
Provides contemporary examples of: Wood engraving, etching, steel engraving, Dickes' & Leighton's colour printing, anastatic printing, chemitype, nature printing, natural illustration, photography, photo-lithography, chromo-lithography, Woodburytype, collotype, photogravure, halftone printing, Evans' colour printing, trichromatic photo-engraving. Each is accompanied by a leaf of explanatory text.

A269 **Woodward, D. Ed.** 1975. Five centuries of map printing: The Kenneth Nebenzahl Jr. lectures in the history of cartography. Chicago, Ill. xi+177pp.
Incl. papers by A.H. Robinson, D. Woodward, C. Verner, W.W. Ristow, E.M. Harris, & C. Koeman on various graphic processes used in map making and especially printing. Emphasises American methods.

A270 **Godfrey, R.T.** 1978. Printmaking in Britain: A general history from its beginnings to the present day. Oxford. 244pp.

A271 **Griffiths, A.** 1980. Prints & printmaking: An introduction to the history & techniques. London. 152pp.

A272 **Wakeman, G.** 1981. Graphic methods in book illustration. Loughborough. 19 fascicles. Limited to 120 copies.
Each describes & illustrates the most common graphic reproduction methods used from the 15th to the early 20th centuries, viz.: Woodcut, wood engraving, etching, copper stipple & steel engraving, aquatint, mezzotint, chalk- & line-style lithography, lithographic & relief colour printing, hand colouring, photography, Woodburytype, collotype, photogravure & photomechanical printing. Each fascicle includes a contemporary example of the process. Intended to assist the user with the identification of book-illustration processes.

A273 **Wakeman, G.** 1976. The production of nineteenth century illustration. Loughborough. vi+17pp. & 17 pls.
Describes graphic reproduction processes and provides contemporary examples under the following headings: Hand colouring; Baxter's process; Charles Knight; Leighton & others; William Dickes; Benjamin Fawcett; Edmund Evans; Nature printing; The tinted lithograph; The first decades of chromo-lithography; Chromo-lithography in the seventies; Turn of the century; Colour printing from Scotland; & Colour printing in Ireland.

Ap General history of colour printing

A great deal of the pioneer work of unravelling the history of colour printing was performed by Burch (A275) in a lengthy and detailed series of articles. They consist of a strightforward narrative written for a readership of practical printers, the final chapters of which are little more than a chronological summary of later 19th century colour-printing patent specifications. Most of the text was edited for publication as a book in 1910 (A278), but the later annals of patents were replaced by a new chapter on photo-mechanical developments by the editor of Penrose Annual. This was somewhat unfortunate since the chapters omitted from the original version contain material not recorded elsewhere. Meantime, in 1906, Hardie's scholarly history had appeared (A277). The work of a printmaker and museum curator it covered much of the same ground as Burch but also described hand-coloured books, based on the rich collection of the Victoria & Albert Museum. Two decades later Lewis, one of the leading enthusiasts in the great Baxter craze, produced a history of Victorian colour printing (A281). It was a natural progression from his elaborate studies of Baxter (A290 A295 A302) and Le Blond (A296) but, although it included much new material, it is distastefully coloured by Baxter hero-worship. It was eventually superseded by McLean's objective and excellently researched history (A286). Wakeman (A286*) provides an exemplar of colour printed specimens in the same manner as the companion work (A266). In another later work (A288) he emphasises the importance of certain technological developments in 19th century colour printing and again includes contemporary examples of several processes.

The early history of colour printing is extremely well documented in Franklin's excellent catalogue (A287) and his accompanying essays. Most 18th and early 19th century work was printed from intaglio surfaces and those methods are treated in section Bm <u>infra</u>. Buday (A285), though not a history of colour printing as such, does demonstrate how extensively it was applied to the burgeoning fancy stationery industry of later Victorian Britain.

A274 **Pingrenon, R.** 1903. Les livres ornés et illustrés en couleur depuis le XVe siècle en France et en Angleterre; avec une bibliographie: Guide du bibliophile et du biblioscope. Paris. 162pp.
Chronological history, pp.5-54; Bibliographie, livres anglais, pp.141-156.

A275 **Burch, R.M.** 1903-06. Some notes on the history of printing in colours. British & Colonial Printer 52: 265-266, 1903; 53: 1-2, 49-50, 65-66, 141-142, 289-290, 393-394, 1903; 54: 33-35, 229-231, 333-335, 461-463, 1904; 55: 65-67, 177-178, 273-274, 289-290, 1904; 56: 49-52, 113-115, 381-382, 1905; 57: 105-107, 153-154, 181-183, 297-298, 345-346, 405-406, 1905; 58: 25-26, 117-119, 225-226, 305-306, 369-370, 1906; 59: 1-3, 1906.

A276 **Paston, G.** 1905. Old coloured books. London. viii+48pp.

A277 **Hardie, M.** [1906.] English coloured books. London. xxiv+340pp. Repr. Bath, 1973.

A278 **Burch, R.M.** 1910. Colour printing & colour printers. London. xviii+281pp. & 23 pls. 2nd edn., 1910. Repr. with an introduction by J. Friedman, New York, 1980. (but without the pls.)
With a chapter on "Modern colour processes" by W. Gamble. The pls. incl. actual examples of Baxter proc., chromo-xylogr., chromo-liths. (2), Rembrandt grav., 3-col. collo., 3-col. proc. engs. (6), 4-col. proc. engs. (2), & 3-col. screenless proc. engs. (2).

A279 **Peddie, R.A.** 1914. The history of colour printing. Journal, Royal Society of Arts 62: 262-270. Also pub. in his: History of printing, together with printing in colours, pp.37-52. London, 1917.

A280 **Clarke, H.G.** 1925-26. Early colour picture printing processes. B.P. Collector & Baxter Times 3: 131-141.

A281 **Lewis, C.T.C.** [1928.] The story of picture printing in England in the nineteenth century, or forty years of wood & stone. London. xxxv+405pp.

A282 ----- 1931. The mystery of oil-colour printing. Penrose Annual 33: 74-78.

A283 **Clarke, H.G.** 1933-34. Early picture printing processes to the time of Baxter. Printing Review 3: 61-62, 131-133, 175-176.

A284 **Rylatt, J.H.** 1937. Colour printing. Proceedings, National Picture Print Society etc. 2: 22-30.

A285 **Buday, G.** 1954. The history of the Christmas card. London. xxiii+304pp. Repr. London, 1964.

A286 **McLean, R.** 1972. Victorian book design & colour printing. 2nd edn. London. xii+241. 1st edn., London, 1963.

A286* **Wakeman, G,** 1976. XIX century colour illustration. Loughborough. 17ff. & 17 pls.
A companion to (A266), this item concentrates solely on colour printed work and is accompanied by contemporary examples of: Hand col., Baxter proc., Knight's proc., Leighton's, Dickes', Fawcett's and Evans' relief printing, nature printing, tinted lith., early 70's and turn of the century chromo--lith., col. printing in Scotland and Ireland.

A287 **Franklin, C.** 1977. A catalogue of early colour printing from chiaroscuro to aquatint. Culham. viii+73pp.
Incl. essays on different methods and practitioners.

A288 **Wakeman, G.** 1981. Victorian colour printing. Loughborough. 30pp. & 8 pls., & various loose specimens. Limited to 141 copies.
Surveys the history and techniques of various commercial methods. Several contemporary printing appliances are illustrated. The various processes are

exemplified by contemporary specimens of Baxter proc., chromo-xylogr. (Knight, Leighton, Dickes & Fawcett), modern printings of 5 colour separations for a chromo-xylogr. of ca.1870 (from the original blocks), chromo--lith., 3-col. proc. eng., together with misc. specimens of commercial colour printing.

Aq History of colour printing: Baxter process

Baxter's colour printing process, which combined an intaglio "key" plate and superimposed colouring from carefully prepared colour wood-block separations, was capable of achieving extremely rich and glamourous effects combined with detail fine enough to bear close inspection. Its success was due in large part to the high standards of craftsmanship of its inventor rather than any innate secret and was, as R.A. Peddie commented (A279), "a personality, not a process."

At the beginning of the present century the enthusiasm of a few collectors backed by the commercial interest of some print dealers was quickly nurtured into a collecting craze of sizeable proportions. A steady flow of literature appeared extolling the virtues of their hero Baxter, and to a lesser extent, his disciples. As a result we have a very detailed, if biassed, account of Baxter's every production and much of the work of his licensees. Most other colour printers were measured, in somewhat disparaging terms, against the "genius" of the Master. This group of studies must, therefore, be used with great caution.

The most extensive study of Baxter is by Lewis (A302) who cumulated much of the material from a variety of earlier studies. The later works of Clarke & Rylatt (A308) and Mitzman (A311) present little new material but have lowered the tone of Baxter adulation to a more bearable level.

Separate monographs on Le Blond (A296), Bradshaw & Blacklock (A299*), and Mansell (A303 A304 A305) were each augmented and incorporated into Lewis's 1928 history (A308). Dickes was given a full-scale treatment by Docker (A301), but the work of Kronheim, perhaps the most underrated of the licensces, was never fully catalogued. His firm's large output was produced in very different qualities to suit to the market at which each was directed, varying from superbly crafted to crudely mass-produced. Unfortunately, Kronheim's work has usually been judged by the standard of the poorer work. A selected list of 1,000 of their Baxter-process subjects, out of a total of 3,000, appeared in 1923 (A298) and a more detailed catalogue was also commenced in 1923 continuing until the demise of the Baxter Times in 1925 and sadly stopping well short of completion (A300).

A289 **Bullock, C.F.** 1901. Life of George Baxter, engraver, artist, & colour printer. Birmingham. 29pp.
The first of many studies on this craftsman including a list of Baxter prints & books containing them.

A290 **Lewis, C.T.C.** 1908. George Baxter (colour printer): His life & work. A manual for collectors. London. xviii+276pp. Repr. 1972.

A291 **Colebrook, F.** 1909. George Baxter: His work & method. London.
Not seen.

A292 **Lewis, C.T.C.** 1911. The colour printer of the XIXth century: George Baxter. London. xxvi+363pp.

A293 ----- 1913. The Baxter year book, 1912. London. 117pp.
Chapter 2 adds detailed notes on various prints described in the previous work.

A294 **Clarke, H.G.** 1919. Baxter colour prints: Their history & methods of production. London & Leamington Spa. 121pp.

A295 **Lewis, C.T.C.** 1919. The Baxter book, 1919. London. xiv+231pp.
Chapter 3 adds detailed notes on numerous prints more briefly described in Lewis (A292).

A296 ----- 1920. The Le Blond book, 1920: Being a history & detailed catalogue of the work of Le Blond & Co., by the Baxter process. London. xv+138pp.

A297 **Clarke, H.G.** 1920-21. Baxter colour prints pictorially presented. London. 292pp. & 136 pls.
Issued in 12 fascicles. The text incl. a detailed account of "The disposal of Baxter's plates & blocks in 1860", pp.22-29, 33-40, 44-51, 55-62, & 66-70. Some ten purchasers acquired the right to print from Baxter's materials but none achieved success. Most of the blocks and plates later passed to Vincent Brooks and Le Blond, some others reverting to Baxter himself.

A298 **Etheridge, E.** 1923. Baxter, Le Blond & Baxter process print values for 1923. Leamington Spa. 170pp.
Useful historical introduction and separate lists of licensees' productions.

A299 **Anon.** 1923-24. Baxter chats, 1-5: Baxter rarities. Baxter Times 1: 14-19, 54-56, 69-73, 118-120, 132-135.
----- -----, 6: Unique items. Ibid. pp.164-167.
----- -----, 7-11: Baxter prints of which his plates & blocks passed into other printers' hands. Ibid., pp.196-199, 227-231, 253, 259-261, 291-293, 323-325.

A299* ----- 1923-25. Bradshaw & Blacklock's colour prints by the Baxter process. Baxter Times 1: 147-150, 173-174, 206-207, 239-241, 270-273, 307-309, 338-340, 1923-24; 2: 67-68, 340-342, 1924-25; 3: 70-71, 1925.

A300 ----- 1923-25. Kronheim & Co.'s colour prints by the Baxter process, 1850-1880. Baxter Times 1: 3-15, 43-50, 77-86, 111-117, 141-146, 168-172, 200-205, 232-237, 263-267, 296-302, 329-337, 361-369, 1923-24; 2: 6-15, 39-48, 75-80, 82, 113-120, 146-153, 177-182, 212-216, 239-242, 278-279, 312-313, 339-340, 372-373, 1924-25; 3: 19-22, 54-55, 85-87, 119-121, 151-152, 1925.

A301 **Docker, A.** 1924. The colour prints of William Dickes. London & Leamington Spa. x+50+[104]pp.

A302 **Lewis, C.T.C.** 1924. George Baxter, the picture printer. London. xxxvi+608pp.
Includes: Ch. 4: A Baxter process print in the making, and Ch. 6: Baxter process prints by licensees and others.

A303 **Anon.** 1923/24. Joseph Mansell's colour prints by the Baxter process. Baxter Times 1: 150-152, 174-176, 208-210, 237-239, 268-270, 304-306, 342-344.

A304 ----- 1923/24. Mansell's prints from Baxter's original plates. Baxter Times 1: 371-374.

A305 ----- 1924/25. Cries of London. Baxter Times 2: 232-233, 274-275, 362-364.
By Joseph Mansell, Baxter process.

A306 **Lewis, C.T.C.** [1928.] The story of picture printing in England in the nineteenth century, or forty years of wood & stone. London. xxxv+405pp.
Incl. detailed treatment of Baxter licensees and their productions.

A307 **Etheridge, E.** [1929.] Baxter prints: A concise guide to their collection, including Baxter licensee prints, etc. London. 54pp.

A308 **Clarke, H.G. & J.H. Rylatt.** 1936. The centenary Baxter book, being an appreciation of George Baxter (1804-1867) the nineteenth century colour picture printer. Together with a catalogue resume of his works. Leamington Spa. viii+176pp.
A limited edn. presentation of much familiar Baxteriana. Incl. a repr. of Baxter's patent, the specification, and the renewal of the patent.

A309 **Cordingley, J.** 1949. Early colour printing & George Baxter, 1804-1867. A monograph produced in the printing department of the North Western Polytechnic. London. 24pp.

A310 **Ball, A. & M. Martin.** 1974. The price guide to Baxter prints. Woodbridge. viii+275pp.
Provides a photograph of every print.

A311 **Mitzman, M.E.** 1978. George Baxter & the Baxter prints. Newton Abbot. 176pp.

Ar History of nature printing

The most significant retrospective survey is by Fischer (A314) who provides a detailed international bibliography of literature about, or containing examples of, nature printing. Nature printing in England is largely identified with the work of Henry Bradbury, whose productions are catalogued by Wakeman (A316). The technicalities of Bradbury's process are fully described by Harris (A322) against the background of various other experimental processes, and his work is also well represented in a wider ranging history of the craft by Cave & Wakeman (A318).

The eccentric craft of making butterfly wing prints, -- a form of "natural illustration" -- is the subject of two historical notes by Cowan (A321).

A312 **Sheridan, F.** 1906. Nature printing: Its history & development through three centuries. Modern Lithographer 2: 330-332.

A313 **Tiberghien, A.** 1931. Phytotypie et phytotypes: Notice sommaire bibliographique et historique sur l'impression des plantes elles-mêmes. Bulletin, Société Royale de Botanique de Belgique 64: 81-91.

A314 **Fischer, E.** 1933. 200 Jahre Naturselbstdruck. Gutenberg Jahrbuch 1933: 186-213.

A315 **Eder, J.M.** 1945. Nature printing. In: History of photography. Translated by E. Epstean. pp.45-51, 796-806. New York. Repr. New York, 1978.

A316 **Wakeman, G.** 1966. Henry Bradbury's nature printed books. Library (5) 21: 63-67.

A317 **Fawcett, T.** 1966. (Correspondence) Nature printing. Library (5) 21: 331.

A318 **Cave, R. & G. Wakeman.** 1967. Typographia naturalis. Wymondham. vii+37, & 5 pls.
The pls. incl. an actual specimen of Henry Bradbury's nature printing.

A319 **Wakeman, G.** 1967. (Correspondence) Nature printing. Library (5) 22: 355.

A320 **Collins, J.** 1967. (Correspondence) Nature printing. Library (5) 22: 355-356.

A321 **Cowan, C.F.** 1968-70. Butterfly wing prints. Journal, Society for the Bibliography of Natural History 4: 368-369, 1968; 5: 389, 1970.

A322 **Harris, E.M.** 1970. Nature printing. In: Experimental graphic processes in England 1800-1859. Part IV. Journal, Printing Historical Society 6: 53-65.

As History of electrotype

Despite the importance of electrotype to both letterpress and picture printing during the 19th century, no adequate history of the craft has yet appeared. The titles listed below provide little more than an outline sketch of developments written too close to the events to have much historical detachment. Harris (A327) gives a detailed account of two specialised applications of electrotype for graphic reproduction.

A323 **Southward, J.** 1897. The history of stereotyping & electrotyping. In: Wilson, F.J.F. Stereotyping & electrotyping. pp.1-24. London.

A324 **Anon.** 1899. Stereotyping & electrotyping. Printers' Year Book & Diary 1899: 62-63.
Brief but informative sketch of some British firms who first specialised in electrotype.

A325 ----- 1904/05. The progress of electrotyping. Collis's Journal 2: 108-109, 126-127, 140-141, 152-153, 166-167.
Historical notes.

A326 **Anon.** 1957. Curiosities of printing history - electrotyping in the nineteenth century. British Printer 70 (10): 77-80.

A327 **Harris, E.M.** 1969-70. Glyphography. Electrotint. In: Experimental graphic processes in England 1800-1859. Parts III & IV. Journal, Printing Historical Society 5: 63-80, 1969; 6: 65-70, 1970.
Both processes relied on the use of electrotype techniques for the production of the printing surface.

At History of equipment & materials

The development of printing presses and machines from their origins to the high level of technological sophistication achieved by the later 19th century is chronicled in Meier (A330) and Moran (A335). Meier deals with hand presses used for relief and intaglio work while Moran concentrates on letterpress equipment and includes the development of power driven machines. Letterpress machine developments led the field but many of their mechanical innovations were later incorporated into the design of powered lithographic and intaglio equipment.

Foreign machinery was imported in significant quantities for use by a wide range of British printers, particularly from American and France. Hoe (A328) describes American developments and Niepp (A332) emphasizes continental work but also mentions some English developments in letterpress and intaglio machines.

The history of the platen press in England is briefly described by Nuttall (A337) and for America by Green (A333). Platen presses acquired considerable importance in the early development of tri-chromatic process printing because of their accuracy in registering finely-screened the colour separations.

Wiborg (A329) and Bloy (A334) both recount the general history of printing ink manufacture, Bloy also includes a retrospective recipe book for every variety of ink used in letterpress or picture printing.

Robison (A336), although merely an annotated exhibition catalogue, about the only attempt to study the aesthetic quality and importance of paper, the support for almost every print and printed picture. A wide ranging general history of paper can be found in Hunter (A331).

A328 **Hoe, R.** 1902. A short history of the printing press & of improvements in printing machinery from the time of Gutenberg up to the present day. New York. 91pp.
Especially good on cylinder, rotary, and web presses of the later 19th century.

A329 **Wiborg, F.B.** 1926. Printing ink: A history. New York. 299pp.

A330 **Meier, H.** 1941. The origin of the printing & roller press. Print Collector's Quarterly 28: 8-55, 164-205, 338-379, 496-527.

A331 **Hunter, D.** 1947. Papermaking: The history & technique of an ancient craft. 2nd edn., rev. London. xxiv+611+xxxviipp. Repr. New York, 1978.

A332 **Niepp, L.** 1951. Les machines à imprimer depuis Gutenberg. Paris. 443pp.
Chap. III: Le presse mecanique en Angleterre; Chap. VIII: Les machines a imprimer les procéses autres que la typographie.

A333 **Green, R.** 1953. A history of the platen jobber. Chicago, Ill. iv+38pp.

A334 **Bloy, C.H.** 1967. A history of printing ink, balls & rollers, 1440-1850. London. xii+147pp.

A335 **Moran, J.** 1973. Printing presses: History & development from the fifteenth century to modern times. London. 263pp.

A336 **Robison, A.** 1977. Paper in prints. Washington, D.C. 62pp. Catalogue to accompany an exhibition at the National gallery of Art, Washington.

A337 **Nuttall, D.** 1979. A brief history of platen presses. 2nd edn. Manchester. 10pp.

Au **Miscellaneous studies on history of printmaking**

A pot-pourri of titles that do not easily fall into the previous sections and including items which lay emphasis on the analytical rather than aesthetic study of prints and printed pictures.

The correct identification of the process by which any printed image was produced is an obvious necessity. In the absence of an exemplar such as Stannard (A34) or Wakeman (A266 A268* A272 A273 A286* A288) one requires a well illustrated analytical guide to the characteristic details of each process. The best, despite its small size, is Ivins (A347) which educates the reader in the art of looking into the print. Hubbard (A343) served the print collector for many years and was only superseded by Brunner's treatise on printmaking (A348) which included a useful series of enlarged photos arranged as a systematic guide to the identification of numerous processes. Salamon (A350) also provided an analytical guide to major processes for collectors or dealers in master prints.

The often imperfectly understood question of "proofs" and "states" is excellently and authoritatively elucidated by Hind (A340) while Grundy (A341) describes the methods for designating proofs used by the Printsellers' Association in the 19th century. The alteration and re-use of previously published engravings formed the special interest of Layard whose 1908 general study (A339) was followed in 1922 by his fascinating analytical history of the several forms of a single portrait engraving (A342).

The problem of the language and syntax of the printmaker is the chief concern of the scholarly and readable study by Ivins (A345), a work described by Griffiths (A271) as "The most brilliant and idiosyncratic book ever written about prints". Extravagant praise, perhaps, but the book was unique in its approach to printmaking history and is the work of a distinguished authority. The interpretive language employed by the printmaker in making copies of other prints, or printed interpretations of paintings and drawings, is the chief concern of three exhibitions whose annotated catalogues make instructive reading (A351 A354 A357). The concept of "facsimile" and its relation to the idea of "copy" is discussed by Weitenkampf (A344).

The problem of making bibliographical descriptions of prints, their states, or other peculiarities, is discussed by Verner (A352) and Bridson (A355), the former in regard to maps, the latter in relation to scientific illustrations. Tanselle (A360) discussed and reviews the various approaches to these problems.

William Blake's artistic genius and uniquely eccentric printmaking skill has stimulated many scholarly studies of his printed work. His methods, which he never described, have been the source of much speculation, in their efforts to unravel his methods, scholars have closely scrutinised his work and examined its relationship to the traditions under which he learnt the craft. The result is some excellent analytical studies which are worthy of perusal even if one is not infected with the Blake mystique; three are selected for inclusion here, Lister (A353), Essick (A358), and Bentley (A359).

A338 **Printsellers' Association.** 1882. A few words on art, which are also words of advice & warning, containing a description of the various states of impressions printed from engraved plates, also information how spurious proofs are made. London. 56pp.
Description of the several "states" accepted by members of the Association, touching upon: Artist's proof, Proof before letters, Proofs on India paper, Signed proofs, Stamped proofs, Remarque proofs, etc. Also discusses the acceptance of photogravure as a creative printmaking process. (For photographic illustrations of the various proof marks see Grundy (A341).)

A339 **Layard, G.S.** 1908. Suppressed plates, wood engravings, etc. London. xiii+254pp.
See also his catalogue of palimpsest portrait engravings (A393).

A340 **Hind, A.M.** 1909. Engravings & their states. [Parts] I & II. Burlington Magazine 15: 25-30, 271-285; also letters from W.G. Rawlinson and M. Hardie, pp.120, 186-187.
Well illustrated with photos of examples.

A341 **Grundy, C.R.** 1910. How to distinguish proof impressions. Connoisseur 28: 93-99; 29: 245-249.
As defined by the rules of the Printsellers' Association.

A342 **Layard, G.S.** 1922. The headless horseman: Pierre Lombart's engraving: Charles or Cromwell? London. xix+132pp.
An intriguing account of some palimpsest portrait engravings.

A343 **Hubbard, H.** Editor. 1926. How to distinguish prints: Written & illustrated by members of the Print Society. Woodgreen Common, Hants. 127pp.
Illustrated by photographic enlargements of surface details of the principal processes.

A344 **Weitenkampf. F.** 1943. What is a facsimile? Papers, Bibliographical Society of America 37: 114-130.
"Every facsimile is a copy, but not any copy is a facsimile".

A345 **Ivins, W.M. Jr.** 1953. Prints & visual communication. Cambridge, Mass. xxv+190pp. Repr. New York, 1969.
"... prints are among the most important and powerful tools of modern life and thought. Certainly we cannot hope to realize their actual role unless we get away from the snobbery of modern print collecting notions and definitions and begin to think of them as exactly repeatable pictorial statements or communications, without regard to the accident of rarity or what for the moment we may regard as aesthetic merit. We must look at them from the point of view of general ideas and particular functions, and, especially, we

must think about the limitations which their techniques have imposed on them as conveyors of information and on us as receivers of that information." Carefully chosen enlargements of print details and comparisons of different printmakers' interpretations of the same image illustrate this scholarly treatise.

A346 **Bland, D.** 1957. The influence of reproductive technique on book illustration. Penrose Annual 51: 16-19.

A347 **Ivins, W.M. Jr.** 1964. How prints look: Photographs with a commentary. New edn. Boston, Mass. 164pp. 1st edn., New York, 1943.

A348 **Brunner, F.** 1964. The identification of printing processes, pp.321-366. The identification of colour prints, pp.318-320. Genuine or false, pp.274-296. In: A handbook of graphic reproduction processes. 2nd edn. London. 379pp.
One of the best books on modern printmaking processes with a strong interest in the historical development of all methods.

A349 **Zigrosser, G. & C.M. Gaehde.** 1966. A guide to the collecting & care of original prints. Sponsored by the Print Council of America. London & New York. vii+120pp. 14th printing, 1979.
Includes an authoritative glossary of terms, pp.37-82.

A350 **Salamon, F.** 1972. A collector's guide to prints & print makers from Durer to Picasso. London. viii+303pp.
Part 1: A short anatomy of printmaking. Incl.: Ch. I: Paper; Ch. II: Watermarks; Ch. III: States; Ch. VI: Copies & forgeries; Ch. VIII: Posthumous impressions.

A351 **Princeton University Art Museum.** 1974. Copies of originals: Translations in media & techniques. Princeton, N.J.. 115pp.
Annotated exhibition catalogue. "This exhibition explores the various facets of the relationship between copy and original, dealing primarily with the copyist's translation of the original into a different medium and technique. ... The line, form, and color of a master, transformed by another artist and transposed into a different medium, provide a valuable illustration of the process of visual interpretation."

A352 **Verner, C.** 1974. Carto-bibliographical description: The analysis of variants in maps printed from copperplates. American Cartographer 1: 77-87.

A353 **Lister, R.** 1975. Infernal methods: A study of William Blake's art techniques. London. xii+102pp.

A354 **Sterling & Francine Clark Art Institute.** 1975. Dürer through other eyes: His graphic work mirrored in copies & forgeries of three centuries. An exhibition. Williamstown, Mass. 99pp.
Incl: The documents and literature on printed copies after Dürer, [&] Techniques of copying, pp.9-17, followed by a systematic study of the work of known and anonymous copyists.

A355 **Bridson, G.D.R.** 1976. The treatment of plates in bibliographical description. Journal, Society for the Bibliography of Natural History 7: 469-488.

A356 **Anon.** 1978. Recognition of photographic processes. History of Photography 2: 34-36.
A descriptive "key" to the various processes of the 19th century for the aid of archivists, librarians and museum curators.

A357 **Alexander, D. & R.T. Godfrey.** 1980. Painters & engraving: The reproductive print from Hogarth to Wilkie. New Haven, Conn. iv+73pp.
Extensively annotated catalogue of an exhibition at the Yale Center for British Art. Devoted to a detailed study of the reproductive engraver in England and his importance in making the work of English painters known to the general public through the medium of prints.

A358 **Essick, R.N.** 1980. William Blake, printmaker. Princeton, N.J.. xxii+283pp.
Chapter 3: Etching & engraving, pp.8-28, provides a very thorough account of procedures at the time Blake was serving his apprenticeship.

A359 **Bentley, G.E. Jr.** 1981. William Blake's techniques of engraving & printing. Studies in Bibliography 34: 241-253.

A360 **Tanselle, G.T.** 1982. The description of non-letterpress material in books. Studies in Bibliography 35: 1-42.

Av History of printmaking: Catalogues of examples

A selection of general, thematic (subject), and special (media), catalogues chosen for their value to the historian of printmaking technique rather than the print connoisseur or collector. Some of these reference works describe prints in great technical detail but most do not and can only be relied upon to provide a simple statement of the process, the printmaker, and perhaps the printer, responsible for each item. However, even this limited information can serve to identify the print as an example of a particular technique or as a specimen of the work of an individual worker in that medium.

The list commences with a number of general print catalogues, including thematic guides defined by the subject of the picture. They are followed by special catalogues distinguished by the form of printmaking process covered.

"Prints" are taken to include both separately published pictures and book illustrations. Consequently, some major bibliographies and bibliographical catalogues are also included.

This section is classified under these headings: General; Colour printing processes; Intaglio plate processes; Relief block processes; Lithographic processes; Photo-mechanical processes.

General

A361 **Le Blanc, C.** 1854-88. Manuel de l'amateur d'estampes, contenant: 1. Un dictionnaire des graveurs de toutes les nations. 2. Un répertoire des estampes dont les auteurs ne sont connus que par des marques figurées. 3. Un dictionnaire des monogrammes des graveurs. 4. Une table des peintres, sculpteurs, architectes et dessinateurs. 5. Une table methodique des estampes precédé de considérations sur l'histoire de la gravure, ses divers procédés, le choix des estampes, et la manière de les conserver. Ouvrage destinés à faire suite au Manuel du Libraire et de l'Amateur de Livres, par

J.C. Brunet. Paris, 1854-88. [Issued in 17 fascicules. Publication of 9-17 delayed for some 30 years.] Repr. Amsterdam, 1970. 2 vols.; New York, 1978.
A pioneer work surveying engraved and other forms of book illustration. Arranged under the names of the printmakers.

A362 **Printsellers' Association.** 1892. An alphabetical list of engravings declared at the office of the Printsellers' Association, London ... since its establishment in 1847 to the end of 1891. Comp. by G.W. Friend. London. Unpaged.
----- 1912. An alphabetical list of engravings ... from 1892-1911 inclusive. Comp. by C.F. Duffell. London. Unpaged.
----- 1912. Index of painters & engravers with the titles of their works ... as described in An alphabetical list ... 1847 to 1911 inclusive. Comp. by C.F. Duffell. London. 112pp.
These "trade" lists include publication information such as the size of the edition, the registered "states", and so forth, in addition to the usual catalogue details.

A363 **Library of Congress.** 1906. A.L.A. portrait index: Index to portraits contained in printed books & periodicals ... edited by W.C. Lane. Washington, D.C. lxxv+1601pp.
Alphabetically arranged by the subject of the portrait, this monumental catalogue gives very brief details for each print, usually mentioning the engraver and the process but, unfortunately, without an index of printmakers. List of books indexed, pp.xi-lxxiv.

A364 **British Museum.** 1908-25. Catalogue of engraved British portraits preserved in the Department of Prints & Drawings in the British Museum. London. 6 vols.
Incl. a list of printmakers, the main body of the work being alphabetically arranged by the subjects.

A365 **Schwerdt, C.F.G.R.** 1928-37. Hunting, hawking, shooting: Illustrated in a catalogue of books, manuscripts, prints, & drawings. London. 4 vols. Catalogue of engravings in vol. 3, pp.1-193 & vol. 4, pp.135-182.

A366 **Siltzer, F.** 1929. The story of British sporting prints. New edn. London. vii+707pp. Repr. 1979.

A367 **Slater, J.H.** 1929. Engravings & their value. 6th edn. by F.W. Maxwell-Barbour. London. vii+707pp. Repr. 1979.
1st edn., 1891. "Prints & their value" would be a more accurate title since lithographs are included. Although intended as a collector's guide to prices it also constitutes a useful biographical dictionary of printmakers with select lists of productions for each.

A368 **Dunthorne, G.** 1938. Flower & fruit prints of the 18th & early 19th centuries: Their history, makers & uses, with a catalogue raisonné of the works in which they are found. Washington, D.C. xiv+275pp. Repr. London, 1970.
The author had an intimate understanding of the process of printmaking which is revealed by his admirable analytical descriptions.

A369 **Abbey, J.R.** 1952. Scenery of Great Britain & Ireland in aquatint & lithography, 1770-1860: A bibliographical catalogue. London. xx+399pp. Repr. London, 1973.
This, and the two succeeding works, provide accurate lists of all illustrations in the books described with transcriptions of the signature line of each. There are indexes of printmakers, printers, and publishers.

A370 ----- 1953. Life in England in aquatint & lithography, 1770-1860; architecture, drawings books, art collections, magazines, Navy & Army, panoramas, etc: A bibliographical catalogue. London. xxi+427pp. Repr. London, 1973.

A371 ----- 1956. Travel in aquatint & lithography, 1770-1860: A bibliographical catalogue. London. 2 vols. Repr. London, 1973.

A372 **Nissen, C.** 1953. Die illustrierten Vögelbucher: Ihre Geschichte & Bibliographie. Stuttgart. 222pp.
This, and the two succeeding works, provide an international bibliography of one of the most richly illustrated literatures -- natural history. For each book described, the printmaking process, the artists, printmakers and printers are all detailed. All three works have indexes of "Kunstler", which include also include printmakers and printers.

A373 ----- 1966. Die botanische Buchillustration: Ihre Geschichte & Bibliographie. 2. Aufl. Stuttgart. 3 vols in one, i.e. the 2 vols of the 1st edn. (1951) with a supplement.

A374 ----- 1966-78. Die zoologische Buchillustration: Ihre Bibliographie & Geschichte. Stuttgart. 2 vols.
The study on bird books (A372) forms an essential complement to this work which cross refers the reader to all its entries.

A375 **Elmes, R.M.** 1975. Catalogue of Irish topographical prints & original drawings. New edn. rev. & enl. by M. Hewson. Dublin. ix+256pp.
With an index of engravers (and lithographers).

A376 **Ray, G.N.** 1976. The illustrator & the book in England from 1790 to 1914. London. xxxiii+336pp.
A valuable descriptive survey based on an exhibition.

Colour printing processes

(N.B. Catalogues of colour prints by Geo. Baxter & his licencees are included in Section Aq <u>supra</u>.)

A377 **Pingrenon, R.** 1903. Les livres ornés et illustrés en couleur depuis le XVe siècle en France et en Angleterre; avec une bibliographie: Guide du bibliophile et du biblioscope. Paris. 162pp.
Bibliographie: Livres Anglais, pp.141-156.

A378 **Darmon, J.E.** 1929. Dictionnaire des gravures en couleurs, en bistre et en sanguine du XVIIIe siècle, des écoles française et anglaise, en circulation dans le commerce des estampes, avec leurs prix. Nouv. edn. Montpellier. 142pp. Repr. New York, 1978.
Lists the works of some 53 printmakers in alphabetical title arrangement.

A379 **Franklin, C.** 1977. A catalogue of early colour printing from chiaroscuro to aquatint. Culham. viii+73pp.
This invaluable catalogue includes a remarkable range of 18th century colour intaglio work.

A380 **Friedman, J.M.** 1978. Colour printing in England: 1486-1870. An exhibition, Yale Center for British Art. New Haven, Conn. ix+72pp.
Well annotated descriptive survey.

A381 **Tooley, R.V.** 1979. English books with coloured plates 1790 to 1860: A bibliographical account of the most important books illustrated by English artists in colour aquatint & colour lithography. Rev. edn. London. x+452pp.
1st edn. entitled: Some English books with coloured plates, London, 1935. Excl. natural history books, placing emphasis on books with hand-coloured rather than colour-printed illustrations. Provides full lists of pls. for each title and mentions artist and printmaker, but sometimes omits mention of the printmaking process. No index of printmakers.

A382 **British Printing Machinery Association.** 1980. Catalogue of exhibitions of British coloured books, 1738-1898. Organised in conjunction with IPEX 80 [International Printing Exhibition]. London. 139pp.
Incl. a ch. on "British Coloured Books 1738-1898" by R. McLean. "Coloured" books is taken to incl. hand-coloured as well as colour-printed works.

A383 **National Library of Wales.** 1980. English colour-plate books, 1750-1880: An exhibition on the occasion of IPEX. Aberystwyth. 27pp.
A companion to the above item.

A384 **Waddleton, N.** 1981. A chronology of books with coloured illustrations or decorations, mainly in relief or planar colour printed: Mainly of the nineteenth century. 3rd edn. London. [225]pp.
A privately issued catalogue of the author's unusually comprehensive collection. The entry for each item within the chronological list includes mention of the colour printer. In this provisional edn. there is no index to printers. Undoubtedly the fullest list of English colour-printed books.

Intaglio plate processes

A385 **Upcott, W.** 1818. A bibliographical account of the principal works relating to English topography. London. 3 vols. Repr. New York, 1968; London, 1978.
A remarkably detailed bibliography for its day. Provides full plate lists for each book and quotes the signature line of each pl. Almost all the illustrations listed at this date are, of course, intaglio.

A386 **Andresen, A.** 1870-73. Handbuch für Kupferstichsammler; oder Lexikon der Kupferstecher ... aller Länder & Schulen ... Auf Grundlagen der zweiten Auflage von Heller's Pract. Handbuch fur Kupferstichsammler. Leipzig. 2 vols.
Suppl. by Wessely (A389).

A387 **Apell, A.** 1880. Handbuch für Kupferstichsammler (oder Lexicon der vorzüglichsten Stecher des XIXten Jahrunderts welche in Linienmanier gearbeitet haben, sowie Beschreibung ihrer besten & gesuchtesten Blätter). Leipzig. xxxvii+478pp.

A388 **Smith, J.C.** 1883. British mezzotint portraits: Being a descriptive catalogue of these engravings from the introduction of the art to the early part of the present century. Arranged according to the engravers, the inscriptions given at full length & the variations of state precisely set forth; accompanied by biographical notes. London. 4 vols. with 125 pls. Repr. New York, 1978.
An elaborate catalogue, replete with information. Suppl. by Russell (A392).

A389 **Wessely, J.E.** 1885. Ergänzungsheft zu Andresen-Wessely's Handbuch für Kupferstichsammler, enhaltend die Seit 1873 erscheinenen hervorragenden Blätter nebst zahlreichen Nachtragen zum Hauptwerke. Leipzig. 120pp.
Forms a supplement to Andresen (A386).

A390 **Lewine, J.** 1898. Bibliography of eighteenth century art & illustrated books: Being a guide to collectors of illustrated works in English & French of the period. London. xv+615pp.

A391 **Victoria & Albert Museum.** 1906. Catalogue of prints II. Modern etchings & aquatints of the British & American schools. London. ii+364pp.

A392 **Russell, C.E.** 1926. English mezzotint portraits & their states, from the invention of mezzotinting until the early part of the 19th century. London. 2 vols.
Forms a suppl. to Smith (A388).

A393 **Layard, G.S.** 1927. Catalogue raisonné of engraved British portraits from altered plates. Arranged by H.M. Latham, with an introduction by the Marquess of Sligo. London. x+133pp.

A394 **Holloway, M.** 1977. A bibliography of nineteenth-century British topographical books with steel engravings. London. vii+205pp.

A395 **Lane, C.** 1978-79. Sporting aquatints & their engravers. Leigh-on-Sea. 2 vols.
A series of monographs on the leading aquatinters in this field. Incl. much new material on the printmakers and very full lists of their productions.

Relief block processes

A396 **Victoria & Albert Museum.** Catalogue of modern wood-engravings in the Victoria & Albert Museum. Compiled by M. Hardie. London. ii+419pp.

Lithographic processes

A397 **Victoria & Albert Museum.** Catalogue of the loan collection of lithographs, 1898-99. London. xvi+264pp.
The exhibition commemorated the first century of lithography.

A398 **Man, F.** 1963. Lithography in England (1801-1810). In: Zigrosser, C. Ed. Prints: Thirteen illustrated essays on the art of the print. pp.97-130. London.
A studiously prepared catalogue of the English "incunabula" of this medium.

Photo-mechanical processes

A399 **Boston Museum of Fine Arts.** 1892. Exhibition illustrating the technical methods of the reproductive arts from the XVth century to the present time, with special reference to the photo-mechanical processes. Introduction by S.R. Koehler. Boston, Mass. xi+98pp.

A400 **Victoria & Albert Museum.** 1901. Catalogue of the loan exhibition of modern illustration, 1901. Introduction by H.B. Wheatley. London. 152pp.
Much of the exhibited work was produced by various photo-mechanical processes and is not documented elsewhere.

A401 ----- 1905. Catalogue of the loan exhibition of process engraving, 1905. Introduction by J. Waterhouse. London. xx+64pp.
An extremely valuable end-of-century review of the state of the art. Much of the exhibited material is not documented in any other catalogue.

A402 **Columbia University Libraries.** 1937. A catalog of the Epstean collection on the history & science of photography & its applications, especially to the graphic arts. New York. [209]pp.
----- 1938. Authors & short-title index, Epstean collection. Corrected with additions to May 1, 1938. New York.
----- 1942. Accessions May 1938 - Dec. 1941, with addenda, 1942. New York. 29 11.
Neither of the addenda has been seen.

A403 **Schultze, R.S.** 1962. Victorian books illustrated with original photographs & by early photomechanical processes: Catalogue of an exhibition at the National Book League. London. 14pp.

A404 **Science Museum.** 1969. The Science Museum photography collection. By D.B. Thomas. London. v+113pp.
Covers photographic material of all kinds incl. a representative collection of pioneer efforts in photo-mechanical printing.

A404* **Haaften, J. van.** 1977. "Original sun pictures": A check list of the New York Public Library's holdings of early works illustrated with photographs, 1844-1900. Bulletin, New York Public Library 80: 355-415.
The collection incl. British books.

Aw **Printmakers & picture printers**

From the 18th century up to the present day there has been an unending succession of biographical dictionaries of artists, many of which include printmakers and some of which are entirely devoted to them. Unfortunately, if one makes a careful comparison of their contents it soon becomes clear that many of them are either drawn from the same sources or else repeat each other's information.

Firstly, the general works of international compass. One of the largest of the older generation is Nagler (A408) which is still of great value today and has been a much plagiarised source book. In addition to biographical accounts it also provides select lists of each printmaker's works. A new, considerably enlarged and improved edition of the whole was commenced by Meyer (A411) but, sadly, progressed no farther than the letter "B". Müller's dictionary (A414) is concise and generally reliable and was edited by Singer, an authority on printmaking history. The last edition of Bryan (A416), which appeared shortly after the commencement of Müller, is widely recommended but has a comparatively poor coverage of printmakers. Thieme & Becker (A417) is the major work in this field and one that can only be found in major libraries. In addition to the sizeable biographical accounts by a variety of authors each includes a good bibliography of other source works, including articles in other biographical dictionaries. Because Thieme & Becker took over 40 years to complete the earlier part of the alphabet is in need of up-dating to match the documentation of later entries. Benezit (A427) is specially comprehensive in its coverage of minor artists but the whole work is presented in a much more succinct form than Thieme & Becker and the information given for each artist is obviously limited.

Of the national general dictionaries, Strickland's (A420) is distinguished by its commendably careful research into unpublished biographical sources. Redgrave's handy dictionary (A412) has surprisingly comprehensive coverage of English artists who had died before its completion and includes many engravers, some quite obscure workers. Rees (A419), on the other hand, is little more than a transcription of relevant D.N.B. material.

The earliest of the special dictionaries of printmakers are now of little more than historical interest today; Strutt (A405) & Walpole (A406). However, the work by Ottley (A407), had he only completed it, would have survived as a distinguished reference work to this day. It was intentionally published as a fragment (Aba - Bal) but one which set a standard so high that no one else completed it or matched it. If any reservoir of material remained for its continuance it was never, apparently, utilised for no subsequent dictionary of British printmakers had similar content. Le Blanc (A409) is still of value and has a higher content of engravers for book illustration than is usual with dictionaries of printmakers. Hind's list (A421) is scarcely biographical but usefully points to other sources of information. Marshall (A410), Fincham (A415), Bushnell (A424), Grant (A425), Engen (A428), Hunnisett (A429), and Guichard (A430) provide the core of specialised reference sources, each containing varying levels of biographical information on different aspects of printmaking. Heal (A422), though a small work, provides the only study of engravers based on their own trade cards and is well worthy of revision and expansion. Hammelmann (A426) concentrates on one class of book-illustration engravers in considerable detail and, despite being incomplete at the author's death, includes a number of engravers who are not documented elsewhere. Levis (A431), Colin (A432), and especially Ludman & Mason (A433), serve to enlarge and update the individual bibliographies in Thieme & Becker. (N.B. A number of the print catalogues in the previous section also contain useful biographical information, e.g. Slater (A367), Smith (A388), Lane (A395), etc.)

Most dictionaries of printmakers are concerned with those who ranked as creative artists but the craft embraced a very large number, perhaps even a majority, who were occupied with reproductive, decorative, or even less ambitious ancillary tasks. Many worked for publishers or stationers preparing book illustrations or decorative stationery. Others applied their craft wherever work could be found and engraved on decorative silver or brass ware, door or coffin plates, etc. Most of the well commissioned engravers employed apprentices and assistants who performed mundane chores under the signature of their master, such as laying grounds for mezzotinters, preliminary biting-in of etched foundation work, machine-ruling expanses of sky, filling in backgrounds, ruling borders, whilst lettering generally the work of specialist letter-engravers. The lithographic trade employed large numbers of skilled litho artists, transfer printers, colour separation draughtsmen, stone preparers, and the like. The person who actually did the printing of the picture might rise to the level of master-craftsman (like Fredk. Goulding who printed for Whistler & others) but most were unsung professionals who worked for larger firms and were never granted recognition.

Recently a number of historians have turned their attention to the brigades of workers who made up the body of the 18th and 19th century picture printing and printmaking industry. The focus has been on the years up to 1850 and a number of useful studies have been completed (A434 - A443). Generally they have little biographical information but they do contain valuable compilations of other facts about business histories, apprentice training, services offered, examples of the work accomplished, etc. However, much remains to be done and for the period from 1850 to 1900 one must go to contemporary sources for information. A selection of references (A444 - A451) draws attention to those which contain classified lists of tradesmen. There is, of course, a vast number of unspecialised street directories that may contain some information on any particular individual for almost every year of the 19th century. Their byways are signposted by Goss (A452) and Norton (A453) while Pollard may be consulted for information on booktrade directories (A454).

This section is classified according to: Biographical dictionaries; Bibliographies on monographs on printmakers; Historical dictionaries of printers, etc.; Contemporary directories of printers, etc.; Guides to directories; Unpublished sources.

Biographical dictionaries

A405 **Strutt, J.** 1785-86. A biographical dictionary; containing an historical account of all the engravers, from the earliest period of the art of engraving to the present time, & a short list of their most esteemed works, with their ciphers, monograms, etc. London. 2 vols. Reprint, 1972.

A406 **Walpole, H.** 1765. A catalogue of engravers who have been born or resided in England: Digested by Mr. Horace Walpole from the MSS. of Mr. George Vertue. 2nd edn. London. 181pp. Also repr. in: Anecdotes of painting in England, with additions by the Rev. James Dallaway, & Vertue's catalogue of engravers who have been born or have resided in England. New edn. Vol. 3, pp.119-267. London, 1888. There were a number of intervening editions of this catalogue.

A407 **Ottley, W.Y.** 1831. Notices of engravers & their works being the commencement (Aba - Bal) of a new dictionary which it is not intended to continue. London. viii+208pp.

A408 **Nagler, G.K.** 1835-52. Neues allgemeines Künstler-Lexicon. Munich. 22 vols. Repr. Leipzig, [1924.]

A409 **Le Blanc, C.** 1854-88. Manuel de l'amateur d'estampes, contenant: 1. Un dictionnaire des graveurs de toutes les nations. 2. Un répertoire des estampes dont les auteurs ne sont connus que par des marques figurées. 3. Un dictionnaire des monogrammes des graveurs. 4. Une table des peintres, sculpteurs, architectes et dessinateurs. 5. Une table methodique des estampes precédé de considérations sur l'histoire de la gravure, ses divers procédés, le choix des estampes, et la maniere de les conserver. Ouvrage

destinés à faire suite au Manuel du Libraire et de l'Amateur de Livres, par J.C. Brunet. Paris, 1854-88. [Issued in 17 fascicules. Publication of 9-17 delayed for some 30 years.] Repr. Amsterdam, 1970. 2 vols.; New York, 1978.
A pioneer work surveying engraved and other forms of book illustration. Arranged under the names of the printmakers.

A410 **Marshall, J.** 1869. Handbook of engravers of ornament. London. viii+39pp.
Based on the collection of ornamental engraving in the South Kensington Museum.

A411 **Meyer, J.** Ed. 1872-85. Allgemeines Künstler-Lexicon. Unter Mitwirkung der namhaftesten Fachgelehrten des In- und Auslandes. 2. gänzlich neubearbeite Auflage von Nagler's Künstler-Lexicon. Aa- (-Bezzuoli). Leipzig. 3 vols.
All published.

A412 **Redgrave, S.** 1878. A dictionary of artists of the English school: Painters, sculptors, architects, engravers & ornamentalists. 2nd edn. London. xvi+498pp. Repr. Bath, 1970.

A413 **Clement, C.E. & L. Hutton.** 1884. Artists of the 19th century. Rev. edn. Boston, Mass. & New York. 2 vols. Repr. St. Louis, Mo., 1969.
Especially useful in that it incl. living artists of the day.

A414 **Müller, F.** 1895-1906. Allgemeines Künstler-Lexicon: Leben & Werke der berühmstehen bildenden Künstler. 3. Aufl. herausg. von H.W. Singer. Frankfurt am Main. 6 vols.

A415 **Fincham, H.W.** 1897. Artists & engravers of British & American book plates: A book of reference for book plate & print collectors. London. xvi+135pp.

A416 **Bryan, M.** 1903-04. Dictionary of painters & engravers. 4th edn. Rev. by G.C. Williamson. London. 5 vols. Repr. New York, 1964.

A417 **Thieme, U. & F. Becker.** Eds. 1907-50. Allgemeine Lexikon der bildenden Künstler von der Antike bis zür Gegenwart; unter Mitwirkung von 300 Fachgelehrten des In- und Auslandes. Leipzig. 36 vols. & suppl. Repr. Zwickau, 1964.

A418 **Imeson, W.E.** 1912. A dictionary of delineators. In: Illustrated music titles & their delineators. pp.22-46. London.
Incl. notes on printers as well as draughtsmen.

A419 **Rees, T.M.** 1912. Welsh painters, engravers, etc., 1527-1911. Carnarvon. 188pp.

A420 **Strickland, W.G.** 1913. A dictionary of Irish artists. Dublin. 2 vols. Repr. New York, 1968.

A421 **Hind, A.M.** 1923. Classified list of engravers: The British Isles. Index of engravers & individual bibliography. In: A history of engraving & etching from the 15th century to the year 1914. 3rd edn. pp.378-388 & 420-484. London. Repr. New York, 1963.

A422 **Heal, A.** 1927. The trade cards of engravers. Print Collector's Quarterly 14: 218-250. Also issued separately, 1928.

A423 **Newbolt, Sir F.G.** 1930. The history of the Royal Society of Painter--Etchers & Engravers 1880-1930. London. 271pp.
Incl. a chronological list of the membership.

A424 **Bushnell, G.H.** 1949. Scottish engravers: A biographical dictionary of Scottish engravers & of engravers who worked in Scotland to the beginning of the nineteenth century. London. xii+60pp.
An earlier version published in: Print Collector's Quarterly 16: 251-277, 1929 & 18: 288-296, 1931.

A425 **Grant, M.H.** 1952. Dictionary of British etchers. London. 232pp.
A very comprehensive list, but with rather brief entries for each.

A426 **Hammelmann, H.** 1975. Book illustrators in eighteenth century England. Ed. & completed by T.S.R. Boase. London & New Haven, Conn.. xiv+120pp.
Ca. 260 illustrators are included.

A427 **Benezit, E.** 1976. Dictionnaire critique et documentaire des peintres, sculpteurs, dessinateurs et graveurs de tous les temps et de tous les pays, par un groupe d'écrivains spécialistes français et étrangers. Nouv. [3rd] edn. entièrement refondu, rév. et corr. Paris. 10 vols.

A428 **Engen, R.K.** 1979. Dictionary of Victorian engravers, print publishers, & their works. Cambridge. 245pp.
Largely based on the Printsellers' Association lists (A362).

A429 **Hunnisett, B.** 1980. A dictionary of British steel engravers. Leigh-on-Sea. 148pp.

A430 **Guichard, K.M.** 1981. British etchers 1850-1940. 2nd edn. London. 82pp.

Bibliographies of monographs on printmakers

A431 **Levis, H.C.** 1912. Catalogues of prints by or after various artists. [&] Biographies & other monographs. In: A descriptive bibliography of the most important books in the English language relating to the art & history of engraving, pp.254-287, 295-326. London, 1912.
----- 1913. ----- In: ----- Supplement & index. pp.16-20, 22-24. London. Both repr. as 1 vol. London, 1974.

A432 **Colin, P.** 1918. La gravure et les graveurs: Les monographies. Bruxelles. viii+344pp. Repr. New York, 1978.
2,659 entries arranged alphabetically by artist.

A433 **Mason, L. & J. Ludman.** 1979. Print reference sources: A selected bibliography, 18th-20th centuries. 2nd edn. rev. & enl. Millwood, N.Y., 1979. xi+363pp.

Historical dictionaries of printers, etc.

A434 **Walton, J.** 1968. A survey of the printing trade & related occupations of Nottingham & Nottinghamshire to 1900. Library Association thesis. 1968. Photocopies are available in a few libraries, e.g. the St. bride Printing Library.

A435 **Todd, W.B.** 1972. A directory of printers & others in allied trades: London & vicinity 1800-1840. London. xxvii+234pp.
Incl. mention of copper-plate and lithographic printers.

A436 **Birmingham Bibliographical Society.** 1975+. Working papers for an historical directory of the West Midlands book trade to 1850. Birmingham. In progress.
No.1: To 1779; No.2: 1780-1789; No.3: 1790-1799 with addenda to nos. 1 & 2; No.4: 1800-1809; No.5: 1810-1819; No.6: ...

A437 **Hunt, C.J.** 1975. The book trade in Northumberland & Durham to 1860. Newcastle. xvii+116pp.
Supplemented by: **Wallis, P.J.** 1981. ----- : A supplement to C.J. Hunt's biographical dictionary. Newcastle. viii+60pp.

A438 **Wakeman, G. & G.D.R. Bridson.** 1975. A guide to nineteenth century colour printers. Loughborough. xii+127pp.

A439 **Twyman, M.** 1976. A directory of London lithographic printers, 1800-1850. Journal, Printing Historical Society 10: 1-55. Also issued separately, 1976.

A440 **Maxted, I.** 1977. The London book trades, 1775-1800: A preliminary checklist of members. Folkestone. xxxv+257pp.
See also (A442).

A441 **McKenzie, D.F.** 1978. Stationers' Company apprentices, 1701-1800. Oxford. xii+514pp.

A442 **Maxted, I.** 1980. The London book trades, 1775-1800: A topographical guide. Including a correction of major errors in the author's "Preliminary checklist of members". Exeter. 16pp. & 5 microfiches.
A companion to (A440).

A443 **Feather, J.** 1981. The English provincial book trade before 1850: A checklist of secondary sources. Oxford. vi+37pp. Publications, Oxford Bibliographical Society, no.16.

Contemporary directories of printers, etc.

A444 **Pendred, J.** [1785.] The earliest directory of the book trade [1785]. Ed. by G. Pollard. London, 1955. xxiv+90pp.
Incl. lists of engravers, copper-plate printers, etc., in addition to letterpress printers. Original edition entitled "The London & country printers, booksellers & stationers vade mecum".

A445 **Anon.** 1830. The literary blue book or kalendar of literature, science & art for MDCCCXXX. London.
Incl. lists of lithographic artists, line, mezzotinto, aquatinta, chalk, and wood engravers, pp.94-115.

A446 ----- 1849. The artists' almanac & handbook for artists & amateurs for 1850. London. 36pp.
Incl. lists of engravers, lithographers, designers on wood, engravers on wood, ornamental printers, copper and steel plate makers, and preparers of box-wood for engraving, pp.33-36.

A447 **Hodson, W.H.** 1855. Hodson's booksellers, publishers & stationers directory 1855. A facsimile of the copy in the Bodleian Library, Oxford. With an intro. by G. Pollard. Oxford, 1972. ix+viii+92pp.
Incl. lists of engravers on wood, lithographers [incl. printers and copper--plate printers], and printers [letterpress].

A448 **Kelly, F. & Co.** 1872+. Post office directory of stationers, printers, booksellers, publishers, & paper makers of England, Scotland, Wales, & the principal towns of Ireland. London.
Revised edns. were published in 1876 (not seen), 1880, 1885, 1889, 1893, 1896 (not seen), and 1900, with slight variations in title. Ireland was omitted from 1885. Incl. lists of copper-plate printers, copper-plate engravers, lithographers, litho-zincographers, draughtsmen (lithographic), photo--lithographers, oil-colour printers, wood engravers, draughtsmen (wood engraver's), automatic and photographic engravers, photographic engravers, process engravers, photographic printers, collotype printers, electrotypers, etc.

A449 **Amalgamated Society of Lithographic Artists, Designers & Writers, Copper-plate & Wood Engravers,** [Founded 1885]. 1888+. Reports. Manchester.
The 5th report for 1888 is the earliest one seen. Each incl. a list of lithographic firms and trademasters, lithographic artists and engravers, for all major towns in Great Britain.

A450 **Amalgamated Society of Lithographic Printers of Great Britain & Ireland,** [Founded 1880]. 1888/89+. Half-yearly report. Manchester.
The report for Sept. 1888 to Mar. 1889 is the earliest one seen. Each incl. a list of lithographic establishments for all the major towns.

A451 **Lamb, A.** [1888.] The British & foreign guide to the printing, stationery & fancy goods trades. Part 1: Paper, stationery, printing, bookbinding & photography. London.
Incl. lists of lithographers, chromo-lithographers, printers, etc.

Guides to directories

A452 **Goss, C.W.F.** 1932. The London directories 1677-1855: A bibliography with notes on their origin & development. London. xi+146pp.

A453 **Norton, J.E.** 1950. Guide to the national & provincial directories of England & Wales, excluding London, published before 1865. London. vii+241pp.
The intro. incl. information on the method of compilation of 19th century directories and advice on their use, together with suggestions for testing their reliability.

A454 Pollard, G. 1955. Appendix. [Guide to booktrade directories down to end of the 19th century.] In: Pendred, J. The earliest directory of the book trade [1785]. Ed. by G. Pollard. pp.49-90. London.
See also: Todd, W.B. 1956. [Review with addenda.] Papers, Bibliographical Society of America 50: 398-402.

Unpublished sources

Guidance on the existence and whereabouts of trade archives can be obtained from the National Register of Archives of the Royal Commission on Historical Manuscripts. Unpublished, and probably untapped, personnel records exist in the past membership records of Trade Unions. A brief list of unions active in the printing trade of the 1890's can be found in :

A455 Anon. 1894. Directory of trade societies, institutions, etc. Printing Times & Lithographer N.S.3: 112-113.

Section B: Intaglio plate processes

Ba Bibliographies

Many of the general bibliographies described in section Aa supra contain extensive listings of books on intaglio processes. Two specialised bibliographies are worthy of mention here. Hind (B1) includes a large number of works in his classified list but the entries are extremely concise and unannotated. Laver (B2) contains a fairly comprehensive general bibliography on etching and also a useful list of monographs on individual etchers.

B1 Hind, A.M. 1923. General bibliography. In: A history of engraving & etching from the 15th century to the year 1914. pp.393-419. London. Repr. New York, 1963.

B2 Laver, J. 1929. Bibliography. In: A history of British & American etching. pp.153-186. London.

Bb Engraving & etching techniques in general

Works in this section describe the whole range of hand-produced intaglio printmaking processes. They are complemented by items included in section Ab supra, several of which provide detailed coverage of engraving and etching techniques.

The great majority of titles listed below deal only with etching processes but there is none that treats solely of line-engraving. The latter process was the medium by which great numbers of prints were produced in the 18th and first half of the 19th centuries. However, most line engravers used etching as an integral part of their work. Preliminary etching of the plate was a normal procedure before "finishing" with the burin and additional strengthening of more forceful lines and tones was often achieved by supplementary biting-in. "Pure" line engraved plates were comparatively rare.

The early English works on engraving and etching are described in some detail by Levis (A7). Although our bibliography takes 1750 as its starting date we commence with some works of older vintage that were still widely used and quoted in the second half of the 18th century. Faithorne (B3), first published in 1662, was based on Bosse's earlier manual of 1645. It was the most authoritative work of its kind, providing comprehensive and practical information on all aspects of etching and line engraving (in that order) and its 2nd edn of 1702 was further enhanced by the addition of instructions on plate printing. The anonymous Sculptura Historico-Technica (B4) and Evelyn's Sculptura (B5) share credit with Faithorne for being widely used, the former going through four edns., the latter two. Evelyn's work was the least technical, paying more attention to history and aesthetics, but is notable for introducing mezzotint to the printmaking world. Dossie (B6) compiled a comprehensive handbook of crafts including a chapter on engraving (which would have merited separate publication) dealing with all the known methods of printmaking, even Le Blon's colour process.

After this impressive quartet the ensuing literature was dominated by works whose principal concern was etching. For a balanced treatment of both etching and line engraving one had to turn to the first three edns. of Encyclopaedia Britannica (A17 - A19), to the very good articles in Rees' Cyclopaedia (A20), to Partington's useful manual (A26), or various other encyclopaedias, until Fielding's comprehensive treatise appeared in 1841 (A28).

In later years the works of Stannard (A34), Hamerton (A42), and Singer & Strang (A52), provided adequate treatment of line-engraving along with the whole range of other graphic processes. Edns 4 to 9 of Encyclopaedia Britannica (A21 to A40) and Encyclopaedia Metropolitana (A32) also included line-engraving amongst their articles but their unwieldy size must have limited their convenience as sources of practical instruction.

Although etching was extensively employed in the commercial production of engraved illustrations there were no "trade" manuals of etching, those that exist were directed at amateurs or artists aspiring to produce works of art. Authors such as Alken, Hamerton, Lalanne, and Short were respected printmakers and their texts reflect the creative individuality of each. The books on etching range from little manuals such as Ashley's (B18) or Short's (B34) to weighty tomes like Koehler's (B33) which included much historical and critical metter in addition to the instructional text. Hamerton's works were apparently widely read, to judge by their several editions, ranging from his first notes on etching in 1866 (B21) through his manuals and treatises published over the next 15 years (B22 B25 B26 & B29). 1880 saw the foundation of the Royal Society of Painter Etchers & Engravers and manuals such as Lalanne (B28), Chattock (B31), Koehler (B33), Short (B34), Herkomer (B37), and Paton (B39) particularly address themselves to those who strove to achieve the society's creative ideals.

In the printing trade, meantime, etching techniques were beginning to take a significant part in the developing photo-mechanical reproduction processes. Etching for its own sake was scarcely mentioned in printing trade journals (B30) though, curiously enough, Paton's manual first appeared as a series of papers in the British Lithographer (B38). To judge by the other "trade" matter in that journal, Paton's work must have been oddly at variance with the likely interest of the readership. If a printer, or any other casually interested amateur, cared to dabble in etching he would be less likely to turn to Paton's detailed treatise than to one of the little practical manuals such as Robertson (B32) or Rhead (B36).

Other engraving processes such as chalk-style, stipple, drypoint, soft-ground etching, and the like are variously treated in a scatter of sources. Guidance on the location of descriptive accounts can be found by looking at the references given for each one in our "Index of processes".

Despite the fact that virtually every print or engraved book illustration within our period has an artist/engraver/publisher signature line, and usually a title also, there is apparently no British work which deals with the ubiquitous craft of letter-engraving. The American manual by Whelpley (B41) is the only work we can suggest for information on this craft.

For literature on photo-intaglio processes see section Ec <u>infra</u>.

B3 **Faithorne, W.** 1702. The art of graving & etching. Wherein is express'd the true way of graving in copper. The 2nd edn: To which is added, the way of printing copper-plates, & how to make the press. London. [vi]+72pp. & 16 pls. Repr. with an introduction by J. Kainen, New York, 1970, (comprising facsim. of the 1662 edn. and the 1702 suppl. on plate printing). 1st edn., 1662.
Largely based on A. Bosse's Traicté des manières de graveur en taille douce, Paris, 1645. Sections 1 to 24 deal with etching, methods of needling (incl. "the use of oval points to make large strokes in etching"), biting-in, etc. Sections 25 to 28 deal with line engraving with the burin. Illustrated by 10 pls., of which 3 demonstrate the grammar of etching & engraving. "The plates were so fundamentally informative, so beautifully engraved, that any reader could grasp their meaning at a glance", Kainen.

B4 **Anon.** 1747. Sculptura historico-technica: Or, the history & art of engraving. Containing, I. The rise & progress of engraving, II. Of engraving in general, III. Of engraving, etching, & scraping on copper, as now practised, [etc.] London. xii+225pp. & 10 pls. 2nd edn., ca. 1768; 3rd edn., 1766, xi+264pp. & 10 pls; 4th edn., 1770, xi+264pp. & 10 pls.
(Notes based on the 3rd. & 4th. edns.) Pp.20-45 deal with directions for conducting the strokes or cuts of the graver, and equality and harmony in the work; pp.47-81 deal with engraving with aqua fortis; pp.82-98 deal with soft varnish; pp.99-108 with the art of engraving; p.109 with mezzotinto. The pls. incl. demonstrations of the kinds of strokes and how to use oval points to make large strokes. The latter half of the book deals with print collecting and incl. lists of printmakers and their monograms.

B5 **Evelyn, J.** 1755. Sculptura: Or the history & art of chalcography & engraving in copper. 2nd edn.: Containing some corrections & additions taken from the margin of the Author's printed copy. London. [iii]+xxxvi+140pp. & 3 pls. 1st edn., 1662; 2nd edn. re-issued in 1759 & 1769 with altered t.p's. Repr. in: The miscellaneous writings of John Evelyn, ... now first collected with occasional notes by W. Upcott. pp.243-336. London, 1825; & again as: Evelyn's Sculptura; with the unpublished second part, edited by C.F. Bell, Oxford, 1906, xxiv+[xxxii]+151+viii+32pp.
(Notes based on the 2nd edn.) Pp.15-94 deal with the history of chalcography; pp.95-126 with drawing & design, and pp.127-129 with mezzotinto. One of the pls. is a copy, by Houston, of the mezzotint done by Prince Rupert for the 1st edn.

B6 **Dossie, R.** 1758. The handmaid to the arts. Vol. 2: Teaching ... Part II. The art of engraving, etching, & scraping mezzotintoes; with the preparation of the aquafortis, varnishes, or grounds etc. ... as also the manner of printing copper plates; ... & of printing in chiaro oscuro, & with colours, in the way practised by Mr. Le Blon. pp.41-218. London. 2nd edn., 1764, pp.43-222; New edn., 1796.
(Notes based on the 2nd edn.) Pp.54-76 describe working with the graver; pp.76-172 with etching, incl. details on the manner of engraving special subjects; pp.172-189 with mezzotinto and colour-printed impressions; pp.190-216 with plate printing; and pp.217-222 with wood engraving. The text of the 2nd edn. is a slightly revised version of the 1758 edn.

B7 **Anon.** 1788. The artist's assistant in drawing, perspective, etching, engraving, mezzotinto-scraping, [etc.] 5th edn. London. vii+48pp. & 2 pls. 1st edn., Birmingham, 1773.
A much reprinted elementary text. An edn. as late as 1814 was published in Gainsborough.

B8 ----- [1791.] Valuable secrets in arts & trades: Or approved directions from the best artists for the various methods of engraving, [etc.] London. v+351pp.
The 1st chapter deals with the art of engraving, incl. etching and line engraving, and details of engraving methods for metal decoration unrelated to printmaking.

B9 **Wilson, P.** 1798. Copy of a letter from Professor Wilson of Glasgow, on the art of multiplying copies of engraved plates & stamps in relief. Journal of Natural Philosophy, Chemistry & the Arts 2: 60-63.
A thin plate of glass has a design etched into it by the action of "fluor acid" and is then cemented to a metal plate ready for printing.

B10 **Hodson, T. & J. Dougall.** 1805. The cabinet of the arts, being a new & universal drawing book, forming a complete system of drawing, painting in all its branches, etching, engraving, ... Illustrated with upwards of sixty elegant engravings. London. vii+367pp. & 67 pls.
Bk. II: Of etching & engraving, pp.110-124; Bk. III: Of mezzotinto & aquatinta, pp.125-132. Bk. II incl. instructions on engraving "in chalk" (most of the plates are chalk-style engravings). 2nd edn., Ed. by J. Dougall, 1819-21, 2 vols. iii+384pp. & 130pls. Comprises a reprint of the 1805 text with the addition of a chapter on lithography, pp.373-384 & lith. pls.

B11 **Hassell, J.** 1811. Calcographia: Or, the art of multiplying, with perfection, drawings after the manner of chalk, black lead pencil, & pen & ink: Exemplified by ... specimens ... from drawings by ... Morland, Ibbetson, ... & Hassell. To which are added practical illustrations of the art of rebiting, [etc.] London. 37pp. & 8 pls.
A form of lift-ground etching.

B12 ----- 1811. Improvement in the aquatinta process, by which pen, pencil, & chalk drawings can be imitated. Transactions, Society of Arts 28: 97-105. Also pub. in: Journal of Natural Philosophy, Chemistry & the Arts 30: 220-226.
Despite its different title this describes the same process as the above item. Given on the occasion of his being awarded the Society of Arts silver medal.

B13 **Martin, T.** 1813. The circle of the mechanical arts: Containing practical treatises on the various manual arts, trades, & manufactures. London. vii+616pp.
Includes various kinds of engraving methods.

B14 **Hassell, J.** 1826. Graphic delineation: A practical treatise on the art of etching, or the manner of copying pictures & drawings, by a method at once scientific, tasteful, & amusing; to which are added instructions, detailing minutely the whole process of representation, from an outline to a finished print, ... illustrated with plates in progress, [etc.] London. 23pp. & 9 pls. Another edn., 1827.
In addition to 8 etchings "in progress" there is one demonstrating the method of "squaring" for copying a picture.

B15 **Hullmandel, C.** 1840. A new mode of preparing certain surfaces for being corroded with acids, in order to produce patterns & designs for the purpose of certain kinds of printing & transparencies. London Journal of Arts & Sciences, conjoined ser. 16: 257-263.
Patent specification for a method of etching by which a soluble mixture was used for making a freehand drawing on bare copper with a camel hair pencil. The plate was varnished, steeped in water which removed the drawn lines and the revealed copper was then etched. Also described a method of producing reticulate tonal effects, by means of a solution brushed over a thinly greased plate, which was used in conjunction with the first process.

B16 **Anon.** 1842. Engraving: Aqua tinta engraving: Aqua & mezzotinting: Line engraving: Engraving in imitation of black-lead or chalk. Magazine of Science 3: 132-133, 174-175, 205-206, 246-247, 277-278, 292, 331-332, 383-384, 398-399.
An informative series of articles dealing with materials and methods. Possibly by G. Francis, editor of the Magazine.

B17 **Alken, H.** 1849. The art & practice of etching, with directions for other methods of light & entertaining engraving. London. 59pp. & 9 pls. 2nd edn., 1851.
The pls. comprise 3 etch., 2 soft-gd. etch., and 4 aquat., and a full description of these processes.

B18 ----- [1849]. The art of etching on copper. London. v+18pp. & 12 pls. Another edn., 1851.
The pls. incl. an illustration of equipment and a series of progressive exercises in etching. Also describes etching on steel.

B19 **[Castle, C.]** 1849. Etching described & simplified, with progressive illustrations. By a practical engraver. London. 24pp.
Not seen.

B20 **Anon.** 1853. Engraving & printing on copper. Illustrated Magazine of Art 1: 168-173.

B21 **[Hamerton, P.G.]** 1866. About etching. Fine Arts Quarterly Review N.S.1: 145-160.

B22 **Hamerton, P.G.** 1868. Etching & etchers. London. xxvi+354pp. & 35 pls.
The pls. incl. original prints by master etchers. Book I deals with "powers & qualities of the art", Book V with processes, and the rest of the text discusses the work of English, French, and Dutch schools of etching.

B23 ----- 1870. Recent improvements in the process of etching. Portfolio 1: 188-189.

B24 **Shrubsole, W.G.** [1870.] Etching, its principles & practice: A book for students & amateurs. London. 68pp. & 2 pls. (Rowney Treatises on the Fine Arts, no. 28). 2nd edn., 18 ?; 3rd edn., [1889].
The pls. are etchings showing work in two states. Apart from the usual technical details Shrubsole gives very detailed notes on working the design on the plate incl. the use of the oval point and auxiliary methods of creating tints.

B25 **Hamerton, P.G.** 1871. The etcher's handbook: Giving an account of the old processes, & of processes recently discovered. London. viii+84pp. & 6 pls. 2nd edn., 1875. viii+94pp. & 6 pls.
The pls. comprise 5 etch. and a drypt. Hamerton's manual is essentially a technical guide, more concerned with materials and methods than with the grammar of etching, and incl. some of his own developments, such as positive (white) etching ground. The 2nd edn. adds a technical note on the preparation of each pl.

B26 ----- 1876. Etching & etchers. New edn. London. xxxi+459pp. & 12 pls. Repr. East Ardsley, 1975. 3rd edn., London, 1880. xxxiii+360pp. & 48 pls.
Appendix: Practical notes, pp.407-444. Incl. basic etching techniques used in making the pls. with special attention to biting, stopping-out and the chemistry of etching. The pls. in the 1876 edn. are all etchings done by the author and each is accompanied by technical notes on mordants used, length of biting, proofing and printing. The 1880 edn. is essentially a "de luxe" re-presentation of the 1876 edn. but with 26 new pls. (original prints by modern etchers and heliogravure copies of old masters).

B27 **Chattock, R.S.** 1880-82. Practical notes on etching. Etcher, Notes 1880: 9-10, 12, 14, 16-22, 24; 1881: 2, 4, 6, 8, 10-12, 15-18, 20, 22, 24; 1882: 2-4, 10, 12, 16, 18.
The first publication of the 1882 handbook (B31).

B28 **Lalanne, M.** 1880. A treatise on etching. Text & plates by Maxime Lalanne... translated from the 2nd French edn. by S.R. Koehler with an introductory chapter & notes by the translator. London. xxx+79pp. & 13 pls. Repr. as: The technique of etching. With an intro. by J.M. Fisher. New York, 1981. xxv+67pp. & 11 pls; 3rd edn., 1884; another edn., 1892. Orig. edn., Paris, 1866.
The pls. incl. a trial of various biting-in procedures, etchings with single and multiple bitings, soft ground etching, drypoint, and an etching printed clean-wiped and with retroussage. A masterly, detailed, account of technical & artistic etching procedures, auxiliary processes, and plate printing.

B29 **Hamerton, P.G.** 1881. The etcher's handbook ... giving an account of the old processes, & of processes recently discovered. 3rd edn., rev. & augm. London. xi+97pp. & 6 pls.
The pls. are the same as in the earlier edns. (B25).

B30 **Anon.** 1882. Etching for copper-plate printing. Printing Times & Lithographer N.S.8: 247-249.

B31 **Chattock, R.S.** 1882. Practical notes on etching. London. [v]+74p. & 8 pls. 2nd edn., 1883; 3rd edn., 1886.
The pls. comprise 7 etch. and a drypt. They incl. demonstrations of 2 etch. in 2 states, and an etch. printed clean-wiped and with retroussage. Good descriptions of methods of working the design on the plate, of auxiliary processes such as dry-point, re-biting and re-etching.

B32 **Robertson, H.R.** 1883. The art of etching explained & illustrated: With remarks on the allied processes of drypoint, mezzotint, & aquatint. London. 64pp. & 2 pls. (Winsor & Newton Shilling Handbooks on Art, no. 33). 2nd edn., 188?; 3rd edn., 188?; 4th edn., 1885.
Fairly elementary instructions directed at the amateur.

B33 **Koehler, S.R.** 1885. Etching, an outline of its technical processes & its history, with remarks on collections & collecting. London. xiv+238pp. & 30 pls.
An English issue of an American publication by the translator of Lalanne's Treatise. The pls. incl. 23 original and copy etch., a drypt., and 4 heliogr. facsims. One pl. demonstrates various etching techniques, 2 others show a print clean-wiped and printed with retroussage. Ch. I: The etching process; Ch. XII: Reproductive or interpretative etching; Ch. XIV: Making a trial plate; Ch. XV: Hints on drawing, biting, finishing, accidents, auxiliary processes, etc.; Ch. XVI: Printing. Other chapters deal with history and collecting. An excellently informative, if unwieldy, volume.

B34 **Short, F.** 1888. On the making of etchings. London. 34pp. & 4 pls. 2nd edn., 1893; 3rd edn., 1898, 43pp. & 4 pls.
A brief but authoritative statement of the method used by a master etcher.

B35 **Anon.** 1889. The art of stipple engraving. Paper & Printing Trades Journal no.68: 16-17.

B36 **Rhead, G.W.** 1890. Etching. London. xiv+77pp.
One of "Darton's Manuals for Home Work", which indicates its level. Incl. brief mention of drypoint, burin, roulette, mezzotint, aquatint, acid tint, sand grain, soft ground etching and flat sulphur tint processes.

B37 **Herkomer, H. von.** 1892. Etching & mezzotint engraving. London. vii+107pp. & 13 pls.
The pls. incl. 7 etch., (2 demonstrating printing with clean-wiping and retroussage), a drypt., a mezzo., and a "Spongotype". Lectures delivered at Oxford, incl. details of the author's invention for positive ground, the transfer, the work on the plate, biting, dry point, and printing. Herkomer's "Spongotype" method is a re-creation of Palmer's Electrotint: see Sampson (A119).

B38 **Paton, H.** 1892-94. Etching, drypoint, mezzotint. British Lithographer 2: 13-15, 49-51, 91-94, 120-123, 169-172, 201-203, 1892-93; 3: 13-15, 41-43, 89-92, 116-119, 145-148, 177-180, 1893-94.
These papers were revised and enlarged to form the following work (B39).

B39 ----- 1895. Etching, drypoint, mezzotint: The whole art of the painter-etcher. A practical treatise. London. xi+182+viiipp. & 12 pls. Another edn., 1909.
The pls. incl. 6 etch., (1 in 2 states and an etch. on zinc), a drypt., 2 mezzos., a soft-gd. etch., and an electrotyped monotype. Comprehensive coverage of "Process" and "Paraphernalia" for all intaglio printmaking processes, supplemented by a good account of plate printing.

B40 **Gamble, W.** 1900-01. A revolution in steel-plate engraving & printing. [&] The "Johnstonia" mechanical engraving process. Penrose Annual 6: 106-108, & 1 pl., 1900; 7: 145-147, & 1 pl., 1901.
By purely mechanical means a sketch or photo. was reproduced on a line engraved steel plate and printed on a power driven plate printing machine equipped with automatic wiping and inking. Printers had long tried to improve the expensive and time consuming hand-operated traditional methods but this solution arrived too late. Photo-mechanical methods totally eclipsed its potential.

B41 **Whelpley, G.F.** 1884. Practical instruction in the art of letter engraving: The gleanings of several experienced workmen. New York. vi+187pp. 2nd edn., 1894.
An American work which had no British edn. and consequently placed out of chronological sequence. There appears to be no British counterpart on this subject and it is not certain that the work was known in britain. Nevertheless, American practice was undoubtedly similar to ours..

Bc **Mezzotint & aquatint techniques**

For technical descriptions of the tonal processes of mezzotint and aquatint engraving it is usually necessary to turn to general works because there are very few specialised manuals.

Mezzotint is well described by Dossie (B6) but without the aid of illustrations of tools or methods. Almost all the encyclopaedias mentioned in section Ab *supra* include articles on mezzotint but they tend to be rather succinct and usually lack illustrations. Until the introduction of steel or steel-faced copper for mezzotints it was not possible to obtain the large numbers of impressions necessary for the edition of a textbook or encyclopaedia. However, by 1841 Fielding was able to provide one (in two states) in his comprehensive treatise (A28), and Encyclopaedia Metropolitana included one in 1845 (A32). Hamerton (A42) includes a fine example in his treatise but his text is principally concerned with aesthetic rather than technical details of the craft.

Harland (A48), in a manual directed at the practical printer, discusses mezzotint from a commercial standpoint and considers its application to photo-mechanical processes. The 1890's saw renewed interest in the creative use of the process and the publication of three useful texts, all illustrated by good examples. Herkomer (B45) devotes half his book to a masterly essay on his method and discusses its relation to printing, Paton (B39) gives a plainly factual account of materials and methods, and Singer & Strang (A52) include an adequate account of the process in their valuable treatise.

Aquatint was treated by most of the encyclopaedias and general treatises and in two special manuals. Spilsbury (B42) and Green (B43 B44) published a detailed description of the process as practised in its heyday. Hodson & Dougall (B10) give only a modest description of the process but their work contains several good examples of aquatint amongst its many plates of drawing patterns. Fielding (A28), Stannard (A34), and Singer & Strang (A52) each have good descriptions of techniques and all illustrate their texts with examples. Hamerton's treatise (A42) provides a fine specimen but accompanied by an untechnical account of the process.

B42 **[Spilsbury, F.]** 1794. The art of etching & aquatint, strictly laid down by the most approved masters, sufficiently enabling amateurs in drawing to transmit their works to posterity: Or, as amusements among their circle of friends. With a specimen of landscape & profile. By F. Yrubslips. London. 34pp., with pls.
Not seen.

B43 **Green, J.H.** 1801. The complete aquatinter; being the whole process of etching & engraving in aquatinta, the use of aquafortis, with all the tools necessary, together with upwards of fifty of the best receipts for grounds, varnishes, [etc.] Hatfield. iv+23pp. & 1 pl.
The pl. shows 9 specimens of aquat. grounds.

B44 ----- 1804. The complete aquatinter; being the whole process of etching & engraving in aquatinta, the method of using the aquafortis, with all the necessary tools; to which are added, upwards of sixty of the best receipts for grounds, varnishes, etc. 2nd edn., with ... improvements & additions. London. vii+27pp. & 4 pls. 3rd edn., 1810, is the same as the 2nd. but with a new frontis.
Incl. receipts for spirit, dust, sulphur and other aquat. grounds and a pl. demonstrating 12 different effects produced with different grounds. Describes etching and aquatint methods and illustrates them with a finished pl. Also soft ground receipts, etching, and methods, accompanied by 2 demonstration pls.

B45 **Herkomer, H.von.** 1892. Mezzotint. In: Etching & mezzotint engraving. pp.79-92, & 1 pl. London.
Good descriptions of the rocking tool, the mezzotint ground, and the interpretation of pictures. (For a fuller description see B37).

Bd Engraving & etching for security printing

The 19th century saw creation of a special branch of the printing industry for the production of bank-notes, security certificates, cheques, and postage stamps. Despite some early efforts to prove the superiority of relief methods intaglio printing proved to be most successful and reliable. Faced with the need for mass production, but hampered by the uneconomically slow traditional methods, inventors devised novel ways to mechanise and accelerate engraving methods, to perfect the creation of intricately inimitable designs, and to improve plate durability.

Several rival schemes were advanced but those of Jacob Perkins and his partners were to win the day. Their contributions included making machine turned engraved designs, the siderographic technique for transferring designs from one metal surface to another, and the use of hardened steel of great durability. These were admirably described and illustrated in their published patent specifications and other writings, viz. Dyer (B46 B47), Anon (B49), Perkins (B50) and Perkins et al. (B51). The measure of success of these methods may be judged from the account of their continued use for postage stamp manufacture over half a century later (B62). Several other early experiments in bank-note engraving were discussed in a Society of Arts report (B48), by Bradbury (B60 B61) and especially in Sharp's comprehensive survey (B59).

Another significant application of mechanical techniques for preparing engraved designs in the 1830's and 1840's was the process known as anaglyptography, or medallic engraving. This technique, by which low relief forms could be translated into flat images whilst preserving the three dimensional light-and-shade effects of the original, was typical of Victorian ingenuity. A special machine was required to "scan" the medal and to repeat each sweep as a transverse line on the engraved copy. The disputed claims and counterclaims of French and British inventors have left us with valuable accounts of methods and examples of their products (B52 to B58). Stannard included the process in his examplar (A34) and the description was reprinted in 1967 (B61*).

B46 Dyer, J.C. 1811. Specification of the patent granted to Joseph C. Dyer ... for certain improvements in the construction & method of using plates & presses, & for combining various species of works in the same plate, for the kind of printing usually called copper-plate printing designed for the object of detecting counterfeits, for multiplying impression, & saving labour. Repertory of Arts, Manufactures & Agriculture (2) 19: 257-267.

B47 ----- 1819. Specimens & description of Perkin's & Fairman's patent siderographic plan to prevent forgery, being the reports as made to the Commissioners for preventing the forgery of bank-notes. London.
Not seen.

B48 Society of Arts. 1819. Report of the committee of the Society of Arts ... together with the approved communications & evidence upon the same, relative to the mode of preventing the forgery of bank notes. London. iii+72pp. & 6 pls.
The "approved communications" are by T.B. Beaumont, T.C. Hansard, T. Ranson, Mr. Solly, and R. Williamson. The pls. incl. specimens of Hansard's typographic bank note, and Ransom's, Solly's, and Williamson's engraved notes.

B49 **Anon.** 1820. On Mr. Perkins's plan for preventing the forgery of bank notes. London Journal of Arts & Sciences 1: 64-66. Also: Messrs's Perkins's & Fairman's plan for preventing the forgery of bank notes, pp.101-108.

B50 **Perkins, J.** 1820. Certain machinery & implements applicable to transferring of engraved or other work from the surface of one piece of metal to another piece of metal; & to the forming of metallic dies & matrices. And also improvements in the construction & method of using plates & presses for bank notes & other papers, ... And also for certain machinery applicable to ornamental turning & engraving. London Journal of Arts & Sciences 1: 159-171, 256-266.
The patent specification.

B51 **Perkins, Fairman & Heath.** 1821. Certain parts of their siderographic process for multiplying copies of engravings, particularly with a view to the preventing of forgery. Transactions, Society of Arts 38: 47-56, & 2 pls. The pls. are specimens of the same engraved work; the first is one of the earliest impressions taken from the plate, the other is worked from the plate after 35,000 impressions had been taken from it, revealing little signs of wear..

B52 **Bate, J.** 1836. An improvement or improvements on machinery, applicable to the imitation of medals, sculpture, & other works of art executed in relief. London Journal of Arts & Sciences, conjoined ser. 7: 33-40, & 1 pl. The patent specification.

B53 **Anon.** 1836. Medallic engraving. Athenaeum 1836: 706-707, & 1 pl. Also pub. in: Mechanics' Magazine 26: 2-5, 1836.

B54 ----- 1836. Engraving medals by machinery. Mechanics' magazine 26: 332-340.
Minutes of evidence heard by the British Museum committee on medal engraving, including technical details.

B55 "H". 1837. Medal engraving by machinery - the English & French processes. Mechanics' Magazine 26: 475-478.
Comment on the minutes of the British Museum committee on medal engraving.

B56 **Nolte, V.** 1838. Memorial of facts connected with the history of medallic engraving & the process of M. Collas. London. 12pp. & 1 pl. Also issued with: The authors of England; a series of medallic portraits ... engraved ... by Achille Collas. London, 1838.

B57 **Anon.** 1842. Bates's Anaglyptography: Or, a machine for medallic engraving. Magazine of Science 3: 378-379.

B58 ----- 1845. Process of engraving by the Anaglyptograph. Art Union 7: 14, & 1 pl.
Bates's patent.

B59 **Sharp, G.** 1854. The Gilbart Prize Essay on the adaption of recent discoveries & inventions in science & art to the purposes of practical banking. 3rd edn. London. viii+365pp. & 100 pls.

1st & 2nd edns. not seen. In addition to much advice on bank buildings and equipment the author includes: Letter copying machines, pp.211-227, and Engraving & printing, prevention of forgery, pp.241-289. The pls. comprise a collection of trade samples and brochures, specimens of security printing by Perkins, Fisher, Jackson, Hawkins, Batho, Nissen & Parker, and Glynn & Appel, the last incl. eng., glyphogr., water-col. printing, anastatic printing, appelotypes, lith., etc. Also samples of bank-note paper.

B60 **Bradbury, H.** 1856. On the security & manufacture of bank notes. Journal, Society of Arts 4: 638-641.

B61 ----- 1856. On the security & manufacture of bank notes. London. iii+30pp. & 2 pls.
Gives a review of progress, strongly advocates line engraving, discusses surface printing, siderography. anastatic printing, photography, etc. and illustrates his ideas with 2 specimens of engraved notes. A new edn. of the above paper, based on a lecture given to the Royal Institution.

B61* **Stannard, W.J.** ca. 1860. Anaglyptography. [Repr. from the Art Exemplar (A34)]. Loughborough, 1967. ii+11pp. & 1 pl.
Accompanied by a contemporary print engr. by Collas' method.

B62 **Anon.** 1878-79. Postage stamps & their manufacture. Printers' Register 17: 128-129, 1878; 18: 74-75, 89-90, 1879.
Reference to methods used by Perkins, Bacon & Co.

Be **Miscellaneous special processes**

Several methods of intaglio plate preparation, based on electro-chemical principles, have already been mentioned in section Af supra and are also treated by Stannard (A34) and Knight (A37).

In the 1840's Palmer's electrotint was one of the most successful and its technique was revived in Herkomer's Spongotype, which he claimed as a new invention (B66). Pring used electricity to produce spark-etched designs on metal but seems to have been its only practitioner (B63). Wallis's process (B64) was a method for impressing an intaglio image into a metal plate from a drawing made with sticky ink dusted over with emery powder. Duchochois (B65) describes the advantages and technique of galvanic etching which, unlike a mordant, does not undercut fine line work and is thus of value in some kinds of photo-engraving.

For intaglio nature printing see section Ae supra.

B63 **Pring, J.A.** 1843. An account of a method of etching or engraving by means of voltaic electricity. London. Another edn., 1848, 16pp. & 2 pls.
"Via sicca" electro-etching, using a spark drawn between the plate and a metal stylus.

B64 **Wallis, G.** 1863. The new art of autotypography. Journal, Society of Arts 11: 374-381; also letters from Wallis & W. Dickes, Ibid: 403, 453.
Also pub. in: Typographic Advertiser 2: 6, 12-13, 1863; & Photographic News 7: 199-200, 212-214, 1863, with an editorial comment, p.193.

B65 **Duchochois, P.C.** 1890. Photo etchings by electricity. Printing Times & Lithographer N.S.16: 93-94.

B66 **Anon.** 1896. Professor Herkomer's new process. Stationery Trades' Journal 17: 63-64.
See also: Bolas, T. Palmer's electrotint of 1841 & Herkomer's "New Art" of 1896. Photographic Journal N.S. 20: 212-213, 1896.

Bf Plate printing

Literature on this most fundamental operation in intaglio printmaking is unusually sparse and one supposes that much was taught by example within specialist printing firms. Many engravers would have kept a simple rolling press in their studios with which they "proved" their own work and most manuals of engraving and etching touch upon printing methods. However, the production of whole editions of prints and the commercial printing of engraved illustrations for books was handled by specialist craftsmen or printing firms.

Faithorne added a good description of plate printing to the 1702 edition of his manual of engraving (B67) which covered all the essentials of the traditional craft. Evelyn wrote a description of the manner of printing which he read to a meeting of the Royal Society. The account was recorded in their Minute Book but not published at the time and it was not until 1906 that it was first printed as an accompaniment to a reprint of his Sculptura (B68). Dossie's 1758 account (B69), slightly enlarged in 1764, was to remain the most detailed text on the subject for several decades. Brief descriptions were included in some of the encyclopaedias (A17 to A40) but no detailed instruction was to appear in the British Isles for over a century. In France a commendably comprehensive manual was compiled by Messrs Berthiau & Boitard and published in 1837 (B71). It bears more than slight relevance for us since the authors visited several commercial printing offices in England whilst gathering material for the book.

By the 1880's the revival of creative etching craft, especially through the stimulus of the Society of Painter-Etchers, called for the publication of textbooks on creative printmaking in which copper-plate printing was given fairly detailed treatment. The Painter-Etchers placed great store on the printer's ability to "bring out" the finer qualities of their etchings and descriptions of plate printing from this period dwell on the niceties of effect that could be produced by carefully varied plate wiping. The accounts provided by Lalanne (B28), Chattock (B27 B31), and Koehler (B33), all reflect this interest and the last two each include etchings which demonstrate different wiping techniques. Many etchers at this time took to printing their own work because commercial printers, in the main, devoted their energies to mass--produced "clean-wiped" printing from steel, or steel-faced, plates. Some firms were experimenting with automatic plate inking and wiping machinery on power driver presses and especially those firms whose trade was in security work such as cheque and bank-note printing. On the other hand a handful of craft-conscious firms grew to specialise in "fine-art" plate printing. One of the most respected of their group was Frederick Goulding who has left us with some details of his approach to creative plate printing (B75). Menpes (B73) and Newbolt (B74), both etchers of note, contributed brief articles on the importance of this process in the furtherance of their art.

As already noted, there was no practical manual of commercial practice published in 19th century Britain. The sheer numbers of engravings printed in during the century indicate that there must have been an army of pressmen at work producing them, but the techniques of their craft were never committed to print. Even the accounts of "fine art" printing are superficial compared with

Berthiau & Boitard's manual. However, with the advance of the 20th century we find the publication of some admirable accounts of the finer points of plate printing. Since they generally appear to employ traditional procedures we may rely on them for information of value for an understanding of 19th century practices. Strang's texts (B77 B78) describe fine-art printing whilst Neale (B76), although American, explains commercial practices that were probably not so different from their English counterparts.

Towards the close of the 19th century a number of photo-intaglio process came into prominence and gave renewed life to the commercial plate-printing industry for a couple of decades (see section Ec infra).

B67 **Faithorne, W.** 1702. The way of printing copper plates, & withal how to make the press. In: The art of graving & etching ... 2nd edn. pp.[49-72], & pls.11-16. Repr. New York, 1970, as a supplement to a facsimile of the 1662 edn.
Gives a detailed description of the rolling press & the method of plate printing with informative illus.

B68 **Evelyn, J.** 1906. The construction of the rowling press & the manner how to work off the plates. In: Evelyn's Sculptura, with the unpublished second part. Ed. by C.F. Bell. Oxford. xxiv+[xxxii]+151+xiii+32pp.

B69 **Dossie, R.** 1758. The handmaid to the arts. Vol. 2: Teaching ... Part II. The art of engraving ... as also the manner of printing copper plates. pp.187-212. London. 2nd edn., 1764, pp.190-216; New edn., 1796.

B70 **Hansard, T.C.** 1825. Of the rolling-press, or copper-plate printing. In: Typographia. pp.801-804. London. Repr. London, 1966.

B71 **Berthiau, -. & -. Boitard.** [1837.] Nouveau manuel complet de l'imprimer en taille-douce. Paris. iv+320pp., & 4 pls. Repr. Paris, 1978.

B72 **Anon.** 1888. Fine art copper & steel-plate printing. Paper & Printing Trades Journal no.62: 9.

B73 **Menpes, M.** 1889. On the printing of etchings. Magazine of Art 1889: 328-333.

B74 **Newbolt, F.G.** 1906. The art of printing etchings. Studio 39: 134-141.

B75 **Goulding, F.** 1910. Theory & practice. A lecture on "Copper-Plate Printing" delivered by Goulding at the Art Workers' Guild, and his "Notes on Printing". In: Hardie, M. Frederick Goulding: Master printer of copper plates. pp.67-104. Stirling. 167pp.

B76 **Neale, H.S.** 1927. The art of plate printing, with an historical sketch by T. A. Isert. Springfield, Mass. 65pp.
Covers the following techniques: Small dry work, Large dry work, Semi-wet work, Small wet work, Large wet work, Parchment, and India proofs. Concerned with commercial rather than artistic printing.

B77 **Strang, D.** 1930. The printing of etchings & engravings. With an introduction by M. Hardie. London. x+230pp.
A detailed treatise on all practical and artistic aspects of the craft.

B78 **Strang, D.** 1939. Etchings: Good proofs & bad. Print Collectors' Quarterly 26: 136-159.

B79 ----- 1941. Etching. Part 3: The printer proves the plate. Print 2 (3/4): 101-112.
With 11 collo. reproductions of the trial proofs pulled before the desired effect was achieved and the edition commenced.

Bg Plate printing in colour

The most sophisticated and elaborate process for intaglio printing in colour dates back to the early 18th century. J.C. Le Blon devised a method of using three mezzotint plates to print the separate colours using the tri-chromatic principle (B80). Although his book appeared well before our mid-century starting date it was discussed by several subsequent writers and provided them with an impressive example of the capabilities of colour printing using advanced colour theory. Mortimer (B81) and the two editions of Dossie (B82) kept Le Blon's ideas alive in print, if not in practice, but no British printer employed his method. Meanwhile Le Blon took his process to France and achieved some success with it there. His book was re-published there in 1756.

Laurie (B38), Paton (B86), and Ligeron (B87) advocated the à la poupée method, though Laurie provided little practical information. Despite the widespread use of this method in the prolific late 18th century period of colour-print production there is no practical account of contemporary techniques. At the end of the 19th century there was a revival of a la poupee printing amongst artist printmakers, as reflected in Paton's manual (B86). However, for the only comprehensive account of à la poupée printing techniques we have to look to the 20th century work of a Frenchman, Blanc (B87).

Presumably in imitation of the ubiquitous tinted lithograph of his day, Griffiths (B84) introduced an unimaginative patent for printing a single-colour tint on engravings which was used for a few mid-century book illustrations.

Die stamped colour printing was quite extensively used for small devices, trademarks, and the like, in later 19th century commercial and fancy stationery production. This form of intaglio work scarcely qualifies as "picture printing" though the term "cameo work" was sometimes applied to it. The methods of working the process are described in some detail by Herrick (B85).

B80 **Le Blon, J.C.** [1723-26.] Coloritto: Or the harmony of colouring in painting; reduced to mechanical practice, under easy precepts & infallible rules; together with some colour'd figures, in order to render the said precepts & rules intelligible, not only to painters but even to all lovers of painting. London. vii+6-27pp. & 9 pls.
Text in English and French. The pls. incl. a series of colour separations and progressive proofs of a 3-col. mezzo. The same text (but not pls.) also pub. as "L'art d'imprimer les tableaux." Paris, 1756. 71+[vi]pp. & 3 pls. Repr. New York, 1980. xx+71+[vi]pp & 1 pl., with an intro. by F. Birren.

B81 **Mortimer, C.** 1732. An account of Mr. James Christopher Le Blon's principles of printing, in imitation of painting, [etc.] Philosophical Transactions, Royal Society of London 37: 101-103.

B82 **Dossie, R.** 1758. The handmaid to the arts. Vol. 2: Teaching ... Part II. The art of engraving ...; & of printing ... with colours, in the way practised by Mr. Le Blon. pp.179-186. London. 2nd edn., pp.182-189, 1764; New edn., 1796.

B83 **Laurie, R.** 1789. Account of a method of printing mezzotinto prints in colours, as communicated to the Society of Arts in the year 1776. Transactions, Society of Arts 2 (2nd edn.): 145-148.

B84 **Griffiths, H.** 1840. Improvements in the process of producing prints or impressions from steel, copper, or other plates. London Journal of Arts & Sciences, conjoined ser. 16: 42-44.
The patent specification.

B85 **Herrick, T.P.** Ed. 1908? Embossing, blocking & die stamping: A practical guide to these processes. 2nd edn. London & Leicester. 76pp.
Compiled from various articles first published in the British Printer.

B86 **Paton, H.** 1909. Colour etching. London. ii+23pp. & 2 pls. Repr. from his: Etching, drypoint, mezzotint. 2nd edn., with an added chapter on colour etching. Ch. XVI, pp.183-205. London, 1909.
The pls. demonstrate à la poupée colour printing of etchings.

B87 **Ligeron, R.** 1931. Original engraving in colours. Translated from the French by F.L. Emanuel. 3rd edn. Paris. [iv]+165pp. & 5 pls.
Describes etching, soft-ground, aquatint, sugar-aquatint, multi-plate colour engraving, single-plate colour printing. The work includes an appendix on printing by Charles Blanc. The pls. demonstrate pure etch., soft-gd., sugar aquat., 7 kinds of aquat. gd., and the monochrome and colour-printed states of an à la poupée colour etch.

Bh Engravers' equipment & materials

Little attention is generally paid to what may be termed "the engraver's secret armoury" of gadgets and equipment. Most modern accounts of 18th and 19th century engraving omit mention of such devices as ruling machines and pantographs, give little information on engraving tools and etching mordants, and (with the exception of Hunnisett (B174)), generally fail to record the efforts that were being made to improve the durability of the engraver's plate. For those who made a living out of engraving these were important to their trade and the contemporary literature, though scattered and sometimes not wholly informative, does indicate the continuing interest in technical aids for the craftsman.

Rees (A20) includes a useful article describing the manufacture of copper-plate as practised at the turn of the 18th century. Further developments are reported by Anon (B107) and Hamerton (B119), while Anon (B129) provides a good account of manufacture at the end of the 19th century. Efforts to improve the durability of plates led to the introduction of steel in the 1820's and Lupton (B94), Warren (B95), "Caelator" (B96), Turner (B97), Anon. (B104), and Hunt (B111) elaborate on the properties and use of steel plates over three decades.

Meanwhile other developments were taking place which were to result in the more sophisticated technique of electro-chemical steel-facing of copper plates. Joubert (B113) introduced the process to England and Meidinger

(B114), Anon. (B121), Richmond (B128), and Waterhouse (B131) chart its progress down to the time when steel-facing became an everyday part of photo--engraving. Bradbury (B116) and Waterhouse (B118) describe the assistance that electro-chemical methods could provide to the engraver's work. The several kinds of burins, etching needles, and other specialised hand tools are described in most treatises and manuals of engraving and etching. The Victoria & Albert catalogue (B130) lists the range used in the heyday of the painter-etcher but for the most detailed and well illustrated account of the variety of forms of the burin one must turn to Haley's illustrated article (B132), although published well outside our period.

One of the most impressive technical gadgets for the engraver was the ruling machine, first designed by Wilson Lowry in about 1790. He prepared many of the plates in Rees's Cyclopaedia with its aid and demonstrated its efficiency for mechanical draughtsmanship. Lowry never published a description of his machine but Nicholson (B88) makes a comparison between Lowry's machine and his own and gives us some hints as to its construction. Over succeeding years others made experimental and functional ruling machines capable of ever more sophisticated work. In the 19th century ruling machines contributed much of the basic background work in engraving (often most evident in the skies of topographical prints) but the extent of their role is rarely acknowledged today. Ruling machines, pantographs, and pattern copying devices are the subject of papers by Nicholson (B88), Harrison (B92), White (B93), Heath (B100), Baggs (B101), "Graphus" (B102), Anon (B103), Warner (B106), Hunt (B108), Swan (B112), and Anon (B124 - B126). They describe a curious diversity of gadgetry extending over nearly a century of the history of craft engraving and commercial printing. Machines capable of impressing intaglio designs are described by Rochon (B89) and Becker (B109 B110). Two different ways of using photography to assist in the preparation of designs on engraving plates are described by Buss (B115) and Waterhouse (B122).

Mordants and etching grounds are frequently described in textbooks on etching and articles by "Caelator" (B96), Humphrys (B98), Anon (B105 B117), and Waterhouse (B123) serve to supplement them, the last one being a particularly scholarly survey.

The copper-plate press, despite its fundamental importance, is usually given rather sketchy treatment in most textbooks. It seems to have undergone relatively slight improvement over many decades. Kirkwood (B90) and Solly (B91) describe improvements to the traditional press which was to remain hand--operated for most of the century. Power driven machines were not introduced until the 1880's and then only in specialised applications. Anon (B120 B127) give little more than tempting glimpses of these developments in the different fields of cartographic and security printing.

For illustrations and other information of a wide variety of equipment reference should be made to several of the trade catalogues described in section Ah <u>supra</u>.

B88 **Nicholson, W.** 1799. Description of a new instrument for drawing equidistant & other parallel lines with great accuracy & expedition; intended principally for the use of engravers. Journal of Natural Philosophy, Chemistry & the Arts 2: 429-431, & 1 pl. Also: On Mr. Lowry's ruling machine. Ibid., p.524.

Instrument consisting of two flat rulers, one of which confines the plate, the other is made to shift through small intervals by means of the screw and gear, while it constantly preserves its parallelism.

B89 **Rochon, A.** 1799. A memoir on the typographic art. Journal of Natural Philosophy, Chemistry & the Arts 3: 61-73, & 1 pl.
Concerning a new machine which was designed to impress letterforms into copper plates, letter by letter - a sort of type engraver.

B90 **Kirkwood, R.** 1803. Certain improvements on the copper-plate press. Repertory of Arts, Manufactures & Agriculture (2) 3: 245-248, & 1 pl.
The patent specification.

B91 **Solly, Mr.** 1819. (Description of the improved copper-plate printing press for bank notes.) In: Society of Arts, Report of the committee ... relative to the mode of preventing the forgery of bank notes. pp.55-59, 1 pl. London.
For a description of the book see (B48).

B92 **Harrison, A.** 1821. A parallel rule for the use of engravers. Transactions, Society of Arts 38: 45-46, & 1 pl.

B93 **White, J.** 1822. Of a retrograph, or a machine to write backwards, for engravers. In: A new century of inventions, being designs & descriptions of one hundred machines relative to the arts, manufactures, & domestic life. pp.164-165, & pl. 19. Manchester.
A form of pantograph designed to produce a reversed copy of a traced handwriting.

B94 **Lupton, T.G.** 1823. Engraving in mezzotinto on steel. Transactions, Society of Arts 40: 41-43.
On the occasion of his being awarded the Society of Arts Medal.

B95 **Warren, C.** 1823. Engraving on steel plate. Transactions, Society of Arts 41: 88-95.
On the occasion of his being awarded the Society of Arts Medal.

B96 **"Caelator".** 1824. (New method of biting etchings on steel.) London Journal of Arts & Sciences 8: 21-25.

B97 **Turner, C.** 1824. On the invention, progress & advantages of the art of engraving in mezzotint upon steel. Transactions, Society of Arts 42: 55-57.

B98 **Humphrys, W.** 1826. Menstruum for biting-in on plates of soft steel. Transactions, Society of Arts 44: 53-55. Also pub. in: London Journal of Arts & Sciences 13: 42-43, 1827.
A mordant composed of corrosive sublimate, alum, and water.

B99 **Christ, J.G.** 1828. Certain improvements in copper & other plate printing. London Journal of Arts & Sciences (2) 1: 229-230. Also pub. in: Repertory of Arts & Sciences (3) 6: 254-256.
The patent specification. Describes the employment of enamelled card for obtaining the sharpest impressions.

B100 **Heath, P.** 1838. Engravers' ruling machine. Transactions, Society of Arts 51: 25-36.

B101 **Baggs, I.** 1841. Improvements in engraving, which improvements are applicable to lithography. Repertory of Patent Inventions N.S.15: 65-71, & 1 pl.
The patent specification. A machine for making simultaneous multiple engravings in exact imitation of a master design.

B102 **"Graphus".** 1841. Ruling machines. Magazine of Science 2: 21.

B103 **Anon.** 1841. MacLaurin's machine for stump engraving. Magazine of Science 2: 210.
A device, with both tracing point and etching needle, for copying a reduced version of an image onto a grounded plate for etching.

B104 ----- 1842. Steel plates for engraving. Magazine of Science 3: 59-61.
Method of manufacture and general history of use.

B105 ----- 1843. Etching ground for engravers. Magazine of Science 4: 127-128.
Possibly by G. Francis, editor of the magazine, who was also an etcher.

B106 **Warner, J.F.** 1843. Improving ruling machine for engravers. Transactions, Society of Arts 54: 3-7.

B107 **Anon.** 1847. Engravers' plates. Art Union 9: 362.
Improved quality copper plates without flaws, manufactured by Sellers of Sheffield.

B108 **Hunt, R.** 1848. On the applications of science to the fine & useful arts. Machine for engraving from the statue. Art Union 10: 363-364, & specimen pl.
Stokes's improved version of Bate's engraving machine; cf. (B58).

B109 **Becker, F.P.** 1849. The respectful remonstrations of Francis Paul Becker, patentee of The Omnigraph for engraving letters etc.; addressed to the Honourable The Board Of Science. n.p. 7pp.
The text indicates that it was accompanied by a "Memorial" which we could not locate for inspection (possibly the following item).

B110 ----- [1850.] Specimens of engraving by the omnigraph. London.
Not seen.

B111 **Hunt, R.** 1850. On the application of science to the fine & useful arts: Steel plates for engravings. Art Journal 12: 230-232.

B112 **Swan, J.** 1853. Improvements in the production of figured surfaces, & in printing, & in the machinery or apparatus used therein. Mechanics' Magazine 58: 37.
Abstract of the patent specification. An engraving machine working on the pantograph principle..

B113 **Joubert, F.** 1858. On a method of rendering engraved copper-plates capable of producing a greatly increased number of impressions. Journal, Society of Arts 7: 15-20; also letters on electro-deposition from: H. Bradbury, G.T. Doo, F. Joubert, F.W. Kirby, H.W. Reveley, pp.172-173, 189,

203, 221, 236-237, 601-602, 612-613, 625. Also pub. (without the letters) in: Photographic News 1: 147-150, 1858-59; & Journal, Photographic Society 6: 31-36, 1859.

B114 **Meidinger, H.** 1859. On the coating of engraved copper plates with iron by the galvanoplastic process. Journal, Photographic Society 6: 36-37.

B115 **Buss, R.W.** 1859. (Letter). Photography applied to engraving. Journal, Photographic Society 5: 301-302.
Note on the engraver's use of photography in preference to "squaring" in making an accurate copy of an image.

B116 **Bradbury, H.** 1860. Electro copies of engraved steel plates. Journal, Society of Arts 8: 444-445.

B117 **Anon.** 1866. On the various methods of engraving photographic pictures obtained upon metals & stone. Photographic News 10: 428-429.
On etching mordants.

B118 **Waterhouse, J.** 1874. On the application of electro-deposition to the correction of engraved copper plates. Proceedings, Asiatic Society of Bengal 1874: 2-7, & 1 pl.

B119 **Hamerton, P.G.** 1875. Technical note. Thin plates for etching. Portfolio 6: 122.

B120 **Anon.** 1880. Messrs. Bradbury, Wilkinson & Co.'s engraving & plate printing works. British & Colonial Printer 4: 24, & 1 pl.
The pl. shows their modified Guy-Marinoni power-driven plate-printing machine, equipped with automatic inking and plate-wiping facilities, and capable of printing between 8 & 15 impressions a minute.

B121 ----- 1882. Steel & iron facing. Printing Times & Lithographer N.S.8: 110-112.

B122 **Waterhouse, J.** 1882. Photographing on copper. Journal, Photographic Society N.S.6: 100-101.
As a means of transferring complicated designs to the plate prior to making the engraving.

B123 ----- 1882. On etching fluids. Photographic News 26: 166-167, 246-247, 370-372.
Mordants for steel, copper and zinc.

B124 **Anon.** 1885. Note of Lotte's ruling machine. Printing Times & Lithographer N.S.11: 120.

B125 ----- 1885. A new engraving machine. Printing Times & Lithographer N.S.11: 176.
Carter's machine.

B126 ----- 1885. The romance of a machine. Modern Printer 1885: 12-13.
Bellman's ruling machine for tint engraving.

B127 **Anon.** 1888. Trade notes: Copperplate printing machine. Paper & Printing Trades Journal no.62: 36.
Describes & illustrates the massive steam powered press, built by Furnival & Co. for the Ordnance Survey Department, for the purpose of printing map sizes up to 38.5 x 26.5 in.

B128 **Richmond, W.D.** 1892. Acierage of copper-plates. Printing Times & Lithographer N.S.1: 34-35, 97-99.

B129 **Anon.** 1899. British copper plate. Process Photogram 6: 33-35.
Method of manufacture.

B130 **Victoria & Albert Museum.** 1904. Tools & materials used in etching & engraving: A descriptive catalogue of a collection exhibited in the Museum. [By F. Short.] London. 16pp.

B131 **Waterhouse, J.** 1906. Steel facing of engraved copper plates. Penrose Annual 11: 53-56.

B132 **Haley, J.** 1939-40. My friend the graver. Proceedings, National Picture Print Society etc. 5: 22-30, 1939-40; 6: 23-30, 1940-41.

Bi Miscellaneous literature

A selection of writings which have little concern with the technique of etching or engraving, but rather illustrate the discussion and argument over such topica as, the claim of engraving to rank as a fine art, the professional status of engravers, the decline of trade engraving and the rise of painter-etching.

Gilpin (B133), Landser (B135), Meadows (B138), and Craig (B139) speak of engraving as a fine art or of the right of engravers to be accorded full membership of the Royal Academy, a disputed question. The Academy's refusal stimulated engravers to gain greater public recognition and to organise their profession as shown by Society of Engravers' rules (B134) and the comments of Landseer (B136), Sharp (B137), and Pye (B142 B144).

The Photographic Protection Society's pamphlet (B145) reveals a concern over the supposed threat that the photographic multiplication of engravings could pose to the print trade.

Later in the century etching underwent a great revival in the hands of a group of creative printmakers who saw the medium as capable of achieving works of equal merit to any of the accepted "fine" arts and once again the question of Royal Academy membership was argued. The champion and chief spokesman for this view was Haden and it was he who was to become founder-member and President of the Society of Painter-Etchers which sought to give proper status to these artists (B147 to B149 & B152). Wallace (B153) also touched upon the question of their status.

Other comment on the position of engravers and appreciations of their contributions can be found in Anon (B140 B141 B150 B151), Burnet (B143), Ruskin (B146) and Wedmore (B154).

B133 **Gilpin, W.** 1768. An essay upon prints, containing remarks upon the principles of picturesque beauty, the different kinds of prints & the characters of the most noted masters: Illustrated by criticism upon particular

pieces. To which are added some cautions that may be useful in collecting prints. London. 260pp. 2nd edn, 1768. xii+257pp.; 3rd edn., 1781. xv+256pp.; 4th edn., 1792, xv+187pp.
Ch. II: Observations on the different kinds of prints, pp.47-60.

B134 **Society of Engravers.** 1804. The rules, orders & regulations of the Society of Engravers; instituted at London, 1802: Under the immediate patronage of His Royal Highness the Prince of Wales. London. 70pp.
Also: Abstract of the Rules ... London, [1805?].

B135 **Landseer, J.** 1807. Lectures on the art of engraving. London. xxxviii+341pp.

B136 ----- 1810. A letter to a member of the Society for Encouraging the Art of Engraving in objection to a scheme of patronage now under consideration & written with a view to its improvement. London. 44pp.
----- 1810. A second & a third letter to a member of the Society for Encouraging the Art of Engraving. London. pp.45-77.

B137 **Sharp, W.** 1810. (Letter to Mr. Charles Warren, 29th May 1810, apropos the plan for the formation of a Society for the Encouragement of Engraving). First pub. in: Levis, H.C. A descriptive bibliography of the most important books in the English language relating to the art & history of engraving [etc.] pp.96-99. London, 1912.

B138 **Meadows, R.M.** 1811. Three lectures on engraving, delivered at the Surrey Institution in the year 1809. London. viii+88pp.

B139 **Craig, W.M.** 1821. A course of lectures in drawing, painting & engraving, considered as branches of elegant education. London. ix+451pp., & 5 pls.
The pls. comprise an aquatint printed in four stages of tinting and hand-colouring. Lecture VII deals with the means, objects, and pretensions of various styles of engraving.

B140 **Anon.** 1832. On etching & the several styles of engraving. Library of the Fine Arts 2: 193-201, 273-277.

B141 ----- 1832. The British school of engraving. Library of the Fine Arts 2: 379-390; 3: 1-16, 67-77.

B142 **Pye, J.** 1836. Evidence relating to the art of engraving, taken before the Select Committee of the House of Commons, on Arts, 1836; & the Committee's report made to the House thereon. Reprinted, together with the petition of engravers which led to that evidence being taken. To which is prefixed, a brief account of the connexion of engraving with the Royal Academy of Arts of London. London. 46pp.

B143 **Burnet, J.** 1839. The comparative merits of line engraving & mezzotinto. Art Union 1839: 57-58. Also repr. in his: Practical essays on various branches of the fine arts. pp.133-148. London, 1848.

B144 **Pye, J.** 1845. Patronage of British art, or historical sketch: Comprising an account of the rise & progress of art & artists in London from the beginning of the reign of George the Second. London. x+422pp. Repr. with an introduction by R.W. Lightbown, London, 1970.

B145 **Photographic Protection Society.** 1865. Copyright in engravings: Or the law & its alleged infringement. London. 19pp.

B146 **Ruskin, J.** 1876. Ariadne Florentina: Six lectures on wood & metal engraving; with appendix. Given before the University of Oxford in Michaelmas Term, 1872. Sunnyside. 263pp. First issued in 7 parts, 1873-76. Repr., with annotations, in: Cook, E.T. & A. Wedderburn, Eds. The works of John Ruskin. Vol. 22, pp.289-490. London, 1906. Various other separate edns.

B147 **Haden, F.S.** 1878. About etching. Part 1: Notes ... on a collection of etchings & engravings by the Great Masters ... to illustrate the subject of etching. Part 2: An annotated catalogue of the examples illustrative of Painter-Engravers' work. London. 78pp. & 16 pls. 2nd edn., 18 ?; 3rd edn., 1881. 59pp.

B148 ----- 1883. The relative claims of etching & engraving to rank as fine arts. Journal, Society of Arts 31: 714-723. Also pub. in: Printing Times & Lithographer N.S.9: 147-149, 176-178, 1883.

B149 ----- 1883. The relative claims of etching & engraving to rank as fine arts & to be represented as such in the Royal Academy of Arts. London. 26pp. & 4 pls.
Incl. a list of painter-etchers, the lecture delivered to the Society of Arts (B148), and 4 pls. providing a comparative study of the handling of foreground, flesh, drapery, stems, foliage, and sky, by different etchers.

B150 **Anon.** 1884. Decay of the art of engraving in England. Printing Times & Lithographer N.S.10: 39-40.

B151 ----- 1884. The decay of the art of engraving. Stationer, Printer, & Fancy Trades' Register 1884 (July): 479-480.

B152 **Haden, F.S.** 1890. The art of the painter-etcher ... being the Presidential Address of the Royal Society of Painter-Etchers for 1890. London. 16pp.

B153 **Wallace, L.** 1895. The position of the painter-etcher. Artist 16: 185-187.

B154 **Wedmore, F.** 1903. Right principles in etching. Printseller & Collector 1: 28-29.

Historical

Bj General history of engraving & etching

Several of the general histories of printmaking listed in section Ao supra complement the special histories mentioned below. We have provided a selection of the many works which exist, emphasizing those which record British contributions. The most comprehensive, authoritative and widely known is that by Hind (B165). Lippmann (B160) and Salaman (B161) are also replete with historical information.

Etching has stimulated several histories, some by authors who were etchers in their own right. Hamerton (B155), Wedmore (B157 B162), Simpson (B163), Pennell (B166), Sparrow (B167), and Laver (B168) provide good coverage of British work. However, most are written from an aesthetic standpoint with interests of the critic and collector in mind rather than the historian of printmaking technique.

Specialised studies on individual printmaking processes can be found in Clulow (B158) and Beck (B173) for line engraving, Hunnisett (B174) for steel engraving, Hind (B164) for soft-ground etching, Harvey (B169) for stipple engraving, and Mackenzie (B171) and Harris (B172) for bank-note engraving.

A wide range of experimental and unconventional methods of intaglio printing are admirably covered in Harris (A265) and Wakeman (A268).

B155 **Hamerton, P.G.** 1880. Etchers & etching. 3rd edn. London. xxxiii+360pp. & 48 pls. 1st edn., 1868; 2nd edn., 1876.
Bk IV: The English school.

B156 **Vacher, F.** 1888. Engravers & engraving. Inaugural address, Birkenhead Literary & Scientific Society, Session XXXI, 1887/88. Manchester. vii+106pp. & 5 pls.

B157 **Wedmore, F.** 1895. Etching in England. London. xiv+184pp.

B158 **Clulow, G.** 1897. A half century of line engraving, 1780-1830. Journal, Society of Arts 45: 604-610.

B159 **Holme, C.** Ed. 1902. Modern etching & engraving (European & American). London. Various paging.
The chapter on Great Britain is by A.L. Baldry.

B160 **Lippmann, F.** 1906. Engraving & etching: A handbook for the use of students & print collectors. 3rd edn., rev. by M. Lehrs. Translated from the German by M. Hardie. London. xvii+319pp.

B161 **Salaman, M.C.** 1906. The old engravers of England; in their relation to contemporary life and art (1540-1800). London. viii+224pp.

B162 **Wedmore, F.** 1912. Etchings. 2nd edn. London. xiii+237pp. & 44 pls. 1st edn, 1911.
The pls. are collo. reproductions. Ch. XVIII to XXVI deal with English etching.

B163 **Simpson, T.** 1919. Modern etchings & their collectors. London. 98pp.

B164 **Hind, A.M.** 1921. Notes on the history of soft-ground etching, [etc.] Print Collector's Quarterly 8: 377-405.

B165 ----- 1923. A history of engraving & etching from the 15th century to the year 1914. 3rd edn. London. xviii+487pp. Repr. New York, 1963. 1st edn., 1908.
Incl. engraving in the widest sense -- line engraving, etching, and tone processes (mezzotint, crayon manner & stipple, aquatint, and colour-prints).

B166 **Pennell, J.** 1926. Etchers & etching: Chapters in the history of the art together with technical explanations of modern artistic methods. 4th edn. London. xxxv+343pp. & 52 pls. Repr. 1929, 1931, 1936. 1st edn. 1919.
The pls. are photogr. and h-tone reproductions.

B167 **Sparrow, W.S.** 1926. A book of British etching from Francis Barlow to Francis Seymour Haden. London. xvi+227pp.

B168 **Laver, J.** 1929. History of British & American etching. London. xiv+195pp. & 84 pls.
The pls. are collo. reproductions.

B169 **Harvey, F.** 1930. Stipple engraving as practised in England, 1760-1810. Print Collector's Quarterly 17: 48-71.

B170 **Williams, I.A.** 1936. English book illustration, 1700-1775. Library (4) 17: 1-21.

B171 **Mackenzie, A.D.** 1953. The Bank of England note: A history of its printing. Cambridge. x+163pp.

B172 **Harris, E.** 1970. Jacob Perkins, William Congreve, & counterfeit printing in 1820. In: Morse, J.D. Ed. Prints in & of America to 1850: Winterthur Conference report, 1970. pp.193-214. Charlottesville, Va.

B173 **Beck, H.** 1973. Victorian engravings. London. 75pp.
Well illustrated survey of line-engraved work with photo-enlargements of details from several prints.

B174 **Hunnisett, B.** 1980. Steel-engraved book illustration in England. London. xvi+263pp.

Bk History of mezzotint & aquatint

Both these processes are included in most of the general histories of engraving already mentioned.

Chelsum (B175) and Russell (B185) cover the earlier period of mezzotint while Whitman (B177) and Davenport (B179) each provide general, well illustrated, histories of the art with emphasis on the needs of print collectors. Salaman (B182) is little more than an introductory essay followed by a gallery of reproductions. Most of the work of the great mezzotinters was focussed on portraiture and the great catalogues of Smith (B176) and Russell (B184), both replete with biographical and other useful facts, form major contributions to the history of this medium. Some further monographic studies of mezzotinters are listed in section Bn _infra_.

Aquatint has not attracted anything like the same quantity or quality of historical research and Prideaux (B181) is the only attempt at a comprehensive history. It is complemented by the same author's study of Ackermann's press (B180) and by Hind's excellent notes (B183). The only other work of value for the history of aquatint is the study of sporting aquatinters by Lane (A395) which presents much new information on their work.

B175 **[Chelsum, J.]** 1786. A history of the art of engraving in mezzotinto from its origin to the present times, including an account of the works of the earliest artists. Winchester. ii+100+2pp.

B176 **Smith, J.C.** 1878-83. British mezzotinto portraits: Being a descriptive catalogue of these engravings from the introduction of the art to the early part of the present century. Arranged according to the engravers, the inscriptions given at full length, & the variations of state precisely set forth: Accompanied by biographical notes, [etc.] London. 4 vols. with 125 pls. Repr. New York, 1978.
The pls. are autotype reproductions. Supplemented by Russell (B184).

B176* **Ball, W.** 1887. Mezzotinto engraving. London. 24pp. & 1 pl.
The pl. is a mezzo. demonstrating the full tone of a rocked plate before scraping and a partly finished illustration. A lecture to the Sette Of Odd Volumes.

B177 **Whitman, A.C.** 1898. The masters of mezzotint: The men & their work. London. x+95pp. & 60 pls.
The pls. are collo. reproductions.

B178 **Rawlinson, W.G.** 1902. Notes, chiefly on the technique of mezzotint engraving. In: Burlington Fine Arts Club. Exhibition of English mezzotint portraits from circa 1750 to circa 1830. pp.15-26. London.
Incl. reproductions of 30 mezzos.

B179 **Davenport, C.** 1904. Mezzotints. London. xlv+208pp. & 40 pls. Repr. New York, 1978.
The pls. are photogr. reproductions.

B180 **Prideaux, S.T.** 1906. Rudolph Ackermann & the work of his press, 1764--1834. Printing Art 7: 85-93.

B181 ----- 1909. Aquatint engraving: A chapter in the history of book illustration. London. xv+434pp. & illus. Repr. London, 1968.
The illus. incl. an original aquat. With several appendixes, incl: Books published before 1830 with aquatint plates, pp.325-357; Biographical notices of engravers whose names appear on the plates, pp.358-371; Publications by Ackermann with aquatint plates, pp.374-378; and Engravers and the books they illustrated, pp.388-405.

B182 **Salaman, M.C.** 1910. Old English mezzotints. London. xii+43pp. With 128 reproductions.

B183 **Hind, A.M.** 1921. Notes on the history of soft ground etching & aquatint. Print Collector's Quarterly 8: 377-405.

B184 **Russell, C.E.** 1926. English mezzotint portraits & their states from the invention of mezzotinting until the early part of the 19th century. London. 2 vols., 64 pls.
A supplement to Smith (B176).

B185 ----- 1929. Some problems of the early history of mezzotinting. Print Collector's Quarterly 16: 56-75.

B1 History of plate printing

The history of plate printing in Britain has yet to be written and until recently no historian showed any inclination to repair this omission. Meier (B189) in a general history of early printing presses devoted a fair proportion of his study to the birth of the roller press. Some valuable notes on a few English copper-plate printers were compiled by Tuer as part of his study of Bartolozzi's work (B187) but no further studies appeared for many decades. Brief notes on the development of copper-plate printing were provided by Anon (B186), who was clearly someone closely involved with the trade, and by Isert (B188). Mackenzie (B190) looked at the specialised field of bank-note printing in some detail while Verner (B192) outlines cartographic applications. Bain (B191) and Dyson (B193) have made the first serious attempt to document and analyse the development of the plate-printing trade as reflected in the remarkable records of a leading practitioner since the early 19th century. Further work on this archive is anticipated.

B186 **Anon.** 1882. Copperplate printing business: Its past, present & future. British & Colonial Printer 8 (Dec. 14): 9; 8 (Dec. 21): 18.

B187 **Tuer, A.** 1882. Copper- & steel-plate printing. Fine art printers. In: Bartolozzi & his works. Vol. 1, pp.96-102. London.

B188 **Neale, H.S.** 1927. The art of plate printing with an historical sketch by T.A. Isert. Springfield, Mass. 65pp.

B189 **Meier, H.** 1941. The origin of the printing & roller press. Print Collector's Quarterly 28: 8-55, 164-205, 338-379, 496-527.

B190 **Mackenzie, A.D.** 1953. The Bank of England note: A history of its printing. Cambridge. x+163pp.

B191 **Bain, I.** 1966. Thomas Ross & Son. Copper- & steel-plate printers since 1833. Journal, Printing Historical Society 2: 1-22.

B192 **Verner, C.** 1975. Copperplate printing. In: Woodward, D., Ed. Five centuries of map printing. pp.51-75. Chicago, Ill.

B193 **Dyson, T.** 1978. The Ross records: 1833 to 1900. Notes on the forthcoming catalogue of a plate-printer's nineteenth century archive. Journal, Printing Historical Society 12: 52-67.

Bm History of plate printing in colour

Historians have paid much attention to the products of colour printers, whether stipple-engraved, mezzotinted or aquatinted, but give scanty information on the means by which they were created. Burch's wide ranging studies (A275 A278) chronicle the development of colour plate printing in outline and Portalis (B195) provides information on the continental background to British progress. Singer published a short but scholarly study of the work of Le Blon (B197) and Franklin's essays and informatively annotated catalogue add to our knowledge on Le Blon and others. Tuer's study of the colour-printed stipple engravings of Bartolozzi's prolific school included some important notes on the nature and practice of late 18th century methods, admirably illustrated by some demonstration prints. Frankau (B196) wrote a general survey of 18th century stipple engravings but was obliged to admit that information on production techniques amounted to little more than oral tradition. Salaman (B198) presents a "gallery" of reproductions preceded by an historical essay on English artists but adds no new information on techniques. Grundy (B199) outlines the similar methods used for producing colour-printed mezzotints and compares them with practices being employed in the colour-printing revival taking place in his day.

B194 **Tuer, A.** 1881-82. Bartolozzi & his works. London. 2 vols.
The work is illus. with some surviving 18th century copper-plates and some specially prepared prints which demonstrate the nature of stipple engraving and the distinction between colour printed and hand coloured work.

B195 **Portalis, R.** 1888-90. La gravure en couleurs. Gazette des Beaux Arts (2) 38: 441-457, 1888; (3) 1: 29-41, 196-212, 322-338, 1889; (3) 2: 118-128, 1890.

B196 **Frankau, J.** 1900. Eighteenth century colour prints: An essay on certain stipple engravers & their work in colour. London. xvii+132pp. & 52 pls.
The pls. incl. some surviving 18th century coppers. Another edn., 1906. xxiv+307pp. without any illus.

B197 **Singer, H.W.** 1903. Jacob Christoffel Le Blon & his three colour prints. Studio 28: 261-271. Also pub. in: International Studio 19: 216-271, 1903.

B198 **Salaman, M.C.** 1909. Old English colour-prints. London. vi+42pp. & 40 pls.
The pls. are colour reproductions.

B199 **Grundy, C.R.** 1922. The evolution of modern mezzotint in colour. Connoisseur 63: 14-20.

B200 **Franklin, C.** 1977. A catalogue of early colour printing from chiaroscuro to aquatint. Culham. [viii]+73pp.
With essays on different artists and their methods. Illustrated with good colour reproductions.

Bn Selected ancillary monographs

The several excellent histories of British engraving are supplemented by a wealth of monographs on the works of individual engravers, the best of which take the form of detailed catalogues raisonnés accompanied by biographical, historical, technical and analytical notes. A selection is given below with emphasis on those which include analytical studies of printmaking techniques.

Hogarth in the 18th and Turner in the 19th centuries dominated the line engraving schools of their day and the legacy of their work has given rise to some excellent studies; Hogarth et alii. (B201) and Paulson (B213) for the former, and Rawlinson (B209) for the latter. Flaxman's distinctive line engraved work stimulated Bentley's informative technical and bibliographical study (B212).

Mezzotinters have attracted much individual study and two series of monographs written or edited by Whitman (B205 B206) add greatly to his general history of this medium (B177). The remarkable interest that attaches to Turner's Liber Studiorum has given rise to studies by Roget (B202), Rawlinson (B208), and Finberg (B210).

The prolific output of Bartolozzi and his school, especially in stipple--engraved style, has been documented with much useful background information by Tuer (B203) to which Anon (B211) has added a note on the distinctive sanguine colour favoured for some of their prints. Other stipple engravers were the special interest of Frankau who prepared magnificent monographs on them (B204 B207).

Numerous monographs have appeared on the great 19th century etchers. Lister's study of Samuel Palmer (B214) is a very good example of this group and provides much useful insight on the artist's techniques.

Levis (A431), Colin (A432) and Mason & Ludman (A433) should be consulted for full lists of monographs.

B201 **Hogarth, W. et alii.** 1833. Anecdotes of William Hogarth, written by himself, with essays on his life & genius ... selected from Walpole, Gilpin, J. Ireland, Lamb, Phillips, & others. To which are added a catalogue of his prints; account of their variations, & principal copies; [etc.] London. xii+416pp. Repr., With an intro. by R.W. Lightbown. London, 1970.
The chronological catalogue of Hogarth's prints, their states and copies, occupies pp.159-348.

B202 **Roget, J.L. Ed.** 1879. Notes & memoranda respecting the Liber Studiorum of J.M.W. Turner, R.A., written & collected by the late John Pye. Ed. with additional observations by J.L. Roget. London. viii+100pp.

B203 **Tuer, A.** 1881-82. Bartolozzi & his works. London. 2 vols. With many pls. 2nd edn., 1885. viii+478pp. (without pls.)
The 2nd edn., though omitting certain sections, includes corrections to the narrative text.

B204 **Frankau, J.** 1902. An eighteenth century artist & engraver, John Raphael Smith, his life & works. London. xiv+259pp. & 30 pls., with an accompanying portfolio of 50 pls.

B205 **Whitman, A.C.** 1902-07. "Nineteenth century mezzotinters." London. 4 vols.
A series of monographs: Valentine Green. 1902. 204pp.; Samuel William Reynolds. 1904. ix+168pp.; Samuel Cousins. 1904. xii+143pp.; Charles Turner. 1907. x+293pp.

B206 **Whitman, A.C.** Ed. 1903-04. "British mezzotinters." London. 2 vols. Two monographs: Goodwin, G. James McArdell. 1903. 168pp; Goodwin, G. Thomas Watson, James Watson, Elizabeth Judkins. 1904. viii+230pp.

B207 **Frankau, J.** 1904. Eighteenth century artists & engravers, William Ward, A.R.A., James Ward, R.A.; their lives & works. London. xvi+333pp. & 30 pls., with an accompanying portfolio of 11 pls.

B208 **Rawlinson, W.G.** 1906. Turner's Liber Studiorum: A description & a catalogue. 2nd edn. London. lvi+244pp.

B209 ----- 1908-13. The engraved work of J.M.W. Turner. London. 2 vols.

B210 **Finberg, A.J.** 1924. History of Turner's Liber Studiorum. London. xciv+373pp.

B211 **Anon.** 1926-27. Francisco Bartolozzi & "red chalk engraving". B.P. Collector & Baxter Times 4: 341-344.

B212 **Bentley, G.E. Jr.** 1964. The early engravings of Flaxman's Classical Designs: A bibliographical study. New York. 63pp. First pub. in: Bulletin, New York Public Library 68 (May/June), 1964.

B213 **Paulson, R.** 1965. Hogarth's graphic works ... with a commentary. New Haven. 2 vols.

B214 **Lister, R.** 1969. Samuel Palmer & his etchings. London. 131pp.

Section C: Relief block processes

Ca Bibliographies

There is apparently no separate bibliography of literature on relief processes. Reference can be made to the relevant sections of the classified bibliographies by Levis (A6) and Ludman, Mason & Sirefman (A16), or the classified library catalogues of the Patent Office (A5 A7), the Newberry Library, Chicago (A11) and Columbia University Libraries (A15).

Cb Wood engraving techniques (xylography)

The ubiquitous employment of wood-engraving throughout most of the 19th century as the medium for illustrating books and magazines (and for acres of advertising graphics) might suggest the existence of an accordingly large number of technical manuals. In fact, the instructional literature amounts to no more than a handful of books and articles and only two of these have any claim to distinction.

The age of wood engraving, introduced to England with such a profusion of excellence by Bewick and his pupils, left us no textbook on the craft and it was not until 1839 -- a decade after Bewick's death -- that Jackson & Chatto's historical and practical treatise appeared (C2). Bewick and most other wood engravers of the later 18th and early 19th centuries would have known of the detailed treatise published by Papillon in 1766-68 and, if they could read French, they would have acquired a great deal of technical "know-how" on all aspects of their craft. Papillon described wood engraving on longitudinal and end-grain blocks, "lowering" the block to enhance tonality, thickening lines to enrich colour, the use of cross-hatching, and even error correction on the block by insertion of a plug. In the almost total absence of any English instructional texts we must assume that, if Papillon was not consulted, the craft was taught entirely by example and learnt by experience. The English writings that did exist before 1839 were confined to elementary accounts, sometimes drawing on Papillon, in works such as Dossie (B6) and the several articles in the general encyclopaedias listed in section **Ab** <u>supra</u>.

Bewick never wrote specifically on his craft, despite bequeathing a whole school of talented engravers to the Victorian age, and such writings as do survive are contained in his posthumously published autobiography. Rae has extracted and edited several of Bewick's notes on engraving (C3) and more recently Bain (C3) has edited and annotated an unexpurgated edition of the Memoir which his daughter published in 1862, thus enhancing the value of this source document.

The most detailed technical description of the whole craft of 19th century engraving can be found in Jackson & Chatto's treatise (C2). They describe traditional processes in great detail but are sufficiently forward-looking to discuss the problems of machine printing of wood blocks and even mention some alternative mechanical and chemical methods of producing relief block illustrations. The later edition of 1861 retains virtually the same instructional text with only a few corrections and additions by Henry Bohn.

The other work of particular note is Linton's manual of 1884 (C6), the work of a creative and influential master of the art and technique of wood engraving. Fielding (A28), Stannard (A34), Hamerton (A42), Hodson (A43), and Singer & Strang (A52), all provide more or less adequate accounts of the craft as part of their general works on graphic reproduction processes. The popular manuals of Gilks (C4), Marx (C5), and Brown (C7) in the 1860's and 1880's provided cheap textbooks for practical workers and amateurs who were probably not able to afford to buy Jackson & Chatto's tome.

Literature on photo-relief processes is included in section **Ed** infra.

C1 **Papillon, J.B.M.** 1766-[68]. Traité historique et pratique de la gravure en bois. Paris. 3 vols.
Tome 1er: Contenant toute la partie historique; Tome 2nd: Contenant tous les principes de cet art; Supplément: Contenant plusiers faits historiques, de nouvelles manières, servant à perfectionner cet art, les arrêts rendus en favour de la gravure, & une table des matières, etc. In addition to many examples of wood engraving the work includes a chiaroscuro illustration in 4 printings with a set of colour separations.

C2 **Jackson, J. & W.A. Chatto.** 1839. A treatise on wood engraving, historical & practical. [Etc.] London. xvi+749pp., & 7 pls. 2nd edn., 1861. xvi+664+(561*-600*)pp. Repr. Detroit, Mich., 1969. "New edn.", [1881].
The bulk of the volume is historical. Ch. IX deals with the practice of wood engraving, pp.635-738. The pls. incl. examples of Knight's and Baxter's colour printing processes. The authors explain not only the basics of wood engraving but also methods of lowering the block, of repairing errors by plugging the block, and the effects of adapting engraving technique to take account of the rigours of early machine printing. Incl. mention of the newest developments in alternative methods for metallic relief engraving, touching on the processes of Lizars, Hancock, Woone, and Collins (whose techniques are treated in section Cc infra). In the 2nd edn. Ch. IX remained virtually unchanged but the colour printed specimens were omitted.

C3 **Bewick, T.** 1961. Some notes on wood engraving selected from his Memoir. Edited by T. Rae. Greenock. 20+vipp.
The Memoir of Thomas Bewick, written by himself, etc. was first published in an edited version by his daughter, Newcastle, 1862. An unexpurgated text has now been published: A memoir of Thomas Bewick; edited with an introduction by Iain Bain. Oxford, 1975. xliv+258pp.

C4 **Gilks, T.** 1866. The art of wood-engraving: A practical handbook. London. 2nd edn, greatly enl., 1867. 84pp.; 3rd edn., 1871; 5th edn., n.d., 58pp.; 6th edn., 1886; 7th edn., ca.1891, 58pp.
2nd edn., only, seen. An elementary manual by an experienced trade practitioner.

C5 **Marx, C.W.** 1881. The art of drawing & engraving on wood. London. 55pp. 2nd edn., 1881.
Another elementary popular manual.

C6 **Linton, W.J.** 1884. Wood-engraving: A manual of instruction. London. x+127pp.
A valuable textbook stating the author's approach to the art and craft of wood engraving. Linton lived and worked in America for many years after establishing himself as a master of the English school. He further enhanced his skill and reputation over there and published this work in Boston in 1879, for the reviewer and the public as much as for the apprentice, in order that all should understand and appreciate his art.

C7 **Brown, W.N.** 1886. A practical manual of wood engraving, with a brief account of the history of the art. London. x+70pp. 3rd edn., 1899. A manual for the amateur.

Cc Alternative methods of block preparation; Stereotype

Almost 20 years before the publication of England's first textbook of wood engraving in 1839, patent specifications and articles on alternative methods for preparing relief-printed illustrations began to appear in technical periodicals. Most of them were intended to replace the wood engraver's slow and skillful craft in labouring to cut away a wood block so as to leave every tiny detail of the required printing surface standing up in relief. The alternative processes usually sought to reverse this approach so that only the lines of the image were incised (often in a softer substance than boxwood) and the sunken parts then cast to form a relief printing surface. They claimed to allow greater freedom of expression and much saving of time and labour. A number of experimental inventions of this kind were described throughout the century culminating, of course, in the satisfactory development of photo--mechanically produced line and half-tone relief illustrations. Many of these inventions were short-lived and commercially unworkable but some were much more widely employed than is generally recognised. Once again Stannard (A34) must be recommended as the only general work which attempts to include these alternative processes, providing examples of several. For later years Hodson (A43) may be relied upon for brief information on some processes.

The use of a mordant to etch a hand-drawn design in relief was the basis of processes described by Lizars (C8) and Pye (C9), both of whom used a metal block, and by Crocker who used glass (C43). Congreve patented a method of multiplying stereotypes in relief by the indentation of a soft plate from a hard master image (C11). Others used the principle of incising a drawing through the thickness of a soft substance, deposited on a hard level plate, which was then cast to produce a relief image. Woone (C13 C13*), Palmer & Anon. (C18 to C22), Schoenberg (C15 C17), Dircks (C23 & C23*), and Linton (C29) used either chalky compositions or waxy substances for their versions of this technique.

The basis of graphotype, the most successful of these alternative processes, was also a compressed chalk-like coating applied to a plate, but the procedure was unique. The method was to draw a design in an ink that "bound" the chalk into a hard substance so that the untouched powdery areas could be brushed away leaving the image standing up in relief and this was cast and re-cast to form a printing surface. This widely employed process is described by Fitz-Cook (C31), R.M.H. (C32), Graphotyping Co. (C33), and Anon. (C37).

The immiscibility of greasy ink with water or fusible metal formed the basis of two processes. Collins (C28), by repeated inkings, built up an image in a greasy ink relief on a lithographic stone and then made a double cast to produce the same image in relief metal. Duclos' process (C30) used a greasy ink image drawn on a silvered plate which was then flooded with a fusible metal and the whole allowed to cool. The boundary meniscus of each "pool" of metal, where it was rejected by the greasy lines of the image, had the effect of producing a recessed image in the hardened metal which could then be cast.

Shanks & Johnson (C39 C39*) employed a unique approach in which they set up a slender rotary drill attached to a pantograph so that the drill, following the motions of the operator's hand as he traced a design, routed a line image in a plaster block that was then cast in relief.

Electro-metallurgical methods were the means of producing relief images used by Jordan (C14) and Piil (C25) while Brazendale used this principle for lowering the "lights" on relief metal blocks produced by whatever method.

The 1870's saw the arrival of a relief etching process that quickly gained popularity and proved itself to be an effective substitute for wood engraved illustration. Invented in France and known there as Paneiconography, or Gillotage (after its inventor, Gillot), it became established in England as zincography or zinco-typography (C36 C38 C40 C43*). A design was transferred to a zinc plate from a transfer-paper drawing, a lithographic stone, or an intaglio engraved plate, or else was drawn direct onto the zinc in a greasy ink or chalk, and the metal was then etched away to leave a relief design. Its closest competitor in the early years was Dawson's Typographic Etching (C35) which involved making a drawing with an etching needle through a blackened wax coating deposited onto a glass plate. The un-incised portions were then built up by a secret process so as to leave the image deeply incised and, when electrotyped, the result was an extremely fine and well defined relief line block. Hodson describes and illustrates both these processes (A43).

Although zincography was chiefly used for line and dot work it was possible to make a transfer onto zinc from a coarsely-grained transfer paper with results that showed similar tonal qualities to lithography. In later years transfers were made by photographic means and photo-zincotypes filled the pages of many illustrated publications (described in section **Ed** infra).

The ever-increasing print runs required for illustrated books and magazines were greatly facilitated by stereotyping the made-up forme, with the wood blocks included, so that two or more impressions could be run concurrently. In fact, wood blocks were often stereotyped before being set with the type so that the original could be spared any wear and tear in machine printing. Most of the alternative illustration processes depended on casting (and re-casting) to create the printing surface and stereotype thus became an important part of much relief picture printing.

Hodgson (C10) described the early methods of stereotyping and Hansard (C12) included a section on the technique in his printers' manual, but it was not until the introduction of the papier-maché method in the 1840's that the process could successfully duplicate finely engraved work without causing damage to the original block. Kronheim (C24) took out an English patent for this continental development in 1845. Stereotype was described in most printing manuals and eventually became the subject of several specialised textbooks and manuals; Anon. (C41), Wilson (C42), Bolas (C44), and Whetton (C45), among them. Electrotype was eventually to displace stereotype in several picture printing applications (see section **Af** supra), not least because it created distortion free images whereas stereotype could warp on cooling.

C8 **Lizars, W.** 1820. Account of a new style of engraving on copper in alto-relievo. Edinburgh Philosophical Journal 2: 19-23. Also pub. in: Gentleman's Magazine 91: 625-627, 1821; & London Journal of Arts & Sciences 1: 78-79, 1820.

C9 **Pye, C.** 1820. On a new process of engraving on metal & stone. London Journal of Arts & Sciences 1: 55-58.

C10 **Hodgson, T.** 1820. An essay on the origin & progress of stereotype printing: Including a description of the various processes. Newcastle. xii+178pp. & 8pp of specimens.

C11 **Congreve, W.** 1823. Certain improved methods of multiplying fac-simile impressions to any extent. London Journal of Arts & Sciences 5: 185-187. The patent specification.

C12 **Hansard, T.C.** 1825. Stereotype printing. In: Typographia. pp.815-887. London. Repr. London, 1966.
Detailed account of the methods used in his day with an account of their development.

C13 **Woone, G.** 1838. An improved method of forming plates with raised surfaces thereon, for printing impressions on different substances. Repertory of Patent Inventions N.S.9: 95-99. Also pub. in: London Journal of Arts & Sciences, Conjoined Series 13: 162-167, 1839.
The patent specification for gypsography.

C13* ----- 1838. Woone's method of engraving. Mechanics' Magazine 29: 236-238; also, letter from T. Oxley, pp.163-165.

C14 **Jordan, C.J.** 1839. Engraving by galvanism. Mechanics' Magazine 31: 163-164.

C15 **[Schoenberg, L.]** 1841. Acrography. London & Edinburgh Magazine 19 suppl: 430-431. Also pub. in his: Metallic engraving in relief, 1842 (C17).

C16 **Brazendale, M.T.** 1842. Method of lowering the "lights" in some particular engravings executed in the wood-cut manner. Mechanics' Magazine 36: 415.

C17 **Schoenberg, L.** 1842. Metallic engraving in relief, for letterpress printing, being a greatly improved substitute for wood engraving, called acrography, by the inventor, etc. London. 2+2+2pp. & 16 pls.
The pls. are specimens of acrography. Incl. a repr. of his 1841 article (C15). Comprises a general description, a scale of charges, and "Directions to artists for acrographic drawing".

C18 **Palmer, E.** 1843. Improvements in producing printing or embossing surfaces. London Journal of Arts & Sciences N.S.22: 279-283.
The patent specification for Palmer's glyphography.

C19 ----- [1843.] Glyphography, or engraved drawing; for printing at the type press after the manner of woodcuts. [Palmer's patent.] With full instructions for the use of artists, engravers, & amateurs, & specimen illustrations. London. 15pp. & 8 pls.
Incl. "Directions for taking proofs".

C19* ----- [1843?] Glyphography, or engraved drawing; for printing at the type press etc. 2nd edn. London. 16pp., & 12 pls.
The text of this edn. has been completely revised and the pls. are mostly new.

C20 **Anon.** 1843. Glyphography. Practical Mechanic 1843 (2 Sept.):468-469, & pls.16-17.

C21 **Palmer, E.** [1843?] Glyphography, or engraved drawing; for printing at the type press etc. 3rd edn. London. 16+xvii-xxivpp., decorative t.p. & 20 pls.
The text is again revised, new pls. provided, and the suppl. pp. are devoted to artists' testimonials.

C22 **Anon.** 1844. Glyphography. Art Union 6: 38-39.

C23 **Dircks, H.** 1845. Ivory engraving, or Dürer-Type. Mechanics' Magazine 42: 20-21; also, letter from C.J. Jordan, pp.74-75.

C23* ----- 1845. Improvements in engraving. Mechanics' Magazine 42: 140-141. Also pub. in: Athenaeum 1845 (8 Feb.).

C24 **Kronheim, J.M.** 1845. Improvements in stereotyping. London Journal of Arts & Sciences, conjoined ser. 26: 161-165, & pl.9.
The patent specification for the papier-maché process of stereotyping introduced by Kronheim from Brussels where he had seen it operated.

C25 **Piil, C.** 1846. Die Chemitypie, oder die Kunst, eine auf einer Metallplatte in gewöhnlicher Weise ausgeführte Radirung oder Gravirung in einen erhabenen Stempel zu verwandeln, der sich auf der Buchdruckerpresse, wie ein Holzschnitt, im Text oder allein, abdrucken lässt. Leipzig. 8pp. & 8 pls.
Although the process was successfully used for English illustrated books no English version of this technical description was apparently published.

C26 **Morse, S.E.** 1849. Improvements in the manufacture of plates or surfaces for printing or embossing. London Journal of Arts & Sciences, conjoined ser. 34: 257-261.
The patent specification.

C27 **Hansen, W.** 1854. Electro-magnetic engraving machine. Journal, Society of Arts 2: 485-486.
See also additional note, Ibid. 6: 106, 1858.

C28 **Collins, H.G.** 1860. On electro-block printing, especially as applied to enlarging or reducing any printing surface or original drawing. Journal, Society of Arts 9: 39-44; also, letters from W. Stones & Collins, pp.66-67, 82. Also pub. in: Journal of Typographic Arts 1861: 145-147; also, editorial comment, p.150.

C29 **Linton, W.J.** 1861. Specimens of a new process of engraving for surface printing. London. 16pp.
Linton's kerography. The specimens incl. medal eng., outline style, etched and line eng. styles, 18 in all.

C30 **Anon.** 1864. M. Duclos' processes for engraving in relief & in intaglio. Art Student 1: 181-182.

C31 **Fitz-Cook, H.** 1865. On the graphotype, a process for producing from drawings, blocks for surface printing. Journal, Society of Arts 14: 51-60, with specimens. Widely re-pub., e.g.: Typographic Advertiser 4: 73, 80-81, 88, 98, 1866; Stationer & Fancy Trades' Register 1866: 12-15; Nature & Art 1: 219-222, 1866; Fine Arts Quarterly Review N.S.1: 231-234, 1866; & Photographic News 9: 591-592, 1865.

C32 **M., R.H.** 1867. New processes for producing illustrations for letter--press printing. Stationer & Fancy Trades' Register 1867: 463-466.
On graphotype.

C33 **Graphotyping Company.** 1868. The handbook of graphotype: A practical guide for artists & amateurs. London. viii+20+ivpp. & 19 pls.

C34 ----- ca.1874. Specimens of the graphotyping process, together with the cost of executing the same subjects on wood, the saving to the publisher, & the profit to be derived by the company. London. 12pp.

C35 **Anon.** 1873. Typographic etching. Lithographer 4: 24-25, with a specimen.
Dawson's process.

C36 ----- 1874. Automatic engraving processes: Gillotype in London. Printing Times & Lithographer 5: 178-179, with line & chalk specimens.

C37 ----- 1875. Graphotype. Printing Times & Lithographer N.S.1: 90-91.

C38 ----- 1875. Automatic engraving for the letter press: Leitch's process. Printing Times & Lithographer N.S.1: 110-112, with line & chalk specimens.

C39 ----- 1875. Automatic engraving for the letter-press: Shanks & Johnson's process. Printing Times & Lithographer N.S.1: 125-127.

C39* ----- 1875. Shanks & Johnson's machine. Printers' Register 15: 12.

C40 **Cattell, A.S. & Co.** ca.1879-81. The process of zinco-typography or the production of relief printing blocks, with instructions for preparing drawings for the same on transfer paper. London. 56pp.
A trade catalogue with fine examples of the process and interspersed instructional notes.

C41 **Anon.** 1880. The practice of stereotyping. Printing Times & Lithographer N.S.6: 1-2, 29-31, 59-61, 79-81, 101-102, 128-130, 188-190, 240-241, 261-264, 284-286.

C42 **Wilson, F.J.F.** 1880. Stereotyping & electrotyping: A guide for the production of plates by the papier-maché & plaster processes, etc. London. xv+195pp. 4th edn., 1882; 6th edn., 1898.
Includes a history of stereotyping & descriptions of the paper and plaster processes.

C43 **Anon.** 1884. Glass printing-blocks. Printing Times & Lithographer N.S.10: 38-39.
The invention of S.H. Crocker of Tasmania.

C43* ----- 1884-85. Chemical engraving on zinc. Printing Times & Lithographer N.S.10: 214-215, 1884; N.S.11: 54-55, 1885.

C44 **Bolas, T.** 1890. Stereotyping. Cantor lectures. Journal, Society of Arts 38: 817-821, 829-845, 849-858.

C45 **[Whetton, H.]** 1901. Practical notes on stereotyping & electrotyping from "The British Printer". Compiled by the Editor. London. vii+140pp.

Cd Phototransfer onto wood blocks

The normal method of commencing a wood engraving was for the artist to make a reversed drawing on the suitably prepared surface of a boxwood block with pencil outlines and half-tones in either pencil shading or Indian ink wash. Some artists drew in every line of hatching while others merely suggested shading with tonal washes and the engraver's job was to cut away the unwanted areas of the block, leaving his interpretation of the original design standing in relief. Thus the original drawing was lost, both as a work of art and as a point of reference against which the fidelity of the engraving might be compared. The problem of having to make a reversed drawing, so as to preserve the proper "handing" of the printed image, presented a real challenge to the artist.

The idea of photographically transferring a drawing made on paper to the surface of the block was one that exercised the minds of many experimenters and engravers during most of the 19th century, though historians would appear to have overlooked its importance. However, the existence of over two dozen articles describing this procedure, spread over some 50 or more years, serves to underline the pre-occupation with the solution of this technical problem. As with most technological innovations in printing, the pressure to achieve a viable commercial process probably came from the several large trade engraving houses and the publishers of mass-circulation illustrated magazines ever eager to produce the greater and speedier output demanded by their readership.

The credit for being the first to demonstrate the potential of this new aid to engraving must go to to Francis (C46), who published an example in 1839 while photography was still in its infancy. Further developments, it appears, proceeded quietly in engravers' studios so that the next announcement was not until 1854 when Beechey (C47) presented a sophisticated example in the prestigious "Art Journal". Thereafter, a steady stream of recipes and instructions appeared in the photographic and other periodicals. In addition, the process was, of course, described in the various photographic textbooks (see section **Eb** infra).

C46 **Francis, G.** 1839. Important application of photogenic drawing. Magazine of Science 1: 25, 28.
With a specimen engraved from a photographically transferred image.

C47 **Beechey, St.V.** 1854. Photography applied to engraving on wood. Art Journal N.S.6: 244.
With a preceding editorial note, a footnote by R. Langton, and an example of a wood-engraved lunar map by Langton based on a photo.

C48 **Hunt, R.** 1858. Application of photography to wood engravings. Photographic News 1: 158. Also pub. in: Art Journal.

C49 **Anon.** 1858. Photography applied to engraving on wood. Photographic News 1: 193-194.
Styled as "xylophotography".

C50 **Spence, W.** 1859. Photography on wood. Photographic News 3: 170.
The patent specification.

C51 **Anon.** 1861. Photography & wood engraving. Photographic News 5: 97.

C52 **Leighton, J.** 1861. Photography on wood. Journal, Photographic Society 7: 76-78; also, letter from T. Bolton claiming priority & Leighton's reply, pp.114-115.

C53 **Baroux, E.** 1863. Photography on wood. Photographic News 7: 438.

C54 **Martel, C.** 1864. Photography on wood. Art-Student 1: 69-70.

C55 **Anon.** 1870. Photography for wood engraving. Photographic News 14: 254-255.
Full description of work by Mr. Loudan for the Graphic and the Illustrated Times using Herr Grune's method.

C56 **Beyersdorff, A.** 1870. Photography & wood engraving. Photographic News 14: 484.

C57 ----- 1870. Photography & wood engraving. Lithographer 1: 78; also, letter from H.N. Smith, p.99.

C58 **Anon.** 1879. Photography on wood. Printing Times & Lithographer N.S.5: 24.
Husnik's process.

C59 **Husnik, J.** 1879. Photography on wood. Photographic News 23: 4, 137.

C60 **Harris, T.C.** 1879. Photographing on wood. Photographic News 23: 275. Repr. from Practical Photographer.

C61 **Anon.** 1882. Photographing on wood. Photographic News 26: 2-3.

C62 **Dawson, G.** 1882. Photography on wood blocks. British Journal of Photography 29: 197.

C63 **Anon.** 1883. "Processes" - photography & wood engraving. British Journal Photographic Almanac 1883: 135-137.

C64 ----- 1883. Production of the photographic image on the wood block of the engraver. Photographic News 27: 402.

C65 ----- 1884. Photographing on the block of the wood engraver. Photographic News 28: 628-629.

C66 **Ives, F.E.** 1885. Photographing on wood. Year Book of Photography 1885: 88-89.

C67 **Frewing, E.** 1886. Photographing on wood. Year Book of Photography 1886 48-49.

C68 **Anon.** 1890. Photographing upon wood. Photographic News 34: 601. Repr. from Wilson's Photographic Magazine.

C69 **Middleton, E.C.** 1895. Photographing on wood. Process Photogram 2: 62-63, 69-70.

C70 Anon. 1896. Photographing on wood: The commercial method. Printing Times & Lithographer N.S.5: 166.

Ce Block printing

The printing of wood engravings to best effect demanded a high standard of craftsmanship with attention to the finer details of presswork. Some of the early printers' manuals touch on the problem of printing "cut work" but it was Savage's masterly, though modestly titled, treatise (C71) which first demonstrated the high standards that could be achieved. He renewed this advice in his dictionary (C72) some years later. Savage's high level of craftsmanship, performed on the hand press, could not be matched by work printed on power--driven machines. With the arrival of machines, speed and quantity of production became the most important consideration and it was some time before printers turned their attention to improving quality of impression. By the 1870's a stream of journal articles began to appear dealing with fine block printing and specifically with the skill of make-ready and the introduction of the American method of hard packing. It was an American printer, De Vinne, who provided some of the most authoritative comments on the printer's contribution to fine wood-engraved illustration (C77 C78 C100), whilst Noble (C79), Bateman (C86 C89 C90), and others spoke for the British trade. In addition the manuals on machine printing by Wilson (A138 A139) and Wilson & Grey (A147) included advice on this craft, the latter also including examples of relief illustrations with progressive stages of make-ready.

Later in the century the introduction of mechanically prepared tint-blocks for decorative work and the invention of photo-mechanical engraving processes for illustrated work stimulated the search for the higher standards of press work that these innovations demanded. In this era of so-called "artistic printing" a less ambitious counterpart to Savage's treatise was produced by Joyner (C94), a work which exemplified the contemporary letterpress printer's highest levels of craftsmanship. Fisher (C91), Jackson (C92), Anon. (C95), Ward (C96), Noble (C97), Morch (C98), and Cox (C99), contributed various pieces of advice on the precise craft of printing good half-tones with the new cylinder and platen machines, so continuing the tradition of fine pressmanship established over 80 years earlier by Savage.

C71 Savage, W. 1819-22. Practical hints on decorative printing, with illustrations engraved on wood, & printed in colours at the type press. London. xix+122pp. & 49 pls.
In this treatise Savage not only instructs on method but, using the Ruthven press, demonstrates by example what results fine pressmanship could achieve.

C72 ----- 1841. Engravings on wood. In: A dictionary of the art of printing. pp.210-215. London. Repr. London 1966.

C73 Read, J.M. ca.1860. Instructions in the art of making ready woodcuts. Reading. 14pp.

C74 Anon. 1864. Bringing up woodcuts at press. Typographic Advertiser 2: 61, 72.

C75 ----- 1878. Woodcuts: Concerning the taking of proofs & prints. Printing Times & Lithographer N.S.4: 197-199, 221-222.

C76 **Anon.** 1879. Hard-packing "make-ready". Paper & Printing Trades Journal no.29: 11-12. Repr., Ibid. no.47: 21-22.

C77 [**De Vinne, T.L.**] 1879. A printer on the limitations of engraving on wood. Printing Times & Lithographer N.S.5: 45-47, 69-70, 94-96.

C78 **De Vinne, T.L.** 1880. The growth of wood-cut printing. II: The modern method by machines. Scribner's Magazine 20: 34-45.
See (C181) for pt. I.

C79 **Noble, F.** 1883. Difficulties in machine printing & how to overcome them. London. 72pp.
Incl. advice on the use of electrotype copies of wood engs., make-ready, registering for a second colour, cut work, etc.

C80 **Hodson, J.S.** 1884. Printing wood-cuts by hand-press or at machine. In: An historical & practical guide to art illustration, etc. pp.109-115. London.

C81 **Anon.** 1887. Tint plates & how to make them for letterpress work. British & Colonial Printer 19: 17, 113.

C82 ----- 1889. Tint blocks. British & Colonial Printer 23: 129-130, 145.

C83 ----- 1889. Artistic printing. British & Colonial Printing 23: 22, 197, 222, 1889; 24: 453, 1889.

C84 ----- 1890. Making ready of press forms. British Printer 4: 27.
Incl. a passage by T.L. De Vinne repr. from "Century Magazine".

C85 ----- 1890. Hints on the making ready of process blocks. British Printer 3: 31-32.

C86 **Bateman, S.M.** 1890. Making ready of picture blocks. British Printer 3: 5-10.

C87 **Anon.** 1890. Tints or ground work. British & Colonial Printer 25: 89, 125, 309, 354.

C88 **Gass, W.H.** 1890. Newspaper illustration. Printing Times & Lithographer N.S.16: 71.
Advice on printing relief illus. on rotary machines.

C89 **Bateman, S.M.** 1893. Hard packing. Printing World N.S.1: 116f-116g.

C90 ----- 1893. Making ready. Printing World N.S.1: 500-502, 553.

C91 **Fisher, C.H.** 1893. Platen machine work. British Printer 6: 84-92.

C92 **Jackson, T.** 1893. Some hints on making ready on cylinder machines. British Printer 6: 157-159.

C93 **Silsbury, J.H.** 1893. Making & printing tint blocks. Printing World N.S.1: 93-94.

C94 Joyner, G. 1895. Fine printing: Its inception, development, & practice. With twelve artistic supplements illustrating the tendency of fine work. London. viii+111pp.
Ch. IV: Fine presswork; its management, its practice. The illus. incl. specimens of: "Circular style of 1877", wood eng., "Ornamental panel style", "Typical German style", "Typical American style", "British new style of 1888", h-tone engs., a chromo-typogr. picture in 8 printings, a specimen of Swain's photo-chromotype, and other typogr. work; also specimen of embossing.

C95 Anon. 1895. Printing from process blocks. British Printer 8: 359-361.

C96 Ward, J.S. 1895. The ideal of half-tone printing. Photographic Journal N.S.19: 268-272. Also pub. in: British Printer 8: 68-70, 1895.

C97 Noble, W.M. 1895-96. Half-tone blocks & their printing. Printers' Register 35: 149-150, 1895-96; 36: 67-68, 87-88, 107-108, 129-130, 149-150, 169-170, 191-192, 1896-97.

C98 Mörch, J.O. 1898. Making ready & printing of process blocks. Process Photogram 5: 102-106, illus.

C99 Cox, A. [1903.] Half-tone printing: A practical work on the printing & making ready of half-tone blocks. Birmingham. 32pp.
Illus. with examples of h-tone printing, both with and without make-ready.

C100 De Vinne, T. 1911. The printing of wood-engravings. Print Collector's Quarterly 1: 365-378.

Cf Block printing in colour (chromo-xylography)

Printing wood blocks in colour was basically very similar in operation to ordinary xylographic work. The additional skills lay in the achievement of accurate register as successive colour printings were added, and in an understanding of the value of colour harmony and the niceties of inking, printing, and over-printing of tint-blocks.

Jackson's essay of 1754 (C101) gave no technical information, claimed that he had invented ten positive tints in chiaro-oscuro, and presented some rugged examples of his colour work. Savage (C102), in contrast, assembled useful information on his approach to colour printing (much of which is repeated in C103) and provided an ambitious collection of examples of his work.

Colour block-printing was the field in which George Baxter excelled; he combined it with an intaglio "key" plate. Literature on his hybrid process is contained in section Ad supra. One of his early rivals was Charles Knight, who made ingenious inventions for the rapid printing of large runs of colour prints as mentioned by Anon. (C105) and Head (C106).

Problems of pictorial colour harmony and the production of secondary colours by the overprinting of primary-colour tint-blocks were addressed by "Walphage" (C109), Noble (C111 C112 C119), and the American printer Earhart (C117), who either discuss colours at some length or provide long runs of printed examples to illuminate their ideas. The best account of the actual preparation and printing of a chromo-xylographic illustration is probably that by Noble (C110), whilst another work by him (C111 C112) describes the method for producing a colour-printed newspaper supplement.

Southward's two text-books (C113 C118) provide good instruction on colour--block work for general letterpress, jobbing, and display applications, a reminder that, in the second half of the century, chromo-relief printing was used as much for ornamental work as for pictorial reproduction. Ornamental colour work at this time was often enlivened by the addition of metallic tints. Literature on the craft of "bronzing" is included in section Ac supra.

C101 **Jackson, J.B.** 1754. An essay on the invention of engraving & printing in chiaro-oscuro, as practised by Albert Dürer, Hugo di Carpi, etc. & the application of it to the making of paper hangings of taste, duration & elegance. Illustrated with prints in proper colours. London. 19pp. & 8 pls.
The prints are coarsely printed in a very oily ink which badly disfigures the image. The text avoids any mention of technique.

C102 **Savage, W.** 1819-22. Practical hints on decorative printing, with illustrations engraved on wood, & printed in colours at the type press. London. xix+122pp. & 49 pls.
About half the pls. are colour printed. Announced in 1815, the work appeared in two parts. It is an exercise in fine pressmanship and the application of Savage's development of oil-less inks (made with copaiba balsam) to print chromo-xylographs in up to 29 colours on a Ruthven press. One print demonstrates the colour separations employed in a 3-colour print. 18 ink specimens are provided and they (and all the prints) have a characteristically "dry" look, thus vindicating Savage's claim to have overcome the oil staining that marred Jackson's work. The text describes his careful approach to colour printing and gives the order of printing for several pls. In an appendix Savage incl. a translation of "The manner of printing engravings in cameo" from Papillon's Traité (C1).
Savage's own copy of Practical Hints is preserved in the Patent Office Library. It contains a proof of every stage of each colour print incl. all 29 separations of the "Ode to Mercy".

C103 ----- 1825. Coloured prints in imitation of drawings. Transactions, Society of Arts 43: 67-79.
Virtually a repr. of the relevant portion of text from the above work.

C104 **Hansard, T.C.** 1825. Decorative printing. In: Typographia. pp.911-918. London. Repr. London, 1966.
A brief description of Savage's colour printing and of other colour work. Illus. with a colour reproduction of the initial letter B from the Mainz Psalter printed from stereotype blocks.

C105 **Anon.** 1838. Knight's illuminated engravings. Mechanics' Magazine 29: 230-231.

C106 **[Head, Sir F.B.]** 1840. The printer's devil. Quarterly Review 65: 28-29. Repr. in: Printing Art Annual 1974: 56-58.
The only eye-witness account of the operation of Knight's four-platen colour printing press, operating at Clowes' works.

C107 **Anon.** 1863. Printing in colours. Typographic Advertiser 1: 92, & 1 pl.
W. Carpenter's process, patent no. 1180 of 1862, with a specimen.

C108 **Wood, J.** 1864. Chromo-typography. Typographic Advertiser 2: 64, & 1 specimen pl.

C109 **"Walphage".** 1870-71. Practical hints by an old hand. Chromatic typography. Printers' Register 9: 197, 1870.
----- ----- II. The theory of colour printing. Ibid. 9: 242-243, 1870.
----- ----- III. Printing colour on colour. Ibid. 9: 268-269, 1870.
----- ----- IV. Coloured inks & how to make them. Ibid. 10: 42-43, 1871.

C110 **Noble, F.** 1877. Block printing. Printers' Register 16: 69-70, 90-91, 109-111.

C111 ----- 1878-80. Colour printing. Printers' Register 17: 137-140, 164-165, 178-180, 199-201, 213-215, 1878; 18: 8-10, 28-30, 47-50, 66-68, 87-89, 106-107, 128-129, 144-145, 165-167, 182-183, 202-204, 221-222, 1878-79; 19: 6-7, 27-28, 46-48, 65-67, 87-88, 107-108, 128-129, 147-148, 166-167, 207-209, 226-228, 1879-80.
This series of articles was gathered together in book form, see following item.

C112 ----- 1881. The principles & practice of colour printing stated & explained. London. vi+174pp. & 50 pls.
Largely concerned with the laws and harmonies of colour. The pls. show the same motif printed in separate 50 colours. Good information on inks, brief instruction on preparation of colour blocks and machine colour printing. The final portion, pp.145-154, describes the production of the colour--printed 1879 Christmas suppl. to "The Graphic", using Hodson's relief aquatint process - a development of Wm. Dickes' chromograph process.

C113 **Southward, J.** 1882. Colour printing. In: Practical printing: A handbook of the art of typography. pp.504-530. London. 2nd edn., pp.510-524. 1884; 3rd edn., pp.469-492. 1887.

C114 **Anon.** 1884-88. Colour work. Modern Printer 1884 (Mar.): 6; (June): 7-8; (Sept.): 7; 1885 (Jan.): 8-9; (Apr.): 6-8; (Aug.): 5; (Dec.): 7; 1888 (Aug.): 6-7.

C115 ----- 1890. Printing with gold leaf. London, Provincial & Colonial Press News 1890 (Apr.): 22.

C116 ----- 1890. Artistic printing. The chaostype & owltype processes. British & Colonial Printer 25: 237-238, 257-258.

C117 **Earhart, J.F.** 1892. The color printer: A treatise on the use of colors in typographic printing. Cincinnati, Ohio. 137pp. & 90 pls.
This American work was widely advertised in the British trade journals and was seemingly well-known to printers over here. It incl. 46 pls. of colour samples and colour combinations (using a uniform motif), 22 examples of colour jobbing work, and a chromo-xylogr. landscape printed in 10 colours with all the separations shown in progressive combination. The text is simply a description of the pls. and colours employed.

C118 **Southward, J.** 1892. Artistic printing: A supplement to the author's work on "Practical Printing". London. viii+149pp. & 4 pls.
This manual is directed at the ornamental and jobbing printer, rather than the picture-printer. Incl. samples of owltype and slenotype (somewhat garish forms of ornamental printing), and 3 pls. of colour samples.

C119 **Noble, F.** 1892-96. Colour printing. Printers' Register 32: 126-127, 149-151, 169-171, 189-190, 209-210, 229-231, 1892/93; 33: 7, 27, 47, 67-69, 87, 107, 129, 147, 167, 187, 207, 227, 235, 1893/94; 34: 7-9, 27, 47-49, 69, 89-91, 109, 133, 149-150, 169, 189, 209-210, 229, 1894/95; 35: 7, 27-28, 1895. Also pub. in: Southward, J. Practical printing. 5th edn. ed. by A. Powell. Vol. 2, pp.1-199. London, 1900.
A revised version of his earlier book (C112). [N.B. We were unable to locate a perfect copy of vols. 33 & 34 of the Printers' Register. As a result only fragments of the text were examined and the paginations for articles in those vols., based on their indexes, probably only indicate the opening page of each article.]

Cg Block printing in colour for security work

The search for a method of producing inimitable bank-notes and other security documents led to some some interesting developments in relief colour printing. Both Ibbetson (C120) and Congreve (C122 C125) suggested the use of compound printing blocks with different sections printed in contrasting colours. Congreve's was the more complicated and sophisticated of the two and, although not accepted for bank-note printing, it was quite widely used for lottery and admission tickets and some examples can even be found in ornamental books and fancy albums. The decorative appeal of Congreve's process was enhanced by his later invention of combined embossing and colour printing (C126). His efforts to have these innovations accepted by the Bank of England, coupled with his anxiety to demonstrate its superiority over any rival, led to his publishing several patent specifications, articles and pamphlets. As a result we have valuable information on his processes and an interesting range of examples of this byway of colour printing.

C120 **Ibbetson, J.H.** 1819. A practical view of an invention for better protecting bank-notes against forgery. London. 2nd edn., 1821. 68pp. & 19 pls. 1st edn. not seen. The 2nd edn. has many examples of relief printing in black and in colours, together with 3 examples of intaglio bank-note printing.

C121 **Congreve, W.** 1819. Principles upon which it appears that a more perfect system of currency may be formed in the precious or non-intrinsic metals. London. 26pp. & 3 pls.
Largely a criticism of the Perkins/Heath siderographic process and a counter recommendation for the author's compound plate printing. One of the pls. is a 2-col. relief eng. example.

C122 ----- 1820. An analysis of the true principles of security against forgery: Exemplified by an enquiry into the sufficiency of the American plan for a new bank note; ... & that the true basis of security is in the due application of relief engraving, & printing in two or more colours. London. [vi]+39pp. & 11 pls.
Incl. an explanation of Congreve's compound plate process and a specimen.

C123 **Anon.** 1820. Messrs Perkins, Fairman & Heath's Siderography, versus Sir William Congreve's "Compound Plate". London Journal of Arts & Sciences 1: 209-213.
A review of Congreve's book (C122).

C124 **Congreve, W.** 1820. An improved mode of combining & inlaying metals or other hard substances applicable to various purposes. London Journal of Arts & Sciences 1: 241-242. Also pub. in: Repertory of Arts & Sciences (2) 42: 272-274, 1823.
The patent specification.

C125 ----- 1822. Certain improvements in printing in one, two or more colours. London Journal of Arts & Sciences 3: 9-16, & 1 pl.
The patent specification.

C126 ----- 1824. An improved method of stamping. London Journal of Arts & Sciences 8: 121-123. Also pub. in: Repertory of Arts & Sciences (3) 6: 141-143.
The patent specification.

C127 **Hunt, R.** 1848. Compound plate printing. With an illustrative specimen. Art Union 10: 194-195.
The specimen is a double-sided, colour-printed, and embossed example of Congreve's process.

Ch **Wood engravers' equipment, materials, etc.**

The Boxwood used for 19th century wood engraving was chiefly imported from the eastern Mediterranean but, as consumption of this raw material threatened to outstrip this source of supply, a search had to be made for alternative resources or substitute woods. Several articles demonstrate the botanical assistance rendered by experts at Kew Gardens and elsewhere in identifying suitable kinds of engraving wood, i.e. Hunter (C128), Jackson (C130* C137), and Anon. (C131 C132 C134 C135). W.G. Smith, himself a botanist as well as accomplished wood engraver, performed some practical tests to prove the acceptability of their recommendations (C130 C133). The production of ever larger illustrations in newspapers and magazines not only consumed more wood but greatly exceeded the girth of the Box tree. The problem was overcome by bolting several small blocks together and this became an everyday procedure in the second half of the century as described by Anon. (C139). The extremes to which it was possible to go are indicated by Anon. (C162)

Wood engravers' tools are described and illustrated in the various trade catalogues listed in section Ah _supra_. Commercial engraving, especially for advertising and ornamental display work, led to the introduction and sophistication of ruling machines, Anon. (C140 C141 C145), just as with plate engraving.

During the 18th and early 19th centuries wood blocks were printed on ordinary platen presses but, by the 1830's, power-driven machines began to take over the everyday printing of illustrated book and magazine work. Most of the literature on their development is contained in section Ag _supra_. Anon. (C136) announced one of new generation sophisticated, close-tolerance, printing machines designed to give better impressions of illustrated work. Even greater speeds were possible on web rotary machines and Anon. (C142 C143) introduces an example designed for printing better quality illustrated work. The interest in very high standard, short run, "artistic work", which developed later in the century, led to the introduction of close register platen machines, chiefly from America, of which the Colt "Armory" (C148) was a popular example. The fine tolerance presswork necessary for printing half-tone photo-mechanical relief illustrations was provided by improvements in platen and cylinder machines as described by Fisher (C146) and Jackson (C147).

Apparatus for stereotyping can also be found in the trade catalogues listed in section Ah supra, and to those we may add the special catalogue produced by Wood (C129).

C128 **Hunter, A.** 1860. On the Indian woods that have been tried for engraving. Edinburgh New Philosophical Journal N.S.12: 163-165. Also pub. in: Transactions, Botanical Society of Edinburgh 6: 358-361, 1860; & Journal, Society of Arts 8: 321-323, 1860.

C129 **Wood, J. & R.M.** 1860. Papier maché stereotyping apparatus. London. A trade catalogue.

C130 **Smith, W.G.** 1873-75. On woods suitable for wood engraving. Gardeners' Chronicle 1873: 1017, also, a note by J. Britten, p.1210; 1875: 585.

C130* **Jackson, J.R.** 1875. On Box and other woods used for engraving. Leisure Hour 1875 (Jan.9): 618, 697.

C131 **Anon.** 1877. Boxwood. Report, Royal Botanic Garden, Kew 1877: 27.

C132 ----- 1878. Boxwood for engravers. London, Provincial & Colonial Press News 1878 (Mar.): 19.

C133 **Smith, W.G.** 1879. Substitutes for boxwood. Indian Forester 4: 343-345.

C134 **Anon.** 1881. Boxwood, Indian. Report, Royal Botanic Garden, Kew 1881: 25.

C135 ----- 1882. Boxwood substitutes. Report, Royal Botanic Garden, Kew 1882: 35-36.

C136 ----- 1882. Printing machinery for fine cut-work. Printing Times & Lithographer N.S.8: 95.
Harrild's "Bremner" Fine Art cylinder press.

C137 **Jackson, J.R.** 1885. Boxwood & its substitutes. Journal, Society of Arts 33: 566-569, 600-602.

C138 **Anon.** 1885. Recent improvements in the art of illustration. British & Colonial Printer 15: 65.
Apropos photographing on wood and the American tint-ruling machine.

C139 ----- 1885. The manufacture of bolted & amalgamated wood blocks. British & Colonial Printer 14: 100-101.

C140 ----- 1885. The romance of a machine. Modern Printer 1885 (Jan.): 12-13.
Bellman's ruling machine for tint engraving.

C141 ----- 1888. Engravers' ruling machine. British & Colonial Printer 20: 1.
Specially designed for wood engraving.

C142 **Anon.** 1889. A new rotary press for illustrated work. British & Colonial Printer 22: 117-119.
Marinoni's web rotary machine.

C143 ----- 1888. New rotary machine for cut work. Printing Times & Lithographer N.S.14: 187.
Marinoni's web rotary machine.

C144 **Wilkinson, W.T.** 1888. Printing on wood blocks. British Journal Photographic Almanac 1888: 431.

C145 **Anon.** 1891. Some types of American machinery: Richards' ruling machines. British & Colonial Printer 28: 343.
Illus. with a specimen of ruled work.

C146 **Fisher, C.H.** 1893. Platen machines & their construction. British Printer 6: 75-84.

C147 **Jackson, T.** 1893. The cylinder machine & its work. British Printer 6: 151-156.

C148 **Anon.** 1899. The "Colt Armory" platens. British & Colonial Printer 44: 52.

C149 **Heathcote, C.** 1907. A plea for wood engraving. Penrose Annual 12: 21-24.
With examples of the work of the Royle Richards engraving machine.

Ci Miscellaneous literature

This is a selection of works which generally have little concern with the technique of relief engraving & printing but, rather, provide contemporary criticism on the progress of the art in the 19th century. Some are broadly historical but, since they include assessments of the work of contemporary engravers, their historical detachment gives way to subjective comment. Jackson & Chatto (C150), Howitt (C153), Chatto (C155 C156), Bohn (in Jackson & Chatto) (C157), Linton (C163 C164), and Ruskin (C159), speak with authoritative, if prejudiced, voices on the work of their day.

The introduction of some alternative processes aroused criticism -- "Observator" (C152) attacked the novelty of Woone's process, and Anon. (C154) compared glyphography with wood engraving and found it wanting.

Late in the 19th century the advancing march of photo-mechanical processes threatened to undermine the livelihood of the whole trade and the comments of Harland (C166 C167), Herkomer (C170), Gardner (C173 C174), Baldry (C177), Spielmann (C178), and others, reflect this concern and chart the decline, whilst optimistically proclaiming the enduring role that they foresaw for the engraver.

C150 **Jackson, J. & W.A. Chatto.** 1839. A treatise on wood engraving, historical & practical. With upwards of three hundred illustrations engraved on wood by John Jackson. London. xvi+749pp. & 7 pls.
The bulk of the work is historical, taking it "up to the present day" with a selection of the work of contemporary engravers.

C151 **Anon.** 1839. Wood engraving. Art Union 1: 25-32.
Incl. 6pp. of examples from contemporary sources.

C152 **"Observator".** 1839. Metallic relief engraving - Woone's process - Jackson's History of Wood engraving. Mechanics' Magazine 32: 66-69.

C153 **Howitt, W.** 1844. The present state of wood engraving as it regards rural subjects. In: The rural life of England. 3rd edn. pp.341-347. London.

C154 **Anon.** 1845. Glyphography. Magazine of Science 6: 153.

C155 **Chatto, W.A.** 1848. The history & art of wood engraving with specimens of the art, ancient & modern, selected from "The Illustrated London News". London. 28pp. & 56 pls.
First pub. in the Illustrated London News between 20th April & 6th July, 1844.

C156 ----- 1849. Gems of wood engraving from "The Illustrated London News", with a history of the art, ancient & modern. London. 28pp. & 94 pls.
The 1848 text re-issued with a larger complement of illus.

C157 **Bohn, H.** 1861. Artists and engravers on wood of the present day. In: Jackson, J. & W.A. Chatto. A treatise on wood engraving, historical & practical. 2nd edn. With ... 145 additional wood engravings. London. xvi+664+(561*-600*)pp. Repr. Detroit, Mich., 1969. "New edn.", [1881].

C158 **Gilks, T.** 1868. A sketch of the origin & progress of the art of wood engraving. With a chapter explanatory of a box of materials used in the process to accompany the work. London. 84pp.

C159 **Ruskin, J.** 1876. Ariadne Florentina: Six lectures on wood & metal engraving; with appendix. Given before the University of Oxford in Michaelmas Term, 1872. Sunnyside. 263pp. First issued in 7 parts, 1873-76. Repr., with annotations, in: Cook, E.T. & A. Wedderburn, Eds. The works of John Ruskin. Vol. 22, pp.289-490. London, 1906. Various other separate edns.

C160 **Anon.** 1878. The engraver: His function & status. Printing Times & Lithographer N.S.4: 107-110.
Incl. repr. of passages from an article by W.J. Linton in "Scribner's Magazine".

C161 ----- 1881. The new school of wood engravings. Printing Times & Lithographer N.S.7: 60-62.

C162 ----- 1884. A large wood engraving. Printers' Register 23: 260-261.
Largest hitherto executed, being 44 x 33 in., or 1,452 sq. in. of engraved area.

C163 **Linton, W.J.** 1889. The masters of wood engraving. London. vi+xv+229pp. & 29 pls.
Pt. II: On graver work; covers the work of the author's contemporaries.

C164 **Linton, W.J.** 1890. Engraving in wood, old & new. Journal, Society of Arts 38: 487-494.

C165 **Anon.** 1891. Will photography kill wood engraving? Photographic News 35: 617-618.

C166 **Harland, J.W.** 1892. The prospects of wood engraving. Printing Times & Lithographer N.S.1: 41-42.

C167 ----- 1892. A suggested competition for engravers on wood. Printing Times & Lithographer N.S.1: 110-111.
Intended to give impetus to the flagging trade.

C168 **Smith, H.W.** 1892. Wood engraving - past & present. Printing World 2: 156-157.

C169 **Anon.** 1893. Colour printing in excelsis. Printing World N.S.1: 579-580.
Apropos Knoefler prints.

C170 **Herkomer, H. von.** 1894. The position of wood engraving. Printing Times & Lithographer N.S.3: 121-122.
Speech at the annual dinner, International Society of Wood Engravers.

C171 **Anon.** 1895. Engraving: Wood or process? British Printer 4: 190.

C172 **"Boxer".** 1895. The position of wood engraving: What will its future be? Art Printer & Lithographer 1: 41-42.

C173 **Gardner, W.B.** 1895. The present & future of wood engraving. Magazine of Art 19 (Dec.): 57-63.

C174 ----- 1896. Wood engraving as compared with other reproductive arts, & its future as a fine art. Journal, Society of Arts 44: 611-619. Also pub. in: Printing Times & Lithographer N.S.5: 122-123, 146-147, 170-173, 1896.

C175 **Anon.** 1896. Some hope for wood engravers. Artist 17: 81-83.
Their role in the face of inceased use of photo half-tone illus.

C176 **Linton, W.J.** 1897. Some practical hints on wood-engraving for the instruction of reviewers & the public. Boston, Mass., & New York. 92pp.

C177 **Baldry, A.L.** 1898. The future of wood engraving. Studio 14 (June): 10-16.

C178 **Spielmann, M.H.** 1895. The present condition of wood engraving in England & America. National Review 25 (Mar.): 48-58.

Historical

Cj History of wood engraving & printing

About half of the histories of wood engraving published to date were written during the 19th century while the craft was still in its heyday and therefore have limited critical value for the modern student. Having regard only to our period, 1750-1900, we find that Chatto (C179), Anon. (C180), Woodberry (C182), Linton (C183 C184) and Cundall (C185), after passing swiftly through the 18th century, proceed to extoll the virtues of Bewick and his pupils, many of whom were their contemporaries. With the advantage of some 30 years hindsight, White (C186) provides a generally comprehensive critique of work published in the prolific years from ca.1855 to 1870. In our own century Reid (C188) has re-assessed the same period in some detail.

The histories of Bliss (C187) and Garrett (C193) devote little space to the great wealth of wood engraving that followed the Bewick era, whereas De Maré (C195) specifically focusses on this period in a balanced and well informed history. Furthermore, his work includes an excellent range of illustrations, detailed enlargements of some works, and a section on the work of those who engraved for colour reproduction. Lindley's short history (C192) pays more attention to technique than most and emphasises the work of the later 19th century "trade" engraver whose chief concern was interpretation rather than creativity.

A very useful history of the craft of printing from woodblocks was contributed by De Vinne (C181) whose account, though short, is well illustrated and carries the authority of a skilled master in this field. Recently Wakeman (C194) has published a historical sketch of the printing of relief illustrations which is unique in that it is illustrated with a valuable series of contemporary examples that demonstrate both their look and "feel". For histories of the relief printing press see Hoe (A328), Green (A333), Moran (A335), Nuttall (A337), and others in section Ag *supra*.

The practice of transferring designs to the block by photographic means is the subject of a short study by Fildes (C190) and is based, in part, on surviving materials left by his father, Sir Luke Fildes.

C179 **Jackson, J. & W.A. Chatto.** 1861. A treatise on wood engraving, historical & practical. With upwards of three hundred illustrations engraved on wood by John Jackson. The historical portion by W.A. Chatto. 2nd edn. With a new chapter on the artists of the present day by Henry Bohn, & 145 additional wood engravings. London. xvi+664+(561*-600*)pp. Repr. Detroit, Mich., 1969. "New edn.", [1881].
1st edn., 1839. Chatto's history remains virtually unchanged and Bohn's contribution is inserted as an inset chapter.

C180 **Anon.** 1839-40. Illustrated papers on wood engraving. Polytechnic Journal 1: 179-180, 298-301, & 11 pls., 1839; 2: 10-16, 85-89, 169-176, 316-321, & 18 pls., 1840.

C181 **De Vinne, T.L.** 1880. The growth of wood-cut printing. I: Early methods on the hand press. II: The modern method by machine. Scribner's Magazine 19: 860-874; 20: 34-45.
With illus. of machinery and techniques.

C182 **Woodberry, G.E.** 1883. History of wood engraving. London. 221pp. Repr. Detroit, 1969.

C183 **Linton, W.J.** 1889. The masters of wood engraving. London. vi+xv+229pp. & 29 pls.
A valuable history by an accomplished master in his own right. Pt.I: Knife--work [down to Papillon]; Pt.II: Graver-work; Pt.III: Chiroscuro.

C184 ----- 1889. Wood engraving. Cantor lectures. Journal, Society of Arts 37: 676-682.

C185 **Cundall, J.** 1895. A brief history of wood engraving from its invention. London. x+132pp.

C186 **White, G.** 1897. English illustration: "The Sixties" 1855-70. London. xix+204pp. Repr. London, 1906; Bath, 1970.

C187 **Bliss, D.P.** 1928. A history of wood engraving. London. xvi+263pp. Repr. London, 1964.

C188 **Reid, F.** 1928. Illustrators of the sixties. London. xv+295pp. Repr. New York, 1975.

C189 **Morris, R.** 1931. Some forgotten wood engravers. Artwork 7 (26): 108-116.
On the Sir Henry Bemrose collection of original blocks in the Derby School of Art. Mostly from the 19th century Derby firm of Mozley & Richardson.

C190 **Fildes, P.** 1969. Phototransfer of drawings in wood-block printing. Journal, Printing Historical Society 5: 87-97.

C191 **De Maré, E.** 1970. The boxwood illustrators. Penrose Annual 63: 49-68.

C192 **Lindley, K.** 1970. The woodblock engravers. Newton Abbot. 128pp.

C193 **Garrett, A.** 1978. A history of British wood engraving. Tunbridge Wells. 407pp.
Biographical notes, pp.374-400.

C194 **Wakeman, G.** 1977. Printing relief illustrations: Kirkall to the line block. Loughborough. 29pp. & 6 orig. wood engs.

C195 **De Maré, E.** 1980. The Victorian woodblock illustrators. London. 200pp.
Ch. II: The craft; Ch.III: The Engravers; Ch. IX: The decade of colour.

Ck History of alternative methods of block preparation & stereotype

The history of the several curious inventions announced or actually in use before 1850 has been treated in Harris's scholarly study (C201), still the only source of information for some processes. In a wider ranging history Wakeman (C202) takes the story beyond 1850 and shows how these experimental processes contributed to the printing industry and eventually led to the age of photo-mechanical reproduction.

The later history of stereotype and its important contributions to many graphic reproduction techniques has yet to be written. The studies of Carter

(C199) and Morris (C200) deal with the infancy of the technique, while Kubler's (C198) is the only general history, though it naturally emphasises American developments. The sketches of Southward (C196) and Anon. (C197) do no more than outline the commercial development of stereotype as a branch of the printing industry.

Literature on the history of electrotype methods is contained in section **As** supra.

C196 **Southward, J.** 1897. The history of stereotyping & electrotyping. In: Wilson, F.J.F. Stereotyping & electrotyping. pp.1-24. London.

C197 **Anon.** 1899. Stereotyping & electrotyping. Printers' Year Book & Diary 1899: 62-63.
Brief, yet informative, historical sketch of the earliest British stereotype firms.

C198 **Kubler, G.A.** 1941. A new history of stereotyping. New York. x+362pp.
A well illus. history, incl.: Ch.II: Invention of stereotyping; Ch.III: The papier-mache or wet mat process; Ch.V: The dry mat or cold stereotyping process; Ch.VII: Machines.

C199 **Carter, J.** 1960-61. William Ged & the invention of stereotype. Library (5) 15: 161-192.
See also: A postscript. Ibid. (5) 16: 143-145, 1961; & also Donaldson, R. William Ged & the invention of stereotype: A second postscript. Ibid. (5) 22: 352-354, 1967.

C200 **Morris, J.** 1965. A note on the first stereotyping in England. Journal, Printing Historical Society 1: 97-98.

C201 **Harris, E.M.** 1969. Experimental graphic processes in England, 1800-1859. III. Metal relief printing. Journal, Printing Historical Society 5: 41-80.

C202 **Wakeman, G.** 1973. Victorian book illustration: The technical revolution. Newton Abbot. 182pp.

Cl History of block printing in colour

There is no separate history of this branch of colour printing and we must turn to the histories of Burch (A275 A278), Hardie (A277), Lewis (A281), McLean (A286), and De Maré (C195) for general information. In this section we have included a number of monographs on individual craftsmen to supplement the general histories.

Kainen (C208) presents a finely illustrated and scholarly study of the 18th century pioneer, Jackson. The ingenious inventions of Congreve, which chiefly found application in security printing, are the subject of studies by Harris (C210 - C212).

The colour-printing scene in the 1830's and 1840's is dominated by the work of Baxter and his licensees, Kronheim, Dickes, Le Blond and others. Literature on their combined relief and intaglio work is contained in section **Aq** supra.

Leighton, another of Baxter's pupils, did not acquire a license to use

Baxter's process but instead relied on straightforward chromo-xylography; Anon. (C204 C207). As Waddleton shows (C214), he achieved great success in adapting the process to long-run magazine work. Dickes was a successful Baxter licensee but also invented his own "chromograph" process, a form of relief aquatint, and details of his output by this process are listed in Docker's catalogue (C203). Edmund Evans' somewhat rambling autobiography, which includes scarcely any technical information, was edited by McLean (C209) who added a useful list of his major colour-printed work. Fawcett holds a singular place in the field of chromo-xylography on account of the character and quality of the work produced in his Driffield printing house. His output is partly catalogued by Anon. (C205) and Desmond (C213), while Morris (C206) contributes an adulatory memoir which gives no more than tantalising glimpses of Fawcett's methods.

Most of the 19th century firms who specialised in block printing in colour are described in Wakeman & Bridson's guide (A438).

C203 **Docker, A.** 1923. The colour prints of William Dickes. London & Leamington Spa. [x]+50+[104]pp.
Includes a lengthy catalogue of all his known productions.

C204 **Anon.** 1924-25. George Cargill Leighton: Colour prints by one of Baxter's apprentices. Baxter Times 2: 336-338.

C205 ----- 1924-25. Sporting prints in colour by Benjamin Fawcett. Baxter Times 2: 52-54.

C206 **Morris, M.C.F.** 1925. Benjamin Fawcett: Colour printer & engraver. Oxford. xi+140pp.

C207 **Anon.** 1925. Colour prints by G.C. Leighton. Baxter Times 3: 82-83, 116-117, 146-147.

C208 **Kainen, J.** 1962. John Baptist Jackson: 18th century master of the colour woodcut. Bulletin, United States National Museum 222: xii+183pp.
With excellent colour reproductions.

C209 **Evans, E.** 1967. The reminiscences of Edmund Evans, wood engraver & colour printer, 1826-1905. And & introduction & checklist by R. McLean. Oxford. xx+92pp.
The checklist does not claim to be comprehensive. Illus., some in colour.

C210 **Harris, E.M.** 1967. Sir William Congreve & his compound-plate printing. Bulletin, United States National Museum 252: 71-87, illus.

C211 ----- 1968. Congreve's compound-plate printing. Journal, Printing Historical Society 4: 56-66, illus.

C212 ----- 1970. Jacob Perkins, William Congreve, & counterfeit printing in 1820. In: Morse, J.D., Ed. Prints in & of America to 1850: Winterthur conference report, 1970. pp.193-214. Charlottesville, Va.

C213 **Desmond, R.G.C.** 1973. Benjamin Fawcett (1808-1893): Printer & engraver of natural history books. In: Geck, E. & G. Pressler, Eds. Festschrift für Claus Nissen. pp.91-135. Wiesbaden.
A bibliographical description of the books to which he contributed colour-printed illus.

C214 **Waddleton, N.** 1978. Colour printed supplements of the Illustrated London News. Private Library (3) 1: 70-82.

Cm Selected ancillary monographs

As the much revered giant who stands at the head of the great stream of 19th century wood engraving, Bewick has naturally been the subject of many special studies. We cannot include more than a brief selection of literature here but a full list of titles published down to 1913 can be found in Levis's bibliography (A7: pp.140-143); (now supplemented by: Howard-Hill, T.H. Bewick, Thomas, etc. #4015-4047. In: Index to British literary bibliography, vol.IV: British bibliography & textual criticism; a bibliography. pp.349-351. Oxford, 1979.)

Of special technical interest are the catalogues of Bewickiana produced by Anderton & Gibson (C216) and Bain (C218), both of which include illustrations and descriptions of surviving tools and other workshop paraphernalia. Kainen provides a perceptive note on the relation between Bewick's refined engraving style and the contemporary introduction of wove paper which enabled him to print fine impressions of minutely engraved blocks (C217).

The monograph on the Brothers Dalziel (C215), who were so important to Victorian wood engraving, is disappointingly vague on technical matters. Nevertheless it provides a useful chronicle of the work of one of the century's great wood-engraving houses.

C215 **Dalziel Brothers.** 1901. The brothers Dalziel: A record of fifty years' work in conjunction with many of the most distinguished artists of the period, 1840-1890. London. xiii+359pp. Repr. 1979.

C216 **Anderton, B. & W.H. Gibson.** [1904.] Catalogue of the Bewick collection (Pease Bequest). Newcastle-upon-Tyne. vi+110pp.
The collection incl. original sketches, wood blocks, personal relics, letters & examples of his engraved work.

C217 **Kainen, J.** 1959. Why Bewick succeeded: A note in the history of wood engraving. Bulletin, United States National Museum 218: 186-201.

C218 **Bain, I.** 1979. Thomas Bewick: An illustrated record of his life & work. Newcastle-upon-Tyne. 112pp.
Incl. useful technical information on his method of preparing preliminary drawings and his engraving technique.

Section D: Planographic (lithographic) processes

Da Bibliographies

The literature of lithography is included in several of the general bibliographies listed in section Aa supra, such as Levis (A6), Ludman, Mason & Sirefman (A16), and the classified library catalogues of the Patent Office (A5 A7), the Newberry Library, Chicago (A11), and Columbia University Libraries (A15).

The centenary of lithography's invention prompted the special lists of Weitenkampf (D1) and Kampman (D2). Comprehensive coverage of the English literature prior to 1850 is provided by Twyman (D3).

D1 **Weitenkampf, F.** 1896. An attempt at a bibliography. In: Catalogue of an exhibition illustrative of a centenary of artistic lithography, 1796-1896, at the Grolier Club ... New York, pp.11-19. New York.

D2 **Kampmann, C.** 1899. Die Literatur der Lithographie von 1798-1898. Vienna. 40pp. Separat-Abdruck aus Freie Kuenste, Jahrg. 1899. Part A: Books; Part B: Periodicals.

D3 **Twyman, M.** 1970. Bibliography. (A) Literature on the history & techniques of lithography 1801-21; (B) Sources for the early history & techniques of lithography; (C) General. In: Lithography 1800-1850. pp.257-277. London.

Db Lithographic drawing & general techniques

If the technical literature of 19th century wood engraving, the century's most widely used graphic medium, is surprisingly sparse, that of lithography, the same century's other great medium, is appropriately plentiful. Twyman (D251) noted that "... within twelve years of Senefelder's discovering lithography the first independent treatise on the new process had been published in Germany, and in the following forty years some fifty further works were produced in France, Germany, England, and Italy, entirely devoted to explaining the process to printers and artists". He further commented that "The comparative wealth of technical literature on lithography can be partly explained by the rather mysterious nature of the process and its novelty; but it can also be accounted for by the fact that lithography appealed to the amateur artist and painter with no previous experience of the graphic arts, whereas the other processes were firmly established as professional crafts". The earlier manuals were, indeed, largely or sometimes wholly concerned with instruction in lithographic drawing but in the later part of the century their contents came to be dominated by the technicalities of printing. Lithographic draughtsmanship had, by then, largely developed into a "trade" occupation in the hands of professional craftsmen who employed a variety of novel studio techniques. Graphic work was most often transferred to stone or zinc from specially prepared paper for chalk-style work, stippling techniques and rub-down mechanical tints were employed on polished stones and, from the 1860's onward, much graphic work was produced by photo-lithographic techniques. Chromo-lithography had also become a highly developed craft and it, and almost all other work, was normally printed on power-driven machines. The authors of instructional works in this period therefore elaborated on the processes of transferring, photo-lithography, colour mixing, ink control and chemistry, and machine management, giving comparatively little attention to traditional draughting methods.

The first English lithographic manual, by Bankes (D8), was published as early as 1813 and devoted most attention to the art of drawing on stone with pen and ink. Despite the appearance of a slightly enlarged edition in 1816 Bankes' work could not be described as influential. It was the publication of the English translation of Senefelder's treatise in 1819 (D13) that first informed the artistic and printing worlds of the nature, practice, and potential of the new invention. His elaborately prepared text incorporated the fullest treatment of every facet of the process and even forecast some future developments that were not to be introduced for several decades to come. After the several ill-informed and sometimes quite uncomprehending references to the curious art of polyautography and Bankes' less than adequate manual, Senefelder's work provided a model for all subsequent treatises and can still be read with profit today.

Whilst Senefelder described all the technicalities of lithography it was Hullmandel who was to prove the greatest influence in establishing the process as a successful illustration medium in England. A skilled lithographic printer and a tireless worker in the improvement of both the artistic and presswork components of the process, his writings occupy a key place in the English lithographic literature. In 1820 he translated Raucourt de Charleville's useful manual (D14) and twelve years later produced an enlarged edition (D26). But it is his own 1824 manual on lithographic drawing (D20) that holds the first place amongst his writings and stands as the most important English treatise on lithography for many years, with further issues appearing in 1833 and 1835. His efforts to eliminate some of the technical difficulties facing the aspiring lithographic artist and his great concern with the development of tonal qualities in artistic lithography led to his introduction of techniques for correcting and altering work on the stone (D21) and the invention of lithotint (D31 D35).

Meanwhile, a stream of manuals and articles of varying merit had begun to appear directed at informing artists, printers, and the general public. They included the Encyclopaedia Britannica Supplement of 1824 (A24), Partington (A26), Phillips (D22), Anon (D23 D25 D29), Fielding (A28), Nichol (D32), Fielding (D34), Lindsay (A32), Stanbury (D48), Mason (D49), Waterlow (D51), Schenck (D53), Cotterell (D54), Stannard (A34), Straker (D55 D59), and Berri (D58), together with the several general encyclopaedias listed in section Ab supra. Some writers were concerned to announce their particular improvements in draughting technique. Gaillot (D19) introduced an idea for a form of lift ground aquatint on stone, Aresti (D52) also used aquatint effects to good effect for chromo-lithographic work, while Schenck (D45) contributed an improved method for handling the middle tones in lithographic drawing which enhanced both artistic effect and speed of execution.

The process of making transfers of drawings and engravings onto stone mentioned in Senefelder's and other treatises grew in importance. Redman was awarded a premium for his demonstration of its technique (D27) and the first separate account of procedures was published by Miller in 1840 (D28). Another special form of transfer, known as anastatic printing, was patented in England in 1844 and aroused great interest in its day, as revealed by the flurry of notices in periodicals (D36 to D43). The first manual was contributed by De La Motte (D44) but the process became fully established when Cowells adopted it and published their own handbook which remained in print for many years (D46). A further guide to its technique was published by Jordan (D50). Anastatic printing lent itself to amateur use, especially for field archaeological and architectural illustration, and remained in limited but steady use for many years, chiefly by Cowells, and was featured in a trade journal as late as 1873 (D66). Various other autographic and transfer processes were developed, such as those described by Bemrose (D60), Grove (D68), Anon (D69), and a survey of the many varieties available by the 1890's can be found in Anon (D70).

The second half of the century saw the appearance of progressively more technical manuals written with the trade audience in mind. Schenck (D53) is a comprehensive, but rather more concise, survey of the process prepared for an encyclopaedia readership by a much respected lithographic artist and printer. Stannard (A34) also benefits from the printer's insight on technicalities but its tiny edition of ten copies restricted its influence to a privileged few, including Queen Victoria! The first really useful trade textbook of these decades was Straker's (D55) which included all manner of lithographic operations and a practical demonstration of chromo-lithography. Its first appearance was amongst the pages of a general printer's manual but its special value to the lithographic trade probably led to its republication in an improved format (D59). Undoubtedly the most important textbook of this half-century was Richmond's Grammar which found its first readership amongst the subscribers to a lithographic trade periodical (67) and, after re-publication in book form (67*), remained in print virtually unaltered as the standard "trade" manual for the next 30 years. Richmond acknowledged the help of four luminaries of the old school, Louis Haghe, Michael Hanhart, William Simpson, and Harry Sandars (i.e. W.J. Stannard, as was), and they no doubt helped him to achieve a balanced coverage of traditional and modern workshop approaches as well as enhancing the work's authority. He was also the author of one signed article in the same periodical and probably of several other unsigned ones that preceded his Grammar (D61 to D65). Another texbook, by Harrap (D71), also appeared in the pages of a trade periodical and provided a very useful state-of-the-art survey of trade lithography in the early 1890's. It was the work of a professional instructor and would have been of much greater value if it had been separately reprinted. It was not until 1903 that the Grammar's monopoly was challenged by the appearance of Seymour's work (D77) which gave full attention to the advanced machines and techniques that had been introduced since the Grammar first appeared. The next year Cumming's handbook appeared (D78) and, although marginally outside our chosen period, was very much a 19th century work, claiming the benefit of 40 years' experience in Edinburgh's famous lithographic trade and with an emphasis on draughting rather than photo-lithographic techniques. It was to prove as long-lived as Richmond's Grammar being adopted as a War Department manual.

Accounts of lithographic methods directed at the artist rather than the printer are included in general treatises by Hammerton (A42), Hodson (A43), Singer & Strang (A52), and Pennell's largely historical work (D74), while the state-of-the-art on the Continent was described by Goebel (A50). In contrast Harland's studies (A44 A48) include revealing accounts of the lithographic draughtsman's role in a strictly commercial situation, treating of such problems as the difficulty of handling the gigantic stones used for poster work.

Lithographic stone was always under some challenge from zinc as a more conveniently handled substitute (Fielding (A28) gave an excellent specimen of zinc work) and it was eventually widely employed. By the end of the century aluminium was also being recommended and statements of its merits are provided by Algraphy (D73) and Weilandt (D76). Finally, and well outside our period, the techniques of lithographic transferring were fully described in a textbook by Harrap (D79). However, since the work described trade practices which dated back over many years it should be mentioned here.

Literature on photo-lithographic processes is included in section Ee *infra*.

D4 **Anon.** 1807. Art of printing from designs made upon the surface of stone. Journal of Natural Philosophy, Chemistry & the Arts 16: 158.
A vague account of lithographic drawing, probably by W. Nicholson, the editor of the Journal.

D5 **Ker, H.B.** 1807. Some account of polyautography; a discovery lately made of printing from stone. Philosophical Magazine 27: 60-61.

D6 **Fisher, T.** 1808. The process of polyautographic printing. Gentleman's Magazine 78 (1): 193-196.
Briefly describes pen & ink, chalk, and engraved work on stone and its preparation for printing. This, and the two previous articles, were stimulated by the publication of "Specimens of Polyautography", printed by Vollweiler, 1806-07.

D7 **Anon.** 1810. Observations on the newly discovered art of printing with stone. European Magazine 58: 114-115.

D8 **Bankes, H.** 1813. Lithography: Or, the art of making drawings on stone for the purpose of being multiplied by printing. Bath. 23pp. & 3 pls. Repr. London, 1876, together with the 1816 edn., (D10) q.v.
Mainly concerned with pen & ink drawing. No useful information on printing.

D9 **Fisher, T.** 1815. Curious specimen of polyautography, or lithography. Gentleman's Magazine 85 (2): 297-298, & 1 pl.
On the early use of lithography for printing military plans.

D10 **Bankes, H.** 1816. Lithography, or the art of making drawings on stone for the purpose of being multiplied by printing. 2nd edn. with considerable additions. London. 28pp. & 6 pls. Repr. in: Henry Bankes's Treatise on Lithography: Reprinted from the 1813 & 1816 editions with an intro. and notes by M. Twyman. London, 1976. xl+23+28pp.
Once again the chief concern is pen & ink drawing.

D11 **Anon.** 1817. Notice on the origin & practice of the new invention of lithography. Philosophical Magazine 49: 215-218.

D12 ----- 1817. Lithography. Philosophical Magazine 50: 464-465.

D13 **Senefelder, A.** 1819. A complete course of lithography: Containing clear & explicit instructions in all the different branches & manners of that art; accompanied by illustrative specimens of drawings, etc. Transl. from the original German by A.S. [= R. Ackermann]. London. xxx+342pp. & 14 pls. Repr. New York, 1968, together with a suppl. of 31 pls. from the 1st German & French edns.
Includes: A history of lithography from 1796 to 1817; details of materials (stones, ink, chalk, etching-ground, colours, acids and other compositions for preparing the stone, instruments and utensils, sorts of paper, and presses) and methods of lithographic drawing (the elevated manner, the engraved manner, and the mixed manner). The pls. show details of the pole and cylinder presses, and examples of lithographic work, viz. pen drawing, chalk manner, transfer drawing, transfer writing, woodcut imitation, sprinkled manner, etching on stone, tint stone, gum-ink drawing producing white-on--black design, and a chromo-lith.

See also: The invention of lithography. Translated from the original German by J.W. Muller. New York, 1911. xii+229pp. Based on the 2nd edn. of Vollstaendiges Lehrbuch der Steindruckerey. Munich, 1821.

D14 **Raucourt de Charleville, A.** 1820. A manual of lithography, or memoir on the lithographic experiments made in Paris at the Royal School of the Roads & Bridges, clearly explaining the whole art, as well as all the accidents that may happen in printing, and the different methods of avoiding them. Transl. from the French by C. Hullmandel. London. xix+138pp. & 2 pls. 2nd edn., 1821.
In four parts: Basic principles of lithography and necessary materials; descriptions of presses, tools, etc.; drawing on stone in chalk and pen & ink, preparation and printing of stones; comparison of costs with intaglio printing. The pls. show tools and printing presses.

D15 **Dougall, J.** Ed. 1819-21. The cabinet of the arts; being a new & universal drawing book, forming a complete system of drawing, painting in all its branches, etching, engraving, [etc.] Illustrated with 130 elegant engravings. 2nd edn., with additions. London. iii+384pp. & 130pls.
Basically a repr. of the first edn. (B10) with the addition of a new section on lithography. We have not been able to locate a copy of the text for examination. The Victoria & Albert Museum has only the pls. which incl. on nos. 100-104: a transfer, a hand-written poem, a chalk-style drawing, an etching on stone, and an illus. of Ackermann's scraper press (who printed the pls.)

D16 **Anon.** 1822. Lithography. Gentleman's Magazine 92 (2): 627-628.

D17 **F., W.** 1824. On lithography: Or, the art of making drawings on stone. Freebooter 16: 241-244.

D18 **Anon.** 1824. A description of that branch of the lithographic art, called transferography. Freebooter 19: 289-291.

D19 **[Gaillot, -.]** 1824. Lithographic pencil drawing, or instructions for imitating aquatinta on stone, by a pupil of Mr. Senefelder, the inventor of lithography. London. [1]+10+[1]pp. & 13 pls.
Handwritten text is an English transl. of: L'Aquatinta lithographique, ou manière de reproduire les dessins faits au pinceau. Paris, 1824. Describes the methods for obtaining flat, shaded, and stopped-out tints and lists the necessary materials. The pls. show specimen tints of various kinds and demonstrations of drawing in tints, with two pairs showing a drawing in two states.

D20 **Hullmandel, C.** 1824. The art of drawing on stone, giving a full explanation of the various styles of the different methods to be employed to ensure success, & of the modes of correcting, as well as the several causes of failure. London. xvi+vii+92pp. & 19 pls. Repr. with an introduction by J. Friedman, New York, 1980. 2nd edn., 1833; 3rd edn., 1835.
Describes chalk drawing in particular, with advice on the dabbing style and pen-and-ink style. Also covers transfer work, the preparation of the tint stone, correcting drawings on stone and some of the causes of failure. The pls. incl. examples of all styles, a tinted lith. (with a separate printing of the tint stone), a machine eng. transferred to stone, tools and implem-

ents, and methods of employing them. The text of the later edns. remains unchanged (but the xvipp. introduction is omitted) and 5 of the pls. are re-drawn or have the figures re-arranged. The most important lithographic manual published in England in the first half of the century with the most explicit illustrated instructions for the artist working in the tonal style.

D21 **Hullmandel, C.** 1827. On some important improvements in lithographic printing. London. 8pp. & 9 pls.
Apropos his advances in the preparation of stones so as to enhance the production of the paler tones and the possibility of re-touching and amending work after it had been drawn on stone. The text is merely a series of testimonials and provides no technical information. The pls. demonstrate corrections showing work before and after alteration (one example is twice altered), a hitherto impossible procedure.

D22 **Phillips, G.F.** 1828. The art of drawing on stone: In which is fully explained the process of chalk drawing, of pen & ink drawing, & of the dabbing system; together with the preparation of the ink & chalks. London. 22pp.
The title accurately describes the content. It is, however, brief and does not touch upon printing. "With or without this work may be had four lithographic prints, by its author ... being sketches of Humourous Groupes, drawn from the celebrated picture of the Village Festival ... painted by David Wilkie, ..."

D23 **Anon.** 1829. Lithographic mezzotinting. Gentleman's Magazine 99 (1): 347.
A brief note on W. Brockedon's demonstration of lithographic chiaro-scuro by scraping out the "lights" on a totally blackened stone.

D24 **Hullmandel, C.** 1829. [On some further improvements in lithographic printing. With Mr. Hullmandel's compliments.] London. 1p. & 8 pls.
Quoted in some bibliographies as though it were a book, but this is no more than a circular letter stitched together with a collection of lithographic samples. The lithographed handwritten letter and the specimens demonstrating several applications for lithography have survived in a few libraries. The letter, which runs: "Sir, I beg leave to request your acceptance of some specimens which I flatter myself will meet with your approbation ...", is dated April 1829.

D25 **Anon.** 1831. History & process of lithography. Library of the Fine Arts 1: 44-56.

D26 **Raucourt de Charleville, A.** 1832. A manual of lithography, ... 3rd edn. corrected. To which is added (now for the first time printed) selections from the work of M. Bregeaut; forming a sequel to the manual, & bringing down the improvements in the art to the present time. Transl. from the French by C. Hullmandel. London. xix+117pp. & 2 pls.
Basically the same text as the earlier edns., see (D14), with the addition of selections from Bregeaut's work covering general topics in lithography.

D27 **Redman, R.** 1839. Transfers from copperplate to zinc or stone. Transactions, Society of Arts 52: 190-192. Also pub. in: Magazine of Science 4: 204, 1843.

D28 **Miller, A.** 1840. The handbook of transfer lithography. Liverpool. 36pp. & lith. t.p.
A brief historical introduction is followed by details on making and printing the transfer and the work concludes with a section of recipes for transfer paper, ink, varnish, lampblack, and pertinent general remarks.

D29 **Anon.** 1841. Lithography. Magazine of Science 2: 93-95, 109-110, 129-131, 175-176, 202-203.
Complete instructions on drawing and printing.

D30 ----- 1841. Autography. Magazine of Science 2: 238-239, 245-247.
On lithographic transfer work.

D31 **Hullmandel, C.J.** 1841. A new effect of light & shadow, imitating a brush or stump drawing, or both combined, produced on paper, being an impression from a plate or stone prepared in a particular manner for that purpose, as also the mode of preparing the said plate or stone for that object. Mechanics Magazine 34: 207.
Abstract of the patent specification.

D32 **Nichol, W.** 1841. Lithographic printing. In: Hansard, T.C. Treatises on printing & type founding ... from the 7th edn. of the Encyclopaedia Britannica. pp.194-221 & 3 pls. Edinburgh. Originally pub. in: Encyclopaedia Britannica, 7th edn., vol. 13, pp.380-386 (see A29).
A brief but comprehensive account of lithographic drawing and printing. The pls. show lithographic presses and facsimile drawings of pages from the Biblia Pauperum and the Mainz Psalter.

D33 **Anon.** 1842. Lithographic printing. Compositors' Chronicle 1842: 191, 198-199.

D34 **Fielding, T.H.A.** 1842. A manual of lithographic drawing & printing. In: On the theory & practice of painting, etc. 3rd edn., pp.123-146. London. Also repr. in: 4th edn., pp.201-228. 1846; 5th edn., pp.209-236. 1854.
Directed at artists and topographical draughtsmen.

D35 **Rotch, B.** 1843. Hullmandel's lithotint process. Transactions, Society of Arts 54: 174-175.

D36 **Anon.** 1845. A new process of copying engravings. Art Union 7: 8, & 1 pl.
An early report on anastatic printing with a facsimile of an engraving.

D37 ----- 1845. Great discovery in printing. Athenaeum 1845: 71. Also pub. in: Mechanics' Magazine 42: 53, 1845.

D38 ----- 1845. Anastatic printing. Magazine of Science 6: 365-366.

D39 **Faraday, M.** 1845. On anastatic printing. Athenaeum 1845: 437. Also pub. in: Mechanics' magazine 42: 308, 1845, & Magazine of Science 7: 58, 1846.
Report of a paper read to the Royal Institution.

D40 **Anon.** 1845. The "Anastatic", or new mode of printing. Printer, no. 19: 201.

D41 **Jardine, W.** 1848. On papyrography. Contributions to Ornithology 1: 18-22.

D42 **Strickland, H.E.** 1848. Anastatic printing. Magazine of Science 10: 216.

D43 ----- 1848. [On anastatic printing.] Athenaeum 1848: 172, 276.

D44 **De La Motte, P.H.** 1849. On the various applications of anastatic printing & papyrography. With illustrative examples. London. 24pp. & 17 pls.

D45 **Schenck, F.** 1850. Explanation of the treatment of an invention in lithography made by Mr. Schenck & Mr. Ghemar, in August 1849. Edinburgh New Philosophical Journal 48: 147-150, & 1 pl.
A demonstration lecture on their innovation. The specimen pl. "was drawn, lithographed, and cast-off in three hours."

D46 **Cowell, S.H.** 1851/52. A brief description of the art of anastatic printing. Ipswich. 8pp. & 5 pls. Various edns. incl.: 1868, 1872, 1874 & 1881.
Brief instructions addressed to amateurs. The 1868 edn. has a frontis. & 7 pls. demonstrating applications in pen sketching, music printing, and handwriting. The text of the 1874 edn. remains basically unchanged but 11 pls. are provided which incl. a tinted lith. and a specimen of the Pentographic process. The 1881 (10th) edn. omits these 2 pls.

D47 **Hullmandel & Walton.** 1851. A few explanatory remarks, addressed to artists & amateurs, on the means by which the plates exhibited by Hullmandel & Walton are executed. London, Exhibition, Hyde Park.
Not seen. Apparently an exhibition "hand-out" describing their lithotint process.

D48 **Stanbury, G.** 1851. Practical guide to lithography, or the art of drawing on stone; & the various uses of the materials supplied by him. London. ii+11pp. Another edn, 1854.

D49 **Mason, C.** 1852. The practical lithographer, dedicated to painters & artists. London. iv+30pp. & 1 pl.
Describes methods of drawing in chalk & ink, transfer work, production of tint stone, and chromo-lithography but no details on printing. The pl. shows methods and manners of drawing.

D50 **Jordan, C.J.** 1853. A treatise on anastatic printing, or the art of reprinting from prints on paper, ... with various applications & modifications, transfers to zinc & stone, invention of litho-cylindrical printing, etching in relief, etc. London. 1+26pp.

D51 **[Waterlow, A.C.]** 1854. Every man his own printer: Or, lithography made easy. Being an essay on lithography in all its branches, showing more particularly the advantages of the Patent Autographic Press. London. viii+50pp. & 10 pls. 2nd edn., 1859.
An admirably useful illustrated text on the elements of lithographic drawing, writing, transferring, engraving and printing for the inexperienced user. The pls. incl. a demonstration of tinted lithography.

D52 **Aresti, J.** 1857. Lithozôgraphia: Or the new art of obtaining aqua--tinta effects upon painted or washed drawings on stone. 2nd edn. London. viii+vii+16pp. & 10 pls.
The 1st edn. of 1856 could not be traced anywhere. The pls. (which incl. the decorative t.p.) provide examples of aquatint tones & the application of these methods in the preparation of tint stones for chromo-lithographic work. Up to 3 "granulations" are demonstrated in illus. which incl. landscape, seascape, architecture, engineering, & figure studies.

D53 **Schenck, F.** 1857. Short treatise on lithography, from the latest edition of the Encyclopaedia Britannica. Edinburgh. 22pp. Originally pub. in: Encyclopaedia Britannica, 8th. edn., vol. 13, pp.510-514 (see A33).
A brief but comprehensive review of all techniques of drawing, transferring, and printing, incl. tinted and chromo-lithography, and photo-lithography, with mention of the new lithographic steam presses.

D54 **Cotterell, J.F.** [1850's.] The art of drawing on stone. London, n.d. 15pp.
Apparently produced to promote the author's printing business. Cotterell appears in Hodson's 1855 directory (A447).

D55 **Ruse, G. & C. Straker.** 1860? Book II: The lithographic printer. Instructions in the art of lithography. In: Printing and its accessories: A comprehensive book of charges for the guidance of letter-press & lithographic printers, engravers & bookbinders, with ... practical instructions in lithography, ink, chalk, & chromo, with descriptive illustrations, etc. pp.155-290, 291-294. London, n.d. xv+319pp. & 16 pls.
A detailed account of all aspects of drawing, transferring, and re-transferring, covering chalk and pen & ink styles, engraving on stone, chromo--lithography and bronze printing, with full instructions for press-work and necessary materials. Leaf metal printing and zincography are also touched upon. The work is illustrated with a chalk-style chromo-lith. with 5 colour separations.

D56 **Anon.** 1863. Lithography. Typographic Advertiser 1: 67, 74, 82, 90, 98-99, & 2pp. of transfer specimens.

D57 **Fuller, E.** 1863. A short history of the art & practice of lithography; with hints to students. London. ii+24pp. & 3 pls.

D58 **Berri, D.G.** 1864. The art of lithography. London. 44pp. & 5 pls. 2nd edn., 1872; 3rd edn., 1879, with 6 pls.
Written to promote the sale of the author's patent "People's Press" (the frontis. shows a lady at work on one). Covers the rudiments of lithography and a "puff" for the patent press, accompanied by a chromo-lith. pl. with the 3 colour separations.

D59 **Straker, C.** 1867. Instructions in the art of lithography. London. iv+89pp. & 6 pls.
Repr. from Ruse & Straker (D55) in a larger format with a new chromo-lith. example, again printed with 5 colour separations.

D60 **Bemrose & Son.** [Late 1860's.] Bemrose & Son's process of fac-simile printing with instructions for using the instantaneous or fac-simile ink. Derby.
7pp. & 8 pls. A variety of anastatic printing.

D61 **Anon.** 1870. A short treatise on lithography. Lithographer 1: 59-60, 74-75.

D62 **Richmond, W.D.** 1870. Practical hints for engravers on stone. Lithographer 1: 90.

D63 **Anon.** 1870/71. On chalk drawing. Lithographer 1: 172-192.

D64 ----- 1871-74. Dictionary of lithography. Lithographer 2: 76, 92-94, 107-109, 123-124, 140-142, 154-156, 180-181, 1871-72; 3: 6-8, 22-23, 38-41, 106-107, 123-125, 138-141, 155-157, 171-173, 1872-73; 4: 2-3, 18-19, 39-40, 65-66, 117-118, 167-168, 218-219, 243-244, 270-271, 1873-74.
An alphabetically arranged miscellany of short articles of uneven quality on the history and technique of lithography. W.D. Richmond may perhaps have contributed some.

D65 ----- 1872. Hints to artists drawing on stone. Lithographer 3: 27-28, 43-44, 63-64.

D66 ----- 1873/74. Anastatic printing. Lithographer 4: 95-96.

D67 **Richmond, W.D.** 1875-78. Grammar of lithography. Printing Times & Lithographer N.S.1: (11 articles), 1875; N.S.2: (10 articles), 1876; N.S.3: (7 articles), 1877; N.S.4: (8 articles), 1878.
These articles were repr. in the following book (D67*).

D67* ----- 1878. The grammar of lithography: A practical guide for the artist & printer in commercial & artistic lithography & chromo-lithography, zincography, photo-lithography, & lithographic machine printing. London.
12 "edns." appeared over the next 30 years, all apparently reprints of the 1st edn. with, at most, very minor alterations. Part I: Drawing, transferring, and printing; incl. theory, tools, the press, stone preparation, lithographic writing, chalk drawing, transferring, printing, engraving on stone, zincography, chromo-lithography, photo-lithography, and miscellaneous recipes. Part II: Lithographic machine printing, machine management, stone preparation, ink control, paper choice and control, and colour printing. Surprisingly, this authoritative text is not accompanied by any specimen pls.

D68 **Pumphrey, A.** 1878. Collography, for autographic printing; by which any one can reproduce writing or other matter to an unlimited extent, in any colour, with perfection. With autographic illustrations. Birmingham. 26pp. & 13 pls.
The pls are specimens of collography, one in colour. A drawing made with a special ink on paper is pressed against another sheet of paper coated with a specially prepared gelatine. When "developed" with a chemical fluid and rolled with ink only the image of the drawing accepts ink and can be printed like a lithograph.

D68* **Grove, W.B.** 1878. Autographic printing. Midland Naturalist 1: 132-133, 165, & 8 pls.
Pumphrey's collographic process.

D69 **Anon.** 1882. M. Magne's autographic transfer process for printing. Printing Times & Lithographer, N.S.8: 117-118.
For lithographic & zincographic printing.

D70 **Anon.** 1891. Reproduction of writings & drawings by the chemical process. British & Colonial Printer 28: 210, 233, 258, 279.
Polygraphy, Photochromotypy, Velotypy, Papi-autograph, Polychrome autography, Polycopy on paper, Papyrography, Bauer autocopier, Pumphrey apparatus, Multiplicator paper, Gazegraphy, Metallotypy, Perrault process, Cyanotypy, Herschel process, Pellet method, Pizzaghilli process, Fisch process, Nicrography, Collas process, Riegel process, Joltrain process, Shawcross process, & Poitevin process.

D71 **Harrap, C.** 1891-95. Practical lithography. British Lithographer 1 (1): 8-10, (2): 13-18, (3): 8-12, (4): 13-15, (5): 7-9, (6): 21-24, 1891-92; 2: 5-7, 41-44, 81-82, 117-119, 153-155, 209-212, 1892-93; 3: 29-31, 49-52, 93-94, 113-115, 140-141, 169-170, 1893-94; 4: 12-14, 42-44, 77-79, 109-111, 141-143, 179-181, 1894-95.
An up-to-date textbook on trade lithography.

D72 **Verneuil, C.** 1893. Mezzotint designs by lithography. Printing Times & Lithographer N.S.2: 135-136, 168-169, 261, 360-361, 390-391.

D73 **Algraphy Ltd.** 1898. Instructions to the trade for preparation of aluminium plates for algraphic printing. London. 8pp.

D74 **Pennell, J. & E.R.** 1898. Lithography & lithographers; ... with technical remarks & suggestions. London. xiii+279pp.
The revival of interest in lithography as a creative medium in the later 19th century and the continuing concern with good hand-presswork are reflected in the technical portion of this work.

D75 **Watt, P.B.** 1899. Notes on lithography; its theory & practice. Printing Times & Lithographer N.S.8: 80-81, 104-105, 119, 120, 132-133.

D76 **Weilandt, C.** 1901. Algraphy: Or, the art of printing from aluminium plates, with complete technical instructions. Adapted from the German with some details as to various rotary & other machines connected with the process by J.S. Morriss. London. 73pp.

D77 **Seymour, A.** 1903. Practical lithography. London. ix+104pp.
Photo-lithography, rotary zincography, powered presses and other machines had become commonplace and are featured in this up-to-date textbook.

D78 **Cumming, D.** 1904. Handbook of lithography: A practical treatise. London. xi+243pp. & 15 pls.

D79 **Harrap, C.** 1912. Transferring: The practice of transferring to stone, zinc & aluminium as applied to planographic printing; with recipes of transfer papers, inks & crayon. Leicester. viii+162pp.
Incl. a short historical section. Covers amphitype, anastatic transfer, Briggs method, Bromoil, Decalcomanie, Huebner-Bleistein method, etc.

Dc Lithographic printing

The printing of lithographs called for the acquisition of new skills that no conventionally trained printer could be expected to have at his command. The most taxing work was the printing of chalk-style lithography, at which

Hullmandel excelled. However, most earlier lithography was printed from line work, such as pen-and-ink sketches, engraved or line-drawn technical diagrams or maps, handwriting, music writing, or transferred engravings and required rather less skill. However, despite the printers' need for guidance in this new craft there is not a great deal of instructive literature, though printing is briefly covered in several of the general works in section Db supra.

The first good account of the lithographic press and the process of printing was published in Senefelder's comprehensive treatise in 1819 (D13). Instruction on printing was also included by subsequent authors such as Raucourt de Charleville (D14 D26), Encyclopaedia Britannica (A24), Barlow (A32), Nichol (D32), and Straker (D55 D59).

Of singular interest is the inclusion of a chapter "On Polyautographic Printing" in Hansard's treatise on letterpress printing (D82). It is based on Senefelder and was intended to show "how far lithography will either interfere with, or be auxiliary to typography." His view was that "The whole process of drawing on stone appears from Mr. Hullmandel's treatise, beset with difficulties and dangers of the most teasing and curious description; and it is continually liable to failure from, apparently, the most trifling and even ludicrous causes..." His disenchantment was clearly not shared by all as lithographic printers grew in numbers and skill.

Several lithographic manuals were written by lithographic printers who had a vested interest in furthering the popularity of the process. Some, such as Ruthven (D80 D81), Waterlow (D51), and Berri (D58) were also manufacturers of patent presses which they were anxious to promote.

Lithographic printers were about 40 years behind their letterpress colleagues in introducing and developing power-driven machines, the first (a German machine) being commissioned in the 1850's. When these faster machines were put to work it was found that chalk-style work could not be satisfactorily printed on them and new draughting styles were perfected to compensate for this. Work was directly stippled or transferred from textured transfer paper onto polished stone for working at the power press. Schenck's treatise (D53) was probably the first to include mention of the lithographic steam press and various journal articles on machine printing followed (D83 to D88) before Richmond's Grammar (D67 D67*) provided printers with the first thorough guide to this rapidly developing field. Powrie (D89), Harrap (D71), and Seymour (D77) took developments up to the beginning of the present century.

D80 [Ruthven, J.] 1820. Short account of lithography: Or the art of printing from stone, with a description of Ruthven's patent lithographic press. Edinburgh. 22pp.
After a brief introduction on the history, utility, and progress of lithography the rest of the work deals with: Directions for the Patent Lithographic Presses, and incl. transferring, materials, printing, de-scumming, etc. An "R. Horsburgh" is credited with authorship by some sources.

D81 ----- 1821. A concise account of lithography: Or, the art of printing from stone, with suitable directions. Ruthven's patent lithographic press. London. i+17pp.
Similar content to the above together with a lengthy "puff" for the Ruthven press and a testimonial from J. Wyld at the Quarter-Master-General's Office.

D82 Hansard, T.C. 1825. On polyautographic printing or lithography. In: Typographia. pp.888-910. London. Repr. London, 1966.
A brief description of lithographic processes and an assessment of production costs in comparison with letterpress.

D83 Anon. 1870/71. Lithographic machine printing. Lithographer 1: 125-126.

D84 ----- 1871/72. A few general principles for lithographic printing. Lithographer 2: 178-179.

D85 ----- 1872/73. Printing from an engraved stone. Lithographer 3: 107-108, 125-126, 141.

D86 ----- 1873. Printing chalk drawings. Lithographer 4: 4-5, 20-21.

D87 ----- 1876. Instructions in machine printing. I: Lithographic machinery. Printing Times & Lithographer N.S.2: 8-10, 30-32, 55-56.

D88 ----- 1876. The comparative speed of litho machines. Printing Times & Lithographer N.S.2: 179-180; & letter from Thomson, pp.243-244. Others from "T.S.J.", "Commercial", & Thomson, N.S.3: 21, 43-44, 1877. Apropos Thomson's double-cylinder machine, see Anon. (D161).

D89 Powrie, W. 1882. Lithographic printing and its mechanical appliances. British & Colonial Printer 8 (Aug. 10): 1-4.

D90 Anon. 1892. Big work and its difficulties. British Lithographer 1 (5): 21-22.

Dd Lithographic printing in colour (chromo-lithography)

Those guardians of Victorian taste who were quick to pass judgement on new innovations were generally vehement in their condemnation of chromo-lithographs as holding any pretensions to consideration as art. But to most of the Victorian public chromo-lithography was one of the wonders of their age and many printers strove to profit from the growing demand for this new form of colour printing.

As might be expected, Senefelder did not fail to discuss this form of lithography in his remarkably comprehensive treatise (D13) and Ackermann's press provided a specimen of printing in red, blue and black by way of illustration. Subsequent authors such as Nichol (D32), Mason (D49), Schenck (D53), and Stannard (A34) included chromo-lithography in their lithographic textbooks, the latter including specimens of its work. In 1857 Aresti gave an impressive demonstration of his special approach to this process in which he used aquatinta tones for his effects (D91) and even attempted a 4-colour illustration. The scarcity of this work and the apparent lack of other examples of the process suggest that this novelty lacked commercial viability. Straker's description of chromo-lithography, and his specimen with its colour separations, reached a much wider trade audience and was probably the first practical demonstration available to many of them (D55 D59).

Thereafter a steady flow of technical articles appeared in the trade periodicals describing basic colour science and printing procedures. Once again it was Richmond who provided printers with a thorough textbook incorporating both theory and practice (D104 D104*) and forming a companion to his Grammar (D67*). However, the most spectacular works were those by Billing (D92), Day (D102), and Audsley (D105), which took the form of great albums of successive colour separations and progressive combinations of tints culminating in suitably impressive chromo-lithographic pictures.

The kind of chromos that most offended high-minded critics were undoubtedly oleographs -- colour reproductions of paintings produced in lurid oily-looking colours and embossed with imitation "impasta". Most were imported from Germany and brief accounts of them can be found in Thrupp (D96) and Anon. (D103), the latter explaining how the embossed effect was obtained.

Chromo-lithographic pictures prepared for framing, or for use as advertising "show cards", were often given a final coating of machine applied varnish, a process described by Anon. (A240). Literature on the process of bronzing, a process common to lithographic and relief printing, is included in section Ac *supra*.

D91 **Aresti, J.** 1857. Lithozographia: Or, the new art of obtaining aqua-tinta effects upon painted or washed drawings on stone. 2nd edn. London. vi+16pp. & 10 pls.
The application of aquatint tones to chromo-lithography is demonstrated in his 4-colour frontis. and in a pl. "showing the effect obtained by graduating the three primitive colours, with the addition of the chiaro-oscuro plate." See (D52) for description.

D92 **Billing, M.** 1860. Plates illustrating the progressive development of a picture executed in a chromolithograph. Birmingham.
An 1860 calendar, printed in chromo-lithography from 18 stones, is shown in all its colour separations and progressive proofs. Only 12 copies were produced.

D93 **Rowney, F.W.** 1862. Chromo-lithography & other processes of colour printing. In: The record of the International Exhibition, 1862. pp.452-455. Glasgow.

D94 **McLure, A. & A.G. MacDonald.** 1864. On chromolithography. Transactions, Royal Scottish Society of Arts 6: 115-120.
Describes the making of an embossed chromo-lithographic copy of an oil painting in 25 impressions.

D94* **Carpenter, J.** 1866. Chromo- and photo-lithography. Once a Week 14: 147-151, & 2 pls.
With specimens of progressive chromo-lith. from 5 stones and a photo-lith.

D95 **Marples, D.** 1868. On picture printing: Chromo-lithography. Proceedings, Literary & Philoosophical Society of Liverpool 22: 193-224, & 10 pls.
The pls. are a chromo-lith. and its 9 colour separations.

D96 **Thrupp, R.W.** 1870/71. Oleographs. Lithographer 1: 143.

D97 **Watt, P.B.** 1870/71. Hints on colours. Lithographer 1: 2-3, 26-27, 106-107.

D98 ----- 1872. A few hints on colour & printing in colours. London. 32pp.

D99 **Anon.** 1872. Chromo-lithography. Lithographer 3: 58-60.

D100 ----- 1872. Tint stones. Lithographer 3: 62-63, 75-76.

D101 ----- 1872/73. Registering for colour printing. Lithographer 3: 89-90, 157-158; also letters from "A.T." & T.S. Johnston, pp.115, 174.

D102 **Day, J.B. & Son.** [1870's.] How a picture is produced in facsimile of the original, by means of chromo-lithography. London. 27pls.
A picture, printed in 14 colours, is printed in all colour separations and progressive proofs.

D103 **Anon.** 1882. Printing in oil colours. London, Provincial & Colonial Press News 1882 (Aug.): 23-24.
The method of obtaining the embossed "impasta" effects of oleographs.

D104 **Richmond, W.D.** 1882-85. Colour & colour-printing as applied to lithography. Printing Times & Lithographer N.S.8: 5-7, 34-35, 86-88, 1882; N.S.9: 9-11, 32-34, 66-69, 90-92, 119-120, 140-141, 170-171, 205-206, 228-230, 255-256, 277-278, 300-301, 1883; N.S.10: 10, 33-34, 56-57, 84-85, 106, 127-128, 150-151, 194-196, 217-218, 240-241, 263-264, 1884; N.S.11: 6-8, 31-32, 79-80, 1885.
These articles were repr. in the following book (D104*).

D104* ----- [1885?] Colour & colour printing as applied to lithography, containing an introduction to the study of colour, an account of the general & special qualities of pigments employed, their manufacture into printing inks, & the principles involved in their application. London. x+169pp.
Undated 2nd & 3rd "edns" were apparently unaltered repr. of the 1885 edn.
A companion to his grammar (D67 D67*). Ch. I-XX deal with colour pigments, laws of harmony, and related matters; Ch. XXI: Transparent printing; Ch. XXII: Varnishing showcards; Ch. XXIII: Mechanical aids to artistic work [Day's shading mediums, etc.]; Ch. XXIV: Machines for enlarging and reducing; Ch. XXV: Substitutes for lithographic stone; Ch. XXVI: The Hoeschotype photo-chromic printing process.

D105 **Audsley, G.** 1883. The art of chromolithography. London. vi+24pp. & 44 pls.
A description and demonstration of the printing of a chromo-lithograph with all the colour separations and progressive proofs. The work was done by Lemercier of Paris.

D106 **Verneuil, c.** 1895. On cameo printing in colours. British Art Printer & Lithographer 1 (2): 86-87, 90.

D107 **Goodman, J.** 1905-06. Practical colour mixing in lithography. Modern Lithographer 1: 145-146, 163-164, 185-186, 239-241, 279-281, 1905; 2: 333-334, 397-399, 418-420, 442-443, 1906.

De Lithographers' equipment & materials

Most lithographic handbooks include details of the required tools and materials and Winstone (D111) and the various manufacturer's trade catalogues include in section Ah <u>supra</u>, provide a wealth of information. These are supplemented by a scatter of articles in trade periodicals some of which provided information on inventions that were rarely mentioned in lithographic handbooks.

Bavarian limestone, the material that formed the basis of lithography, is the subject of articles by Lord (D110), Spargo (D132), and Anon. (D136). As previously remarked, zinc was used as a more conveniently handled substitute for stone from comparatively early days and its later improvement can be traced in articles by Anon. (D120 D126), and particularly Harrap (D130), whilst the arrival of a further competitor, in the form of aluminium, is described by Waterhouse (D133).

Much graphic work was drawn on specially coated transfer paper rather than directly onto stone or zinc. When this image was placed face down onto the stone and passed through the press it was transferred to the stone and could be prepared for printing. Rival claims existed for priority in this invention the these disputes, together with details of later improvements, are recorded by Anon. (D112 to D115). Transfer designs were sometimes required in a larger or smaller size than the original, a problem that was solved with typical Victorian ingenuity. Pantagraphs and other forms of reducing and enlarging machines were devised and are described by Anon. (D117 D118 D124), but for a really detailed survey of their variety and uses Anon. (D137) must be consulted.

In the later decades of the century the tremendous growth in lithographed commercial graphic and ornamental work called for speedier techniques for preparing designs. The lithographic chalk and pen gave way to such inventions as the rub-down shading medium, a technique that won widespread acceptance, if the several periodicals reports are any guage, Anon. (D116 D119 D121-D123 D127). Another solution was the mechanical stippling pen, described by Anon. (D129), but it was soon superseded by the aerograph, or air-brush, which has survived in common use to this day. This American invention was first reported in 1886 by Anon. (D125) and accounts by others, Anon. (D128), Burdick (D131), Yendis (D134), & Anon. (D135), soon followed.

For information of the special papers used for lithography one must consult the general handbooks on paper listed in section Ak <u>supra</u>. In the earlier years of lithography so-called "India" paper was generally chosen for taking the finest impressions of chalk-style work. The only separate account of its manufacture and use that has come to notice is the French article by Desportes (D109).

D108 **Anon.** 1821. Lithography. Gentleman's Magazine 91 (1): 544.
A report of Senefelder's recent progress in perfecting "stone paper". The development was somewhat ahead of its time and didn't appear as a manufactured material until the present century.

D109 **Desportes, J.** 1839. Papier de Chine, son origine, sa fabrication et sa préparation pour la tirage. Le Lithographe 2: 328-335.

D110 **Lord, W.B.** 1866. Lithographic stone. Nature & Art 1: 74-75.

D111 **Winstone, B.** ca.1867. Price list of lithographic presses, inks, & materials manufactured by B. Winstone. London.

D112 **Anon.** 1870/71. [A series of articles and letters on grained transfer papers, together with discussion of Nelson's patent no.2844 of 1867.] Lithographer 1: 6, 52, 60, 64-65, 67, 82-83, 99, 109, 115.

D113 ----- 1873/74. Autographic paper. Lithographer 4: 138-139.

D114 ----- 1875. The right to use grained paper. Printing Times & Lithographer N.S.1: 211-213; also letters from J. Lewis, "Delta", & "Fairplay", pp.248-249, 266.

D115 Anon. 1880. Improvements in lithography: Grained plates for lithographic drawing & colour printing. British & Colonial Printer 4: 334.
Geo. Cochrane's patent grained transfer paper.

D116 ----- 1883. A new invention in lithography. British & Colonial Printer 9: 4.
On Ben. Day's shading mediums.

D117 ----- 1883. Fougeadoire's machine for enlarging & reducing. Printing Times & Lithographer N.S.9: 61.

D118 ----- 1883. Peiper's precision-pantograph. Printing Times & Lithographer N.S.9: 114.

D119 ----- 1883. Day's lithographic shading mediums. Printing Times & Lithographer N.S.9: 171-172.

D120 ----- 1883. A new substitute for lithographic stone. Printing Times & Lithographer N.S.9: 275-276.
Zinc plates, Moeller's patent.

D121 ----- 1884. Day's shading mediums. Printing Times & Lithographer N.S.10: 7, & 1 pl.
The pl. is a specimen of work.

D122 ----- 1884. Day's shading mediums. Printing Times & Lithographer N.S.10: 175-176.
Progress in acceptance by the trade.

D123 ----- 1885. Day's shading & printing mediums. Paper & Printing Trades Journal no.51: 35.
An advert. appeared in Sept. 1885 in the same periodical with testimonials from several users, the earliest dated Feb. 1884.

D124 ----- 1886. Fougeadoire's reducing & enlarging machine. British & Colonial Printer 17: 331.

D125 ----- 1886. The air-brush -- a new lithographic tool. Printing Times & Lithographer N.S.12: 140-141.
L. Walkup's invention.

D126 ----- 1887. Preparation of plates for zincography. Printing Times & Lithographer N.S.13: 29-30, 135-137.
Zinc plates for lithography.

D127 ----- 1887. Day's shading mediums for lithography, zincography & zincotype. Printing Times & Lithographer N.S.13: 65-66.

D128 ----- 1889. The air-brush. Photographic News 33: 2.

D129 ----- 1892. Hand versus machinery in litho stippling. British & Colonial Printer 29: 82.
On a mechanical stippling pen. An advert. for it in the suppl. to Mar. 17 issue, p.viii.

D130 **Harrap, C.** 1892. Practical lithography. Ch. III: Substitutes for lithographic stone. British Lithographer 1 (4): 13-15, (5): 7-9, (6): 21-24, (7): 5-7.
Provides details of all existing patents.

D131 **Burdick, C.L.** 1894. The fountain air-brush. Journal, Society of Arts 42: 344-350.

D132 **Spargo, E.** 1898. The natural history of lithographic stone: Where & how it is quarried & prepared for printing purposes. British & Colonial Printer 42: 373-374.

D133 **Waterhouse, J.** 1899. Aluminium for lithography. Process Photogram 6: 119-121, 129-132.

D134 **Yendis, M.** 1900. The aerograph & its inventor. Poster 4: 21-23.

D135 **Anon.** 1905. The aerograph, or air brush. Modern Lithographer 1: 153-156.

D136 ----- 1906. Bavarian lithographic stone trade. Quarry 11: 172.

D137 ----- 1907-08. The "Pantagraph" & its use: Mechanical contrivance for enlarging or reducing lithographic designs. Modern Lithographer 3: 777-778, 803-804, 870-872, 1907; 4: 71-72, 95-96, 127-128, 1908.

Df Lithographic presses & machinery

A variety of lithographic presses and machines are described in treatises and manuals from Senefelder onwards. Supplementing these is a useful, if scattered, series of periodical articles and announcements for new machines and attachments. Some are complete transcriptions of patent specifications but most are brief editorial reports which lack any technical details. The trade periodicals which carry these articles usually have ample quantities of advertisements which can be consulted for illustrations, and further information is available in the trade catalogues described in section Ah supra.

The introduction of the first English power driven machines gave rise to a group of articles in the mid. 1860's and by the end of the decade we find an interesting discussion about the requirements in machine capability as seen by the trade (D153). Two further articles supplement this discussion (D155 D157) but in the main the arrival of mechanisation produced surprisingly little comment or debate in the trade journals, editors being content to publish brief announcements of new presses or innovations. Furthermore, a study of advertisements of the period reveals that many litho machines were introduced without any journalistic comment at all so that the literary record is sadly incomplete.

Not until the end of the century do we find a general survey of the variety of machines available to the trade but the booklet, by Powrie, is disappointingly brief (D184)

D138 **Ackermann, R.** 1820. Portable lithographic press, the invention of M. Senefelder. Transactions, Society of Arts 37: 131-132, & pl.22.

D139 **Anon.** 1820. Lithography. Gentleman's Magazine 90 (2): 156, illus. On the Ruthven portable press.

D140 ----- 1822. New lithographic printing press. Gentleman's Magazine 92 (2): 359, illus. Also pub. in: Philosophical Magazine 60: 325, 1822, illus. On the Taylor & Martineau press.

D141 **White, J.** 1822. Of a copper-plate press, with curious & useful properties. In: A new century of inventions, being designs & descriptions of one hundred machines relating to arts, manufactures, & domestic life. pp.230-233, & pl.28. Manchester.
"This machine ... was invented expressly for the use of the lithographic art, as an improvement on the roller press used in Paris when that process was first invented there."

D142 **Day, W.** 1832. Certain improvements in the construction of printing presses. London Journal of Arts & Sciences, conjoined ser. 1: 341-342, & pl.16.
The patent specification for the top-lever lithographic press.

D143 **Baker, E.W.** 1837. Grant's improved lithographic press. Mechanics' Magazine 28: 65-66, illus.

D144 **Nichol, W.** 1844. Improvements in lithographic & other printing presses. London Journal of Arts & Sciences, conjoined ser. 25: 103-108, & pl.6.
The patent specification.

D145 **Scholefield, G.** 1847. Certain improvements in machinery or apparatus to be employed in lithographic printing. London Journal of Arts & Sciences, conjoined ser. 29: 395-398, & pl.20.
The patent specification.

D146 **Smart, W.** 1847. Smart's patent lithographic printing press. Mechanics' Magazine 47: 587-592.
Detailed illustrated specifications.

D147 **Waterlow, A.C.** 1850. Improvements in the means & apparatus for obtaining copies of writings, drawings, & other designs. Repertory of Patent Inventions, enlarged ser. 16: 80-83, & 1 pl.
The patent specification.

D148 **Anon.** 1864. Conisbee's new fast litho printing machine. Typographic Advertiser 2: 34.

D149 ----- 1865. The Conisbee cylindrical lithographic machine. Printers' Register no.25: 7-8.

D150 ----- 1865. The Conisbee machine. Printers' Journal & Typographical Magazine 1: 246-247.

D151 ----- 1867. Litho-typography. Printers' Register 1867 (June 7) suppl: 151-152.
Nicholson's machine.

D152 Anon. 1867. Patent litho-typographic printing machines. London, Provincial & Colonial Press News 1867 (June 15): 13.
Nicholson's machine.

D153 Lewis, J. & others. 1870. [A series of letters on the need for the development of efficient lithographic printing machines & the special features that they should possess.] Lithographer 1: 36, 51-52, 68, 81-82, 100; also editorial comment, pp.125-126.

D154 Anon. 1871. Furnival's "Express" machine. Lithographer 2: 7.

D155 ----- 1871. Is it possible to print in lithography by the platen action? Lithographer 2: 8.

D156 ----- 1871. Wolstenholme's rotary lithographic machine. Lithographer 2: 31.

D157 ----- 1871. What constitutes a good machine. Lithographer 2: 55.

D158 ----- 1872. The Lewis rotary lithographic machine. Lithographer 2: 138.

D159 ----- 1875. The "Leeds" machine. Lithographer N.S.1: 12.
Newsum, Wood & Dyson's machine.

D160 ----- 1875. The Quebec lithographic machine. Printing Times & Lithographer N.S.1: 142-143.
Roxby's machine.

D161 ----- 1876. The new double-cylinder litho machine. Printing Times & Lithographer N.S.2: 119-120.
Thomson's machine. For a discussion of its speed of operation, see Anon. (D88).

D162 ----- 1879. Furnival's new chromo-lithographic machine. Printing Times & Lithographer N.S.5: 25.

D163 ----- 1879. Mann's taking-off apparatus for litho-machines. Printing Times & Lithographer N.S.5: 50.

D164 ----- 1879. Hird's pneumatic deliverer. Printing Times & Lithographer N.S.5: 77-78.
For litho machines.

D165 ----- 1882. Improvements in lithographic machinery. Printing Times & Lithographer N.S.8: 268.
Newsum, Wood & Dyson's Anglo-American machine.

D166 ----- 1882. Schlotke's zincographic perfecting machine. Printing Times & Lithographer N.S.8: 289-290.

D167 ----- 1882. The Anglo-American rotary. London, Provincial & Colonial Press News 1882 (May): 15-16.
Newsum, Wood & Dyson's machine.

D168 Anon. 1884. The single cylinder machine & its essentials. British & Colonial Printer 12 (Mar. 3): 1-2.

D169 ----- 1885. Koenig & Bauer's new lithographic machine. British & Colonial Printer 14: 225.

D170 ----- 1887. A new rotary machine. British & Colonial Printer 18: 263. T. Ruddiman Johnston's machine.

D171 ----- 1887. Paton's new litho machine. Printing Times & Lithographer N.S.13: 215-216.

D172 ----- 1891. Trade notes [On Seggie's "Edinburgh" litho machine]. British Lithographer 1 (1): 32-33.

D173 ----- 1891. The single cylinder machine & its essentials. British & Colonial Printer 27: 233-234, illus.
On Furnival's very large machine for production of oleographs.

D174 ----- 1891. The "Reliable" litho machine. British & Colonial Printer 27: 370, 372.
Ratcliff's machine.

D175 ----- 1891. Some types of American machinery: The "Huber" zincographic press. British & Colonial Printer 28: 387, illus.

D176 ----- 1891. Some types of British machinery: The "Express" litho printing machine. British & Colonial Printer 28: 431.
Furnival's machine.

D177 ----- 1892. Trade notes [On Charlesworth's "Advance" litho machine]. British Lithographer 1 (4): 36.

D178 ----- 1892. Some types of British machinery: Hughes & Kimber's latest litho. British & Colonial Printer 30: 253, illus.

D179 ----- 1894. McAleese's rotary zincographic machine. British & Colonial Printer 33: 247.

D180 ----- 1894. A pioneer rotary zincographic machine. British & Colonial Printer 34: 401-402.
Tuke's machine.

D181 ----- 1894/95. The rotary zincographic printing machine. British Lithographer 4: 153-155, illus.
T. Ruddiman Johnston's machine.

D182 ----- 1895. Rotary printing from the zinc plate; some details of McAleese's patented machine. British & Colonial Printer 34: 97-98.

D183 ----- 1896. The remodelled Anglo-American litho machine. Printer's Register 36: 95-96.

D184 Powrie, W. 1900. Lithographic printing machinery & appliances. Deptford. 16pp.
An illustrated paper first read to the London Association of Foreman Engineers & Draughtsmen.

Dg Miscellaneous literature

This section includes a miscellaneous collection of periodical articles that provide background comment on the growth of lithographic craft and the changing state of the lithographic trade.

Croker (D187), and Anon. (D189 D190) provide decidedly biassed reviews of progress over the first few decades of the century. New inventions, such as Hullmandel's lithotint, later engaged the public's attention. Lithotint was introduced with a flourish only to face such a challenge to the Hullmandel's claim to priority that an interesting legal action ensued; as recorded in Anon. (D191), Hullmandel (D192), Hancock (D193), Hullmandel (D194), & Anon. (D196). Another invention, anastatic printing, was introduced from Germany in 1844 and it also draw a challenge, this time from an amateur botanist, Cocks, who claimed ten years priority (D195).

Wyatt (D197) gave a fascinating behind-the-scenes glimpse of the gargantuan scale of labour and materials that went into the making of his splended chromo--lithographed folios (a feat surpassed by Waring's counterpart a decade later). The progress of lithography in the middle years of the century as it changed from hand-press to powered machine operation is revealed the Society of Arts catalogue (D196*), and in studies by Williams (D198), Sala (D199), and Anon. (D200 D202 D203), while Anon. (D201) voiced thoughts on likely competition that were to have prophetic significance. The state of the trade, its fears and prospects, were vividly portrayed in two series of articles, one in the 1870's, Anon. (D204), and the other some 13 years later, "B" (D208). There were grumbles about foreign competition and pleas for a more progressive outlook from the trade in a number of editorials and articles, viz. Anon. (D205 D207 D211-D214), Müller (D216), and Colebrook (D219). By the 1880's lithography had become an industry with large numbers of personnel who grouped themselves into trade unions such as ASLA (D206) and ASLP (D209), and in 1896 international congresses were commenced which served to bring the trade organisations into contact with their overseas counterparts (D218).

The 1870's had seen the revival of interest in artistic lithography and old-style chalk drawing and hand-printing were discussed, or strongly advocated, by Anon. (D203), Simpson (D210), Rothenstein (D215), Spielmann (D217), and Pennell (D222). At the close of lithography's first century Dolby (D220) looked back to the days of old, whereas Morriss (D221) looked forward to lithography's newest advance -- a new substitute for stone.

D185 Hullmandel, C. 1820. [Communication to accompany:] The best specimens of lithography executed on German stone. Transactions, Society of Arts 37: 53-57. Also pub. in: Repertory of Arts & Sciences (2) 37: 18-22, 1820, & Philosophical Magazine 41: 282-285, 1820.
Notice of an award of the Society's silver medal.

D186 Redman, D. 1820. [Communication to accompany:] A specimen of lithography ... executed on English stone. Transactions, Society of Arts 37: 58. Also pub. in: Repertory of Arts & Sciences (2) 37: 22, 1820, & Philosophical Magazine 56: 285, 1820.
Notice of an award by the Society.

D187 [Croker, C.] 1829. History of lithography. Foreign Review & Continental Miscellany 4: 41-58.

D188 **Hullmandel, C.** 1829. Reply to some statements in an article entitled "The history of lithography" published in the Foreign Review, No.VII, for July 1829. London. 11pp.
Not seen: cf. Bigmore & Wyman (A2), p.349.

D189 **Anon.** 1831. A view of the present state of lithography in England. Library of the Fine Arts 1: 201-216.

D190 ----- 1839. The state & prospects of lithography. Art Union 1: 97-98.

D191 ----- 1842. Lithotint in chancery. Art Union 4: 105-106.

D192 **Hullmandel, C.** 1843. The inventor of lithotint. Art Union 5: 290-292.

D193 **Hancock, C.** 1843. The "Inventor" of lithotint. Art Union 5: 312-313.

D194 **Hullmandel, C.** 1844. The invention of lithotint. Art Union 6: 19.

D195 **Cocks, W.P.** 1845. [Letter.] Anastatic printing. Mechanics' Magazine 42: 307-308.

D196 **Anon.** 1847. Mr. Hullmandel's new process. Art Union 9: 229.

D196* **Society of Arts.** 1848. Catalogue of the specimens illustrative of the progress of lithography & chromatic printing in England, exhibited at the Society's house from Dec. 27, 1847, to Jan. 8, 1848. Chiswick.
Not seen.

D197 **Wyatt, M.D.** 1851. [Prefatory note on methods & scale of operations for producing:] Industrial arts of the XIXth century. Vol. 1, pp.ix-xii. London.
A similar statement can be found in: Waring, J.B. Masterpieces of industrial art & scultpure at the international exhibition of 1862, Vol. 1, p.[i]. London, 1863.

D198 **Williams, W.S.** 1852. On lithography. Transactions, Society of Arts, 1847-48 suppl. vol: 226-250, & 2 pls.

D199 **Sala, G.A.** 1852. Stone pictures. Household Words no.111: 179-180.

D200 **Anon.** 1870/71. Lithography past & present. Lithographer 1: 4-5, 28-29, 43-44, 140-141, 174.

D201 ----- 1870/71. Photography versus lithography. Lithographer 1: 62-63.

D202 ----- 1871/72. Lithography in London. Lithographer 2: 35-37.

D203 ----- 1873/74. Recent progress & present position of artistic lithography. Lithographer 4: 161-163, 190-192, 212-214, 237-239.

D204 ----- 1873-74. The lithographer. Printing Times 1 & 2.
Monthly reports on the lithographic trade in Britain, Jan. 1873 to Feb. 1874.

D205 **Anon.** 1881. Lithographic notions. British & Colonial Printer 5: 265-267.
An editorial pressing for more progressive ideas in the trade.

D206 **Amalgamated Society of Lithographic Artists, Designers & Writers, Copperplate & Wood Engravers,** [Founded 1885]. 1888+. Reports. Manchester.
The 5th report for 1888 is the earliest one seen.

D207 **Anon.** 1887. Lithography in America, & its future influence upon English trade. Printing Times & Lithographer N.S.13: 46-47, 66-68.

D208 **"B".** 1887-88. Art-litho gossip. Printing Times & Lithographer N.S. 13 & 14.
Monthly comment & reports on the trade in Britain, Sept. 1887 to Oct. 1888.

D209 **Amalgamated Society of Lithographic Printers of Great Britain & Ireland,** [Founded 1880]. 1889+. Half-yearly reports. Manchester.
The report for Sept. 1888 to Mar. 1889 is the earliest one seen.

D210 **Simpson, W.** 1891. Lithography: A finished chapter in the history of illustrative art. Journal, Society of Arts 39: 189-201.

D211 **Anon.** 1892. Foreign competition. British Lithographer 1 (5): 11-12.
Specifically, American competition.

D212 ----- 1893. Colour printing in England. Printing Times & Lithographer N.S.2: 430.
Discussion of the effects of foreign competition on the litho trade.

D213 ----- 1893. The lost enterprise in British lithography. British & Colonial Printer 32: 347.
On the problem of foreign competition.

D214 ----- 1894. A new departure in the litho trade: Three things needful -- capital, energy, & common sense. British & Colonial Printer 33: 60.

D215 **Rothenstein, W. & T.R. Way.** 1894. Some remarks on artistic lithography. Studio 3: 16-20.

D216 **Müller, S.** 1895. British lithography: Its present & probable future. Art Printer & Lithographer 1: 49-52, 121-123.

D217 **Spielmann, M.H.** 1896-97. The revival of lithography. Introduction: Its rise & first decline. Original lithography: The present revival in England. Magazine of Art 1896 (Dec.): 75-79; 1897 (April): 289-296.

D218 **International Congress of Lithographers.** 1897-1903. Reports.
1st, London, 1896. Manchester, 1897.
2nd, Berne, 1898. Berne, 1898.
3rd, Paris, 1900. Manchester, n.d.
4th, Berlin, 1902. London, 1903.

D219 **Colebrook, F.** 1897. Lithography: Past, present, & future. British & Colonial Printer 40: 381-383.

D220 **Dolby, E.** 1897. Recollections of an old lithographer. Art Journal 1897: 346-347.

D221 **Morriss, J.S.** 1899. Algraphy v. lithography. Poster 2: 54-59. Report of a lecture.

D222 **Pennell, J.** 1899. The truth about lithography. Studio 16: 38-44. Comparative merits of work drawn direct onto stone or prepared on transfer paper.

Historical

Dh General history of lithography

Well before the centenary of the invention of lithography several writers had attempted brief chronicles of its history, usually based on their own or their acquaintances' experience in the trade. Senefelder's work (D13) contained a narrative of progress from 1796 to 1817 and in 1829 Croker wrote a subjective history (D187) which elicited a rejoinder from Hullmandel (D188). Williams contributed a general survey of the early decades down to the mid century (D198) and others, such as Anon. (D200) and Simpson (D210), followed with personal recollections down to the 1870's. The pioneer patent documents were reviewed by Anon. (D223).

But it was not until the 1890's that Watt (D225 D227 D230 D232), Green (D226 D229), and Burch (D233), with the advantage of greater distance from their subject, commenced detailed historical survey of English lithography, while Murdoch (D234 D235) and Canning (D236) wrote on the Scottish trade. All were, to a great extent, anecdotal and biographical in flavour.

The completion of lithography's first century was apparently the stimulus for the first book length histories by Curtis (D228) and Pennell (D231), both of whom displayed a critical concern with the medium's aesthetic contribution to creative graphic art. Pennell's work was almost entirely revised in 1915 (D239) and was followed by the general histories of Halbmeier (D240) and Weber (D248). A close study of lithography's earliest years is made by Emanuel (D242) and Man (D246), the latter adopting a detailed bibliographical approach. Twyman (D251) examines literary and graphic sources down to 1850 in a scholarly survey of both technical and aesthetic aspects of the medium's development in England and France. Brief, but technically informative, histories which include developments beyond 1850 can be found in Mosley (D244) and Samson (D245).

The curious history of anastatic printing is the special concern of Stoyle (D247) and Wakeman (D249 D252). Victorian illustrated music covers, a fertile field for the application of lithographic art, are given biographical and critical study by Imeson (D238) and King (D243). Another less obvious, but similarly prolific, field for lithography existed in the printing of maps and is the subject of an historical essay by Ristow (D254).

The history and geography of the London lithographic trade is documented in a historical directory by Twyman (A439). Finally, Sproat chronicles the history of one of lithography's most important trade unions (D241).

D223 **Anon.** 1873-74. The history of lithography as written in the records of the Patent Office. Lithographer 4: 139-140, 216-218, 245-246, 1873-74; 5: 120-121, 181, 220-221, 246-247, 1874.

D224 ----- 1881. Senefelder & lithography. Printing Times & Lithographer N.S.7: 62-63, 114-116.

D225 **Watt, P.B.** 1891/92. The rise & progress of lithography in Britain. British Lithographer 1 (1): 21-23; (3): 13-17; (4): 22-25; (5): 29-31. (An incorrect portrait of Michael Hanhart was included. The proper one appeared in (6): 29.)

D226 **Green, E.** 1894. The beginnings of lithography. Archaeological Journal 51: 109-119.

D227 **Watt, P.B.** 1896. Early English lithography. Artist 1896 (May): 224-226.

D228 **Curtis, A.** 1897. Some masters of lithography. New York. xvi+187pp. & 22 pls.
A series of monographic studies of lithographers, incl. R.P. Bonington & J.D. Harding. The pls. are photograv. reproductions.

D229 **Green, E.** 1897. Bath & early lithography. Proceedings, Bath Natural History & Antiquarian Field Club 8: 23-35.

D230 **Watt, P.B.** 1897. The centenary of the art of lithography. Stationer & Fancy Trades' Register 1897: 452-455.

D231 **Pennell, J. & E.R.** 1898. Lithography & lithographers: Some chapters in the history of the art. London. xiii+279pp.

D232 **Watt, P.B.** 1898-99. The exhibition of lithography at South Kensington. Printing Times & Lithographer N.S.7: 169-170, 188-189, 1898; N.S.8: 9-10, 30, 45-46, 1899.
For a catalogue of the exhibition, see Victoria & Albert Museum (A397).

D233 **Burch, R.M.** 1899-1900. Some notes on early lithography. British & Colonial Printer 45: 325, 1899; 46: 13-14, 25-26, 37-38, 61-62, 97-99, 1900.
Takes the history down to 1830 with particular attention to the early patents.

D234 **Murdoch, T.** 1902. The early history of lithography in Glasgow. Glasgow. 23pp.

D235 ----- 1906. The early history of lithography in Glasgow, 1860-1902. Modern Lithographer 2: 365-369.
Largely the same text as the above.

D236 **Canning, D.** 1906. The rise & progress of lithography in Glasgow. Modern Lithographer 2: 489.

D237 **Goodman, J.** 1907. Some old landmarks of lithography. Penrose Annual 12: 105-109.

D238 **Imeson, W.E.** 1912. Illustrated music titles & their delineators. London. 46pp.

D239 **Pennell, J. & E.R.** 1915. Lithography & lithographers: Some chapters in the history of the art by E.R. Pennell together with descriptions & technical explanations of modern artistic methods by J. Pennell. [New edn.] London. xx+319pp.
A largely re-written version of the 1st edn. (D231).

D240 **Halbmeier, C.** 1926. The history of lithography. New York. 216pp.

D241 **Sproat, T.** 1930. The history & progress of the Amalgamated Society of Lithographic Printers & Auxiliaries of Great Britain & Ireland, 1880-1930. Manchester. ix+92pp.

D242 **Emanuel, F.L.** 1934. Some sidelights on early lithography. Print Collectors' Quarterly 21: 337-352.

D243 **King, A.H.** 1950. English pictorial music title-pages 1820-1885. Their style, evolution, & importance. Library (5) 4: 262-272.

D244 **Mosley, J.** 1961. Lithography's first century: The decades of development. British Printer 74 (7): 101-108.

D245 **Sansom, B.W.** 1961. The historical background to lithography. British Printer 74: 107-109.

D246 **Man, F.H.** 1963. Lithography in England (1801-1810). In: Zigrosser, C. Ed. Prints: Thirteen illustrated essays on the art of the print. pp.97-130. London.

D247 **Stoyle, F.W.** 1965. Michael Faraday & anastatic printing. British Ink Manufacturer 8: 46-51.

D248 **Weber, W.** 1965. A history of lithography. London. 259pp.
Translated from the German, Saxa loquuntur: Steine reden. Heidelberg & Munich, 1961-64. 2 vols.

D249 **Wakeman, G.** 1969. Anastatic printing for Sir Thomas Phillips. Journal, Printing Historical Society 5: 24-40.

D250 Deleted.

D251 **Twyman, M.** 1970. Lithography 1800-1850. The techniques of drawing on stone in England & France & their application in works of topography. London. xxi+302pp.

D252 **Wakeman, G.** 1970. Aspects of Victorian lithography. Anastatic printing & photo-zincography. Wymondham. 63pp. & 2 pls.
The pls. are specimens of Victorian anastatic printing & photo-zincography.

D253 **Twyman, M.** 1971. The art of drawing on stone. Penrose Annual 64: 97-124.

D254 **Ristow, W.W.** 1975. Lithography and maps 1796-1850. In: Woodward, D. Ed. Five centuries of map printing. pp.77-112. Chicago, Ill.

Di History of lithographic printing in colour

Most of the historical studies of chromo-lithography are included as part of general histories of colour printing. Apart from the brief notes of Anon. (D255) and Prideaux (D257) the first detailed technical survey was compiled by Burch (A275 A278) and the earlier, and fuller, version of his history is still an unrivalled source for technical aspects of the subject. Lewis's book (A281) dealt with a rather narrower spectrum of chomo-lithography and, despite its tedious style, is still a useful source of general information. Shorter contributions by Gray (D258), Scott (D259), and Sharp (D260) each include interesting technical observations on different aspects of the craft.

In recent decades some scholarly studies have considerably widened our knowledge of the history of chromo-lithography. In earlier years of the century the single- or double-tinted lithograph formed the bulk of colour lithographic work and has been the subject of an excellent history by Twyman (D261). As part of a wide survey of Victorian book design and colour printing McLean provides a fully illustrated and readable history of chromo- lithographed book illustration (A286), and more recently his survey has been supplemented in technical detail by Wakeman (A288), who includes contemporary examples of the art. Special applications of chromo-lithography are surveyed in Nelson's study of Arundel prints (D256), Imeson's guide to music covers (D238), and Buday's history of the Christmas card (A285). Finally, Wakeman & Bridson provide a firm-by-firm survey of the producers of chromo-lithography in nineteenth century Britain (A438).

D255 Anon. 1873. A glance at the history of chromo-lithography. Lithographer 4: 17-18.

D256 **Nelson, H.H.** 1905. Arundel prints. In: Deane, E. Ed. The collector, containing articles & illustrations reprinted from The Queen newspaper, &c. Vol. 2. London.

D257 **Prideaux, S.T.** 1907/08. Color lithography in England, a chapter in the early history of book illustration. Printing Art 10: 305-312.

D258 **Gray, N.** 1938. The nineteenth century chromo-lithograph. Architectural Review 84: 177-178, 187.

D259 **Scott, E.K.** 1939. Renaissance of lithographic colour printing. Proceedings, National Picture Print Society, etc. 4: 37-51.

D260 **Sharp, R.** 1962. The development of chromolithography in the nineteenth century. A brief history of lithography & its association with colour in Germany, France & England over a hundred years. Manchester. 53pp.

D261 **Twyman, M.** 1965. The tinted lithograph. Journal, Printing Historical Society 1: 39-56.

Dj History of lithographers' equipment & materials

Twyman's several historical writings on English lithography include the only study on lithographic stone, so fundamental to the whole industry (D266). Hohenthaner (D264) briefly covers the development of the zinc plate which was to replace stone for most commercial work in the later nineteenth century.

The first half-century's developments in the lithographic hand-press are admirably illustrated and chronicled by Twyman (D265) but, unfortunately, the very brief sketches by Anon. (D262) and Goodman (D263) are all that we have on the later introduction and developments in power-driven lithographic machines, first introduced in the early 1890's.

D262 Anon. 1870. History of the lithographic machine. Lithographer 1: 29-31.

D263 **Goodman, J.** 1905. The evolution of lithographic printing machinery. Penrose Annual 10: 41-46.

D264 **Hohenthaner, R.C.** 1937. Development of the zinc litho plate. Share Your Knowledge Review 18 (12): 26-27.

D265 **Twyman, M.** 1967. The lithographic hand press, 1796-1850. Journal, Printing Historical Society 3: 3-50.

D266 ----- 1972. Lithographic stone & the printing trade in the nineteenth century. Journal, Printing Historical Society 8: 1-41.

Section E: Photo-mechanical processes

Ea Bibliographies

From the 1830's to the end of the century the literature of photography and photo-mechanical printing grew to remarkable proportions, ranging from small popular manuals to extensive files of periodicals. In the mid 1880's Harrison, an early historian of photography, compiled a commendably detailed and comprehensive bibliography of the books and periodicals (E1), a pioneer effort which deserved to be separately published in a more conveniently usable form. The library catalogues of the Patent Office (E3 A6 E4) and the Royal Photographic Society (E5) both complement and supplement Harrison. The recent bibliography by Boni and others (E7), despite its great size, is disappointingly patchy in its coverage of 19th century literature, though it does include periodicals articles which its predecessors all omitted.

The specialised lists of Bolas on colour work (E2), Berry & Thomson on collotype (E6), Gernsheim on early periodicals (E8), together with the catalogues of the St. Bride Foundation (A10), the Newberry Library (A13), and Columbia University Libraries (A15), all add to the coverage of 19th century literature. However, there is still a great need for a thorough retrospective guide to photographic books and periodicals. In particular, the multitude of periodical articles in which are recorded the current advances in research and technical innovation -- week-by-week in some cases -- need proper documentation if one is to gain an accurate picture of these developments and their exploitation by both the amateur photographer and the photographic printing industry.

E1 **Harrison, W.J.** 1886-88. Contributions to the bibliography of photography. Photographic News 30: 9-10, 65-66, 113-115, 242-243, 274-275, 361-363, 436-438, 749, 779-780, 1886; 31: 214-215, 1887; 32: 53-54, 75-76, 107-108, 154, 210-211, 397, 423-424, 1888; & letters relating to the bibliography 31: 270, 284, 365-366, 1887.

E2 **Bolas, T.** 1897. Contributions towards the bibliography of photography in colours. Journal, Society of Arts 45: 531-540.

E3 **Patent Office.** 1900. Subject list of works on photography & the allied arts & sciences in the library of the Patent Office. London. 62pp.

E4 ----- 1914. Subject list of works on photo-mechanical printing & photography in the library of the Patent Office. London. iv+121pp. (Patent Office Subject List, N.S. CA-CC.)

E5 **Royal Photographic Society.** 1939. Library catalogue. Part 1: Author catalogue. London. 52pp.
----- 1952. ----- Supplement. London. 48pp.
----- 1953. ----- Second supplement. London. 28pp.
----- 1953. ----- Part 2: Subject catalogue. London. [iii]+105pp.
----- 1953. ----- ----- Supplement, (1950-1952). London. 43pp.

E6 **Berry, W.T. & M.C. Thomson.** 1958. Collotype printing processes: A special subject list. London. 13pp. (Library Association Special Subject List, no.25.)

E7 **Boni, A. & others.** 1962. Photographic literature: An international bibliographic guide to general & specialised literature on photographic processes, techniques, theory, chemistry, physics, apparatus, materials & applications, industry, history, biography, aesthetics. New York. xvi+333pp.
----- 1972. Photographic literature, 1960-1970; etc. New York. xv+535pp.

E8 **Gernsheim, H. & A.** 1969. The first decade of photographic journals. In: The history of photography from the camera obscura to the beginning of the modern era. 2nd edn. pp.586-588. London.

E9 **Gauntlett, M.D.** 1971. Some aids to retrospective searches of the literature of photographic science. Journal of Photographic Science 19: 21-22.

Eb Photographic & photo-mechanical processes in general

The announcements, in 1839, of photographic processes by Talbot (E10), Daguerre (E11-E13), and Niepce (E17) heralded the start of a technology that was to revolutionise the graphic arts industry over the next sixty years. Within a relatively short span of months the public was provided with a dozen separate published accounts of this new "wonder" and the stream grew to a flood as the decades passed. We have listed only the earliest general photographic works and a small selection of succeeding literature in which the beginnings of photo-mechanical technology is recorded.

It was Talbot's process which first suggested new means of providing book illustrations and in 1844 be commenced publication of the "Pencil of Nature" illustrated with his "sun pictures" (E20). In 1846 one of his photographs was published in an issue of the leading art periodical of the day (E21).

The first practical manual of photographic principles and applications was produced by Hunt in 1841 (E19) and served to bring this novelty to the people at large, including, of course, artists, engravers, lithographers and printers. His successful manual went through several revisions and in the 1854 edn. was the first book to include details of Talbot's new photo-engraving technique (E23), the first true photo-mechanical process. Thus began a long and many branched stream of invention whose goal was to produce photographically created images on chemically or mechanically formed surfaces that could be printed with normal ink onto normal paper.

In 1855 the first of many editions of Hardwich's textbook appeared (E24), and for the next forty years it kept photographers and printers up-to-date with chemical developments. The 1860's saw the publication of a few booklets each of which dealt with an individual photo-mechanical invention such as photo-zincography, photo-lithography, Swan's carbon process, and so forth. But there was no attempt to produce a comprehensive survey of these processes until 1884 when Hodson's guide appeared. Some general treatises on photography appeared in the intervening years such as Vogel (E35 E36), Tissandier (E34 E39), and Abney (E37), all of which included sections on photo-mechanical developments. Vogel's work, which went through six editions in 20 years, was probably the most authoritative, up-to-date, and influential of this group and had the advantage of including 5 actual examples of the new processes.

Hodson's Guide (E44), apart from being the first of a new class of photo-mechanical textbooks, also deserves mention for its splendid series of examples of the processes described. Two years later Wilkinson produced the first edition of his Photo-Engraving (E47), a practical modern technical manual which went through five fully-revised editions by 1894. It eventually became incorporated in his other successful work, Photo-Mechanical Processes (E64), which reached its 3rd edition by 1904. Two other outstanding textbooks of this period were Burton (E49 E61) and Brothers (E60 E69), both appearing in revised editions before 1900. Burton's was the most comprehensive manual of its period while Brothers' was the best illustrated with 24 examples of photo--mechanical processes.

The second part of Brothers' 1892 book was an alphabetical survey of all known photographic and photo-mechanical processes and in the same year Woodbury published his comprehensive encyclopaedia (E65). The earliest dictionary of photo-mechanical terminology is by the American, Baker (E71), but since much trans-Atlantic expertise went into the development of certain photo--mechanical processes in England there was also much shared terminology.

From 1864 onwards photographers and printers were provided with a series of state-of-the-art surveys of developments and applications in photo-mechanical printing in Britain by Crookes (E28), Anon. (E33), Bolas (E38 A41 E43), Anon. (E45), Bolas (E57), Waterlow & Geddes (E62), and Ward (E70). Progress in Germany and Austria, both in the forefront of development, was reviewed by Gunther (E52 E58). Cartographers had been among the first to experiment with the sucessful application of photo-mechanical printing and Waterhouse, taking note of European advances in the field, provided two excellent reviews of cartographical applications in 1870 (E31) and 1878 (E40).

E10 **Talbot, W.H.F.** 1839. Some account of the art of photogenic drawing or the process by which natural objects may be made to delineate themselves without the aid of the artist's pencil. Privately pub. 13pp.
A paper read to the Royal Society of London. Abstracts of it also pub. in: Proceedings, Royal Society of London 4: 120-121, 1839, & Philosophical Magazine 14: 196-211, 1839.

E11 **Daguerre, L.J.M.** 1839. History & practice of photogenic drawing. On the true principles of the daguerreotype, with the new method of dioramic painting. Transl. from the original by J.S. Memes. London. xii+76pp. & 6 pls. Extracts also pub. in: Polytechnic Journal 1: 148-154, 1839.
This translation, pub. by Smith, Elder, was published in three "edns", (actually re-impressions), in the same year. It was the first of three independent English edns. pub. in 1839.

E12 ----- 1839. The history & process of photogenic drawing by means of the daguerreotype. With notes & explanations by M. Arago. London. 46pp. & 6 pls.
This edn. pub. by Strange.

E13 ----- 1839. An historical & descriptive account of the various processes of the Daguerreotype & the diorama. London. [iv]+86pp. Repr., With an intro. by B. Newhall. New York, 1971.
This edn. pub. by McLean.

E14 **Anon.** 1839. Photogenic drawing. Magazine of Science 1: 18-20, 26-28, 34-35, 59-60.
Review of history and progress.

E15 **Anon.** 1839. Principle of the Daguerreotype. Magazine of Science 1: 174-175.
Report of D.F.J. Arago's description of the process as delivered in August to the Académie des Sciences, Paris.

E16 **Talbot, W.H.F.** 1839. Remarks on M. Daguerre's photogenic process. Report, British Association 1839 (2): 3-5. Also pub. in: Magazine of Science 1: 182-184, 1839.
Read at the meeting of the 26th August.

E17 **Niepce, J.N.** 1839. Heliography. Magazine of Science 1: 215-216.
A translation of his "Notice sur l'héliographie" of 1829.

E18 **Berry, M.** 1840. An invention of a new or improved method of obtaining the spontaneous reproduction of all the images received in the focus of the camera obscura, being a communication from a foreigner, residing abroad. London Journal of Arts & Sciences, conjoined ser. 16: 1-25.
On Daguerreotype.

E18* **Talbot, W.H.F.** 1841. On calotype photogenic drawing. Philosophical Magazine 19: 88-92.

E19 **Hunt, R.** 1841. A popular treatise on the art of photography, including Daguerreotype, & all the new methods of producing pictures by the chemical agency of light. London. 96pp. Repr., With intro. by J.Y. Tong. Athens, Ohio, 1973. lxxv+96pp.

E20 **Talbot, W.H.F.** 1844-46. The pencil of nature. London. xxvi+24pp. & 24 pls. Repr., With a new intro. by B. Newhall. New York, 1969. xii+94pp.
Incl. a "Brief historical sketch of the invention of the art" forming an introduction.

E21 **Anon.** 1846. The Talbotype - sun pictures. Art Union 8: 143-144, with a specimen pl.

E22 **Hunt, R.** 1851. Photography: A treatise on the chemical changes produced by solar radiation, and the production of pictures from nature, by the Daguerreotype, Calotype, & other photographic processes. London. 234pp. & 2 pls.

E23 ----- 1854. A manual of photography. 4th edn., rev. London. 329pp.
Incl: Talbot, W.H.F. Photographic engraving, pp.313-319.

E24 **Hardwich, T.F.** 1855. A manual of photographic chemistry, including the practice of the collodion process. London. xvi+384pp. 2nd edn., 1856. xvi+390pp.; 3rd edn., 1856; 4th edn., 1858. xvi+390pp.
Pt. I: The science of photography; Pt. II: Practical details of the collodion process; Pt. III: Outlines of general chemistry. The edns. vary only slightly.

E25 **Hunt, R.** 1857. A manual of photography. 5th edn., rev. London. viii+342pp. & 1 pl.
Pt. I: History of the early discoveries in photography; Pt. II: Practice of photography; Pt. III: Scientific investigations on photography; Ch. XII: On photographic engraving. The pl. is a photo-galvanograph.

E26 **Hardwich, T.F.** 1859. A manual of photographic chemistry, [etc.] 5th edn. London. xvi+516pp.
An enlarged version of the 1855 text with brief sections on photo-galvanography, photo-lithography, photoglyphy, and carbon printing.

E27 ----- 1861. A manual of photographic chemistry, [etc.] 6th edn. London. xvi+571pp.
A further revision of this, by now, standard textbook.

E28 **Crookes, W.** 1864. Photographic printing & engraving. Popular Science Review 3: 1-5, & 1 pl.
Review of photo-engraving and photo-lithography with a specimen of photo--lith.

E29 **Morvan, A.G.** 1867. Photographic transfers for photo-engraving or photo--lithography. Journal, Photographic Society 12: 105-107. Also pub. in: Photographic News 11: 419-420, 1867.
The patent specification.

E30 **Courtenay, R.H.** 1870. On photo printing & heliographic processes. Journal, Photographic Society 15: 5-7. Also pub. in: Photographic News 14: 136, 1870.
Apropos his patent of Dec. 1869.

E31 **Waterhouse, J.** 1870. Cartographic applications of photography -- photo--mechanical printing processes on the Continent. Photographic News 14: 183-184, 198-199, 225-226, 236-237, 247-248, 285-286, 346-347, 389-390, 416-418.
Describes printing offices and the processes used in France, Holland, Germany, Bavaria and Austria.

E32 **Hardwich, T.F.** 1873. A manual of photographic chemistry, [etc.] 8th edn. London. xvi+276pp.
A shortened and re-cast version of his text. Now includes sections on printing in pigments, mechanical printing, photo-lithography, photo-zincography, photo-relief printing, and collotype printing.

E33 **Anon.** 1873-75. The correlation of photography, lithography & typography. Lithographer 4: 115-117, 144-145, 164-165, 187-190, 210-212, 239-241, 265-267, 1873/74; 5: 114-115, 1875.
This series of articles comprises: [Introduction]; Woodbury process; The Autotype Company's process; The heliotype and Albertype processes; Kindred printing processes based on lithography; Photographic processes in France and Germany; The systems of Baldus, Du Motay and Placet; and Sundry foreign processes.

E34 **Tissandier, G.** 1875. A history & handbook of photography. Transl. from the French. Ed. by J. Thomson. London. xvi+326pp.

E35 **Vogel, H.** 1875. The chemistry of light & photography in their application to art, science & industry. London. xii+288pp. & 5 pls.
The pls. are: A Woodburytype, an electro. from a heliograph, a copper plate from a heliograph, a photo-lith., and a comparative pair of photos from untouched and re-touched negatives.

E36 **Vogel, H.** 1876. The chemistry of light & photography, [etc.] New & thoroughly rev. edn. London. viii+280pp. & 5 pls.
Pls. are the same as in (E35).

E37 **Abney, W. de W.** 1878. A treatise on photography. London. xvi+326pp. 2nd edn., 1883, unaltered.
Incl. a historical sketch and chapters on photo-lithographic transfers, photo-engraving and relief processes, and photo-collotype processes.

E38 **Bolas, T.** 1878. Application of photography to the production of printing surfaces & pictures in pigment. The Cantor lectures. Journal, Society of Arts 26: 789-790, 804-805, 818-820, 831-833, 845-847, 853-856. Also pub. separately: London, 1878. 16pp. Also pub. in: Photographic News 22: 352-353, 365, 375-377, 387-388, 399-401, 410-413, 1878.
Comprises: 1. Photo-lithography and photo-zincography; 2. Phototypic or raised printing blocks by swelled gelatine process, zinc etching, and other methods; 3. Line engraving on metal plates; 4. Printing half-tone subjects from metal. Application of Asser's process. Talbot's photo-engraving. Woodbury's methods of engraving and printing; 5. Collotypic printing; 6. Other methods of producing photographs in pigment. Dusting-on process. Autotype printing.

E39 **Tissandier, G.** 1878. A history & handbook of photography. Transl. from the French. Ed. by J. Thomson. 2nd & rev. edn. With an appendix by W.H.F. Talbot. London. xx+400pp. Repr. New York, 1973.

E40 **Waterhouse, J.** 1878. The application of photography to the reproduction of maps & plans by photo-mechanical & other processes. Journal, Asiatic Society of Bengal 47: 53-124, & 1 pl. Also pub. separately, Calcutta, 1878. 76pp. Most of the text also pub. in: Photographic News 22: 380-381, 487-488, 500, 512-513, 521, 557, 585-586, 591-592, 1787; 23: 17, 26-27, 39-40, 111-112, 141, 1879.
In addition to details on the preparation of the drawing and the negative also describes photo-lithography and photo-zincography, collotype, Woodburytype, photographic engraving, photo-typography, and miscellaneous other processes.

E41 **Hardwich, T.F.** 1883. A manual of photographic chemistry, [etc.] London. viii+464pp.
A fully revised version of this textbook, with sections on platinotype printing, carbon or pigment printing, photo-lithography, photo-zincography, Woodbury's process, Stannotype, photo-block printing, collotype printing.

E42 **Vogel, H.** 1883. The chemistry of light & photography, [etc.] 5th edn. London. ix+302pp. & 5 pls. 6th edn., 1892, unaltered.
With a new chapter, "The latest improvements in photography down to 1883", which incl. a section on book illus. by photography.

E43 **Bolas, T.** 1884. Recent improvements in photo-mechanical printing methods. The Cantor lectures. Journal, Society of Arts 32: 1077-1080, 1087-1092, 1099-1101. Also pub. separately, London, 1884. 14pp. Also pub. in: Printing Times & Lithographer N.S.10: 220-221, 245-246, 268-270, 1884.
Comprises: 1. Woodburytype developments [i.e. stannotype]; 2. Line and half-tone, relief and litho; 3. Photogravure and collotype.

E44 **Hodson, J.S.** 1884. An historical & practical guide to art illustration, in connection with books, periodicals, & general decoration: With numerous specimens of the various methods. London. vii+224pp. & 24 pls.
Pt 2 comprises: Engraving by chemical or mechanical processes, and Photographic processes. It incl. photo-lithography, process of M. Baldus, MM. Garnier and Salmon, Albertype, heliotype, photoglyptie, or Woodbury process, stannotype, Ives's process, Moss's new process, photogravure, direct photo-engraving process, photo-relief engraving, Autotype, etching upon glass, Bruce's white-line etching, chromo-photo-lithography, stenochromy, and Hoeschotype, together with the ancillary chemical and mechanical engraving processes. The pls. incl. specimens of: zincogr., typogr. etch., photo-lith., heliot., photoglyptie, Ives's photo-rel., photogr., Direct Photo-Engraving Co. photo-rel., etch. on glass (Hancock's process), & photo-chromo-lith.

E45 **Anon.** 1885. Photo-mechanical processes of illustration. British & Colonial Printer 14: 337.
Brief descriptions of Albert-type, autotype, photogravure, heliogravure, Braun's reproduction process, and Woodburytype.

E46 **Hodson, J.S.** 1885. Modern processes of automatic engraving. Art Journal 1885: 58-60, 182-184, 332-335.
A general view of recent advances incl: Zincography (Gillotage), Dawson's typographic etching, Ives' half-tone, Meisenbach process, Boussod, Valadon & Co's. photogravure.

E47 **Wilkinson, W.T.** 1886. Photo-etching on zinc & copper, in line & half-tone, & photo-lithography: A practical manual, with an appendix. London & Otley. iv+116pp.
The appendix provides general hints and extracts from the Photographic News. Touches upon virtually every process known at this date.

E48 ----- [ca.1887.] Photo-engraving & photolithography in line & in half-tone, also collotype & heliotype. 2nd edn., rev. & enl. London. viii+196pp. & 2 pls.
Largely re-written. The pls. are collos.

E49 **Burton, W.K.** 1887. Practical guide to photographic & photo-mechanical printing. London. xiv+355pp.
Incl. historical sketch of photo-mechanical printing and instructions on the carbon processes, platinotype process, photo-mechanical printing processes, and much general photographic material. Unillustrated.

E50 **Wood, H.T.** 1887. Modern methods of illustrating books. London. viii+247pp.
A non-technical explanation of photo-mechanical processes for the general reader but unfortunately without any illustrations. There were several later reprints.

E51 **Abney, W. de W.** 1888 A treatise on photography. 5th edn., rev. & enl. London. xvi+368pp.

E52 **Gunther, H.E.** 1888. The progress of photo-mechanical processes in Germany & Austria. Photographic News 32: 98-100, 155-156, 197.

E53 **Waterlow, G.S.** 1888. Modern photographic engraving & printing. Photographic News 32: 187, 197-199.
Review of various processes by a member of one of the industry's most progressive photo-mechanical businesses.

E54 **Wilkinson, W.T,.** 1888. Photo-engraving, photo-etching, & photo-lithography in line & half-tone, also collotype & heliotype. Rev. & enl. by E.L. Wilson. American edn. New York. xvi+188pp. & 2 pls.
There was apparently no English 3rd edn., this American edn. standing in its stead. (See the author's preface.) Contents: Pt.1: Photo-engraving in line; Pt.2: Photo-engraving in half-tone; Pt.3: Photo-engraving on copper; Pt.4: Photo-lithography in line; Pt.5: Photo-lithography in half-tone; Pt.6: Collographic printing; Supplement: Swelled gelatine process of making photo-relief plates. The pls. are examples of h-tone proc. eng. (This text was re-issued in re-numbered "editions" with different pls., e.g. American (6th edn.), ca.1899.)

E55 **Winstanley, D.** 1888. Photo-mechanical printing. Photographic News 32: 482-484, 731, 745-746.
A series which was, apparently, abandoned before completion.

E56 **Wood, H.T.** 1888. Photography & the printing press. Photographic News, 32: 73-75, 86-88.

E57 **Bolas, T.** 1889. The photo-mechanical printing methods as employed in the jubilee year of photography. British Journal of Photography 1889: 588-590, 600-602. Also. pub. in: Photographic News 33: 566-567, 578-582, 1889.
A useful state-of-the-art survey.

E58 **Gunther, H.E.** 1890. The progress of the photo-mechanical printing processes. Photographic News 34: 396-397, 471-472, 548-549, 608, 684.
In continuation of his earlier survey (E52). Deals with Germany and Austria.

E59 **Wilkinson, W.T.** 1890. Photo-engraving, photo-litho & collotype. 4th edn. London. viii+162pp. & pls.
The pls. incl. a photo-lith. and a collo.

E59* ----- 1891. Photomechanical processes. Effective Review 1891: 103-123.

E60 **Brothers, A.** 1892. Photography: Its history, processes, apparatus, & materials, comprising working details of all the more important methods. London. xiii+364pp. & 24 pls.
The pls. incl. photogravures, Woodbury-grav., photo-zincographs, typogr., Meisenbach & other h-tone proc. engs., photo-chromo-typogr., photo-liths. in line & h-tone, chromo-lith., collos., chromo-collo., & Woodburytype. Pt.2 comprises an encyclopaedia of processes.

E61 **Burton, W.K.** 1892. Practical guide to photographic & photo-mechanical printing. 2nd edn. London. xviii+415pp.
Fully rev. & updated version of the 1887 edn., (E49).

E62 **Waterlow, P. & J.D. Geddes.** 1892. Photography & photo-mechanical printing. Photographic News 36: 243-245, 267-270.
Incl. photo-lithography, photogravure, zinc etching, half-tone, Woodbury printing and collotype.

E63 **Wilkinson, W.T.** 1892-93. Photo-etching - litho & collotype - gravure. Printing Times & Lithographer N.S.1: 37-39, 101-104, 175-178, 237, 293-296; 1892; N.S. 2: 35-39, 83-86, 133-136, 216-220, 360-362, 1893.

E64 ----- 1892. Photo-mechanical processes: A practical guide to photo--zincography, photo-lithography, & collotype. London. iv+148pp.

E65 **Woodbury, W.B.** 1892. The encyclopaedia of photography: Containing over one thousand five hundred references. London. 755pp.
Alpabetically arranged articles incl. photo-engraving, photogravure, photo--lithography, photo-mechanical processes, photo-zincography, stannotype, and Woodburytype.

E66 **Wilkinson, W.T.** 1894. Photo-engraving, photo-litho, collotype & photo-gravure. With a note on the preparation of drawings for reproduction by G.C. Harper. 5th edn., rev. London. 169pp. & pls.
The pls. incl. a collo., a photo-lith., & a swelled gelatine line-block.

E67 **Abney, W. de W. & others.** 1896. Six lectures on photography with the bichromate salts. Photographic Journal N.S.20: 254-281.
I. Abney, W. de W. Scientific & historical preliminary. pp.254-259.
II. Sinclair, J.A. Carbon printing. pp.259-265.
III. Debenham, W.E. Collotype. pp.265-270.
IV. Geddes, J.D. Woodbury printing. pp.270-273.
V. Wilkinson, W.T. Photo-lithography & photo-zincography. pp.273-277.
VI. ----- Process applications of the bichromate salts. pp.277-281.

E68 **Wilkinson, W.T.** 1897. Photo-mechanical processes, [etc.] 2nd edn. London. 174pp.

E69 **Brothers, A.** 1899. Photography: Its history, processes, apparatus, & materials, [etc.]. 2nd edn. rev. London. xviii+368pp. & 37 pls.
The pls. incl. photograv., Woodbury-grav., photo-zincogr., Dallastype, swelled gelatine rel. block, Meisenbach & other h-tone proc. engs., photo--chromo-typogr., heliochrome, photo-liths. in line & h-tone, collos., Woodburytype, etc. An updated version of the 1892 edn., (E60).

E70 **Ward, W.H.** 1900. The printing arts: A description of the methods now in use, more particularly with regard to illustration. Paris. 16pp. h-tone illus.
A review of current photo-mechanical and other illustration processes prepared for the Exposition Universelle of 1900.

E71 **Baker, W.H.** 1908. A dictionary of engraving (particularly of the modern commercial processes), together with terms used in related branches as electrotyping, lithography, advertising, printing, art, photography, etc. - idiomatic & technical. Cleveland, Ohio. 108pp.
"Primarily this is a dictionary of photo-engraving", the only one published within a decade of the 19th century.

Ec Photo-intaglio processes

The use of mounted photographs as book illustrations was fairly common in the early decades of photographic history despite the fact that each copy had to be separately printed out and mounted at a considerable cost of time and labour. The production of a printing surface from a photograph -- one which could be printed by conventional methods -- was obviously the desired goal.

The earliest efforts were directed towards "engraving" photographic images onto copper or steel similar to the commonplace intaglio plates produced by hand-engraving. As early as the 1840's French experimenters had achieved modest success with etching Daguerreotype plates to produce intaglio printing surfaces and reports of these were published in England by Grove (E72) and Anon. (E73). However, these had no success over here and it was Talbot who made the first successful photo-engravings in the 1850's; the product of his first patent being a steel plate capable of printing scores of impressions (E74 ER75). Talbot used a form of etching to create his plates but soon afterwards another worker, Pretsch, announced a process which relied on an electrotyped copy of a swelled gelatine photo-image which he called photo-galvanography (E77). Photo-mechanical printing had arrived and its progress over the ensuing years was to be a rapid one.

Talbot improved his process and re-named it photoglyphic engraving (E78), Pretsch, another pioneer, described several of his experiments (E82 E83), while Swan announced a new process which he called "photo-mezzotint" (E89). Talbot had discovered the need to introduce "grain" into his process to enable the darker areas to hold ink which the action of plate wiping would otherwise have removed. He first employed a woven silk screen but later changed to a sprinkled resin-dust grain as the means of breaking up the etched image. Pretsch's process relied on hand-engraving for the improvement of the less successful passages in his images -- his process is fully described by Leipold (E91) -- but it was Swan who made the revolutionary advance of using a hand--ruled "screen" on the film (E89). The commercial failure of Pretsch's company enabled a former employee, D.C. Dallas, to introduce "Dallastype"; Pretsch's process re-named (E84-E86). The ingenious Woodbury also developed a photogravure process in which a gritty powder was mixed with the gelatine and the resulting relief image pressed into a soft metal leaving a grainy intaglio image that could be converted to a printing plate by double electrotyping (E90).

Swan's process used his famous carbon tissue which greatly enhanced the middle, or "half"-tones, of the image. Later, Sawyer, who held the license to manufacture this tissue, developed a technique for sprinkling powdered glass over the wet gelatine and, when it had dried, brushed the powder away to leave a pitted electrotypable image (E97), a process he later called "Autogravure". Both Swan's photo-mezzotint and Woodbury's process were very successfully adopted by French firms who called their versions "Heliogravure" or "Goupil-gravure". Their developments are described in Anon. (E93) and Reinbold (E96).

Leitch, a pioneer British photo-mechanical printer, adopted a sophisticated development of Talbot's original process, as perfected by Garnier (E94). Various developments and improvements in etched or electrotyped photogravure process are chronicled in the articles of several authors but it was not until 1890 that Wilkinson published the first separate manual (E102). The work of one of the most successful photogravure firms working in England at this time was A. & C. Dawson whose methods are described in Anon. (E101) and Dawson (E103). Various reviews of progress and descriptions of improved methods of photogravure printing occupied the technical periodicals.

On the Continent, meanwhile, developments were being made by the Czech printer, Karl Klič, which were to lead to the perfection of photogravure processes that would to be employed well into the twentieth century. Using an aquatint grain and a carbon tissue for image transfer he etched his plates in graded strengths of iron chloride to produce very delicate and beautiful prints. Denison's treatise (E110) made this process known to British printers, a happy combination of Talbot's pioneer method with Swan's carbon process. But the most important improvement made by Klic was in the field of rotary gravure. Abandoning the aquatint grain he instead printed a positive cross-lined screen onto the carbon tissue and then etched a printing cylinder through his screened image to produce cells of variable depths. By means of a "doctor" blade, similar to that utilised on intaglio textile printing machines of the day, he was able to achieve a continuous "wipe" of the cylinder whilst printing was in progress. His "Rembrandt" gravure process was described in Huson's little manual (E112) and was accompanied by a fine example printed by the Lancashire firm with whom Klic had perfected his rotary gravure.

Information on photogravure processes can also be found in the works of Bolas, Waterhouse, Hodson, Wilkinson, Burton and Brothers listed in section Eb supra. Before the introduction of rotogravure all photo-intaglios were printed by the conventional plate-printing methods, literature on which is described in section Bf supra; and see also Wilmer (E115).

E72 **Grove, W.B.** 1842. Etching Daguerreotype plates. Magazine of Science 3: 189.
Use of voltaic etching to produce a printing surface.

E73 **Anon.** 1845. Engraving Daguerreotype plates. Magazine of Science 6: 247-248, 251-252.
Claudet's patent process for etching Daguerreotype plates.

E74 **Talbot, W.H.F.** 1853. Photographic etching. Athenaeum 1853 (Apr. 9): 450-451; (Apr. 16): 481-482; (Apr.30): 532-533.

E75 ----- 1854. Photographic engraving. Journal, Photographic Society 1: 42-44, 62-64.

E76 ----- 1854. Photographic engraving. In: Hunt, R. A manual of photography. 4th edn. pp.313-319. London.

E77 **Pretsch, P.** 1856. Photo-galvanography, or engraving by light & electricity. Journal, Photographic Society 3: 58-63. Also pub. in: Journal, Society of Arts 4: 385-389, 1856.

E78 **Talbot, W.H.F.** 1857. Photoglyphic engraving. Journal, Society of Arts 6: 697-698.
The patent specification.

E79 **Malone, T.A.** 1858. On the application of light & electricity to the production of engravings: Photogalvanography. Notice of the Proceedings at the Meetings of the Members of the Royal Institution 2: 343-350, 1854/58.

E80 **Talbot, W.H.F.** 1858. Specification of the patent granted to W.H.F. Talbot for improvements in the art of engraving. Journal, Photographic Society 5: 58-61.

E81 ----- 1858. Description of Mr. Fox Talbot's new process of photographic engraving. Photographic News 1: 73-75.

E82 **Pretsch, P.** 1858/58. Two main points in photography. II: Photography subject to the press. Journal, Photographic Society 5: 109-111, 132-136.

E83 **Pretsch, P.** 1859. Photogalvanography, or nature's engraving. Journal, Photographic Society 6: 29-31.

E84 **Anon.** 1863. Photo-engraving. Photographic News 7: 363-364.
Dallas's process.

E85 **Dallas, D.** 1863. Photo-electric engraving. Photographic News 7: 439-441.
Abstract of a paper read to the British Association but not published by them.

E86 **Anon.** 1864. Our photo-electric engraving. Photographic News 8: 1-2, & 1 pl.
Dallas's method described and demonstrated.

E87 **Lacan, E.** 1864. M. Eugene Placet's process of heliographic engraving. Photographic News 8: 53-54.
From an article in "Moniteur de la Photographie".

E88 **Placet, P.E.** 1864. Improved process of photographic engraving. Photographic News 8: 477.

E89 **Swan, J.W.** 1866. Photo-mezzotint, photo-engraving, photo-lithography. Photographic News 10: 65-67.
The patent specification.

E90 **Woodbury, W.B.** 1870. New photo-engraving process. Photographic News 14: 110.
The patent specification.

E91 **Leopold** [i.e. **Leipold**], J. 1875. Photo-electric engraving. Photographic News 19: 10-11, 16.
Pretsch's photo-galvanographic engraving described.

E92 **Bradley, H.** 1874. Obtaining photographic impressions on copper plates for engraving. Photographic News 18: 521.
The patent specification.

E93 **Anon.** 1877. M. Rousselon's photo-gravure process. Photographic News 21: 379-380.
Goupil's photogravure.

E94 ----- 1877. Photo-gravure: Its antecedents & capabilities. Printing Times & Lithographer N.S.3: 6-7, & 1 pl.
Garnier's process, as practised by Leitch, with a specimen.

E95 **Waterhouse, J.** 1881. An improved method of photo-engraving. Year Book of Photography 1881: 111-112.

E96 **Reinbold, H.** 1884. Heliogravure. British & Colonial Printer 13: 156.
The method used by Goupil of Paris and Schuster of Berlin.

E97 **Sawyer, J.R.** 1885. On a new method of photographic engraving, with a demonstration of the process. Photographic Journal N.S.10: 28-32.

E98 **Waterhouse, J.** 1889. Photo-etching in India. Photographic News 33: 713-714. Repr. from: Annual Report, Survey of India Department, 1887/88.
Heliogravure process worked by A.W. Turner.

E99 **Anon.** 1887. Making intaglio copper plates by the etching process. Photographic News 31: 49-51.
By various methods.

E100 **Hamerton, P.G.** 1889/90. Photogravure & heliogravure. Photographic Quarterly 1: 217-223.

E101 **Anon.** 1890. The photogravure process. Photographic News 34: 625-626, & 1 pl.
As practised by A. & C. Dawson, with a specimen.

E102 **Wilkinson, W.T.** 1890. Photogravure, with illustrations by A.L. Colls. London. 40pp.

E103 **Dawson, A.** 1890/91. Photogravure. Photographic Journal N.S.15: 290-297.

E104 **Corbould, V.A.L.** 1891. Photo-etching upon copper plates. British Journal Photographic Almanac 1891: 657-659.
The heliogravure process.

E105 **Denison, H.** 1892/93. Photogravure, or photographic etching on copper. Photographic Journal N.S.17: 131-137, 175-182.

E106 **Wilmer, H.** 1893/94. Photogravure. Photographic Journal N.S.18: 237-243.
A demonstration, chiefly concerned with printing, supplementing Denison's paper (E105).

E107 **Wilkinson, W.T.** 1895. Photogravure. 2nd edn., re-written to date. London. 48pp.
Incl. sensitizing the carbon tissue, making the transparency, laying the etching ground, printing the resist, etching the plate, other methods of printing the resist, printing from the plate.

E108 **Wilmer, H.** 1895. Modern photogravure methods. Journal, Society of Arts 43: 463-469. Also pub. in: Printing Times & Lithographer N.S.4: 102-104, 132-134, 1895.

E109 **Anon.** 1896. Photogravure. Printing Times & Lithographer N.S.5: 191-192, 234, 296-297.

E110 **Denison, H.** 1896. A treatise on photogravure, by the Talbot-Klic process. London. 140pp. & 1 pl. Repr. Rochester, N.Y., 1974.
Detailed account of line and tone methods. Incl. a chapter on the history of photogravure by T. Bolas.

E111 **Anon.** 1897. Machine-printed photogravure. Process Photogram 4: 129-132.

E112 **Huson, T.** 1897. Photo-aquatint & photogravure: A practical treatise ... to which is added a treatise on machine printed photogravure ... by A. Villain & J.W. Smith. London. 116pp. & 2 pls.
The pls. are specimens of photo-aquat. and photograv.

E113 ----- 1897. Notes on photo-aquatint & on some of the apparatus used in working the process. Photographic Journal N.S.21: 223-232, & pls.45-47. Also pub. in: Process Work & the Printer 5: 64-67, 1897, without the pls.

E114 **Lambert, F.C.** 1897. A few notes on photogravure for amateurs. Penrose Annual 3: 67-72.

E115 **Wilmer, H.** 1897. Printing from intaglio plates. Photographic Journal N.S.21: 160-167.
The printing of photogravure plates.

E116 ----- 1899. Photogravure with a screen grain. Penrose Annual 5: 39-40.
Experiments with a 130 line screen.

Ed Photo-relief processes

The exceptional advantage that any relief process offered to the printer -- as so successfully proved by wood engraving -- was that of being able to machine illustrations and letterpress at one operation. With the invention of photography and the modest success of Talbot's photo-engraving invention, it was natural that this new field should engage the attention of those seeking to develop faster, cheaper, and more "autographic" processes than the wood engraver's slow traditional craft would allow.

An early suggestion for the use of photography to produce relief printing surfaces came from Field (E117) but his process apparently disappeared without trace. It was in 1860 that Pretsch achieved one of the first successes with photo-relief printing (E118) and presented an impressive demonstration of its tonal quality. He used the swelled gelatine principle, first demonstrated by Poitevin, and succeeded in imparting a characteristic worm-like grain to it before electrotyping the image to create a relief printing block. The same principle was used in several later processes. An alternative technique was to wash away the swelled gelatine leaving a lower relief image in insoluble hardened bichromated gelatine that could also be electrotyped. In either case there was a serious need to enhance the depth of the photo-image so that the relief block would print clearly and without clogging, no matter how fine the lines. Many later processes did little more than improve the depth of the printing block formed from the swelled or hardened bichromated gelatine.

From the mid 1860's onwards new "inventions" came thick and fast and the existence of several photographic journals, some of them weeklies, resulted in great competition to be first to publish news of them, usually before their true worth had been demonstrated. A few are worth singling out for special mention. Ramage & Nelson (E122) were early in the field, employing a gutta percha cast of a swelled gelatine image that could be electrotyped in relief or intaglio. From the later 1860's onward, Nelson demonstrated the practicability of the process in a prolific series of local views published over many years. They were printed from an intaglio in heliotrope coloured ink and overprinted with blue and beige ruled or grained relief tints; always on enamelled paper. Dallas succeeded in producing true letterpress relief illustrations using a swelled gelatine process that involved building up the thickness of the gelatine under repeated exposures before making a cast. This was electrotyped to create a printing block with really deep "lights" (E123 E133 E134). In 1867 Courtenay devised a process (E124) in which a photographic image was produced on litho-transfer paper, transferred to a zinc-coated copper block and then electro-chemically etched to leave a relief image, a process that presaged some of the features of Gillotage. Fruwirth (E125) used a relief plaster cast of a bichromated gelatine image and then proceeded to build up the lines and broad spaces on the block with varnish or wax before electrotyping it to form the printing block. Later, working with Hawkins (E126), he developed a different process using a hardened gelatine image on a metal plate which was built up with copal or other varnish and electrotyped in the old manner of glyphography, Hawkins's former speciality.

Roper & Shaw's six part patent (E131) revived another old process -- graphotype. Their suggestions included making an electro of a bichromated gelatine relief image, pressing the electro into compressed chalk with a hydraulic press and, after coating the chalky relief with silicate of potash, brushing away the soft interstices before electrotyping in the usual manner for graphotype. In another version they coated a plain chalk surface with a special waterproof substance, coated it with bichromated gelatine which was exposed and then washed. The broad spaces of the image were washed away with a solvent and the chalk brushed out leaving a relief image for electrotyping. Banks (E137) used a gelatine coated glass plate onto which he put a bichromate of potash, exposed it, washed the image into relief and made a plaster cast, the height of the lines were enhanced by rolling the plaster with copal varnish and ink. The plaster was then placed in a soft soap solution so that the hollows could be brushed out or gouged to the required depth, a wax mould made, and that electrotyped.

In the early 1870's Gillot applied photography to his process of relief line etching using a bichromated albumen coating which was exposed and the unexposed portions etched leaving a relief block ready for printing. In later years it became usual to make an electrotype copy in a more durable printing metal. Hornig (E139) and Anon. (E140) record the earlier methods used in England but for fuller information on photo-zincography and the other photo--relief processes the general manuals described in section Eb <u>supra</u> should be consulted.

One other process from the earlier period that deserves mention is Hancock's hyalographic method of preparing the drawing. A hand "scratched" negative was prepared by drawing through a blackened glass plate with an etching needle and printing the image down onto photo-emulsion coated zinc which was then etched in relief (E121) with results that look very much like Dawson's typographic etching (C35). This, and almost all of the processes described, were only suitable for artwork drawn in line and dot. The early tonal achievements of Pretsch were not to be successfully repeated for some years, despite the claims of Dallastint (E141) which proved itself to be an inadequate imitation.

Woodbury experimented with the creation of tones by pressing mosquito netting into the gelatine, by photographing negatives through the net, or by making an impressed copy of a hardened gelatine relief image in a soft metal plate that had been patterned with an indented mesh pattern and electrotyping the patterned image to form a tonal relief block (E136). The excellent Luxotype process invented by Brown, Barnes & Bell also relied on similar devices, using fine wire mesh or glued and dried muslin, either pressing this "screen" into the gelatine image before electrotyping or else making the first exposure through the mesh (E152 E157 E159 E160).

Ruled screens were to prove better than any other pattern and led to the relief half-tone that achieved such a high degree of perfection by the end of the century. Meisenbach used cross-ruled screens and after exposing and developing the gelatine image on zinc he etched and rolled-up with ink in alternative stages, relying on stopping-out and local etching for the improvement of any tonal imbalance on the block (E162). Meisenbach blocks were very successful and in a very few years they were being used to illustrate a wide range of books, magazines, and newspapers.

However, the most significant refinements came from America and were largely the results of the work of Ives. He also used extremely finely drawn glass screens, not cross- but single-ruled and placed at 90 degrees to each other. He photographed through this screen onto a glue-enamel coated copper block and, after burning the image to hardness, etched with an iron chloride solution (E154 E161 E184). The precision of his screens, the use of copper, and the care in etching produced half-tones of great subtlety, high definition, and full tonal range that came as close to the qualities of a photographic print as was possible with relief printing. One other later 19th century development that deserves mention is Leimtypie, the invention of Husnik of Prague, in which a chromated sheet of gelatine was fixed to the surface of a zinc plate with resin and, after exposure, was developed with a special fluid. The resulting relief gelatine image in line or half-tone is printed by normal letterpress methods (E175). Sometimes known as gelatinotype, the process was very simple to operate, capable of printing long-run work, and formed a competitor to Meisenbach's process for medium quality work.

Much of the news of these diverse processes was contained in reprinted patent specifications or uncritical articles in photographic and printing trade periodicals. With the reviews of Bolas (E38 E43) and the textbooks of Hodson (E44), Wilkinson (E47 E64), Burton (E49) and Brothers (E60), evaluative assessments began to be made and sometimes actual specimens were presented for comparison. The first specialised textbook on line photo-relief work was Boeck's little manual (E173) and in the mid 1890's Farquhar (E186), Gamble (E187 E191), and Cronenberg (E188), added excellent textbooks on British and American half-tone methods.

Photographically produced blocks were printed by normal relief printing methods and literature on those methods is described in section Ce supra.

E117 **Field, J.** 1853. Improvements in transferring & printing. Mechanics' Magazine 58: 374-375.
Abstract of patent specification.

E118 **Pretsch, P.** 1860. New process for photographic pictures reproduced by the ordinary letter-press. Journal, Photographic Society 6: 274-275.

E119 ----- 1860. Printing blocks & plates produced by photography & electrotype. Journal, Photographic Society 7: 36-38, & 1 pl.
The pl. is a fine specimen of the process.

E120 **Lewis, J.** 1863. Photo-block printing. Photographic News 7: 461-462.

E121 **[Hancock, C.]** 1864. Electro-photography; or etching on glass. A ... new process for the production of ... drawings upon surafce-printing electro--plates. London. 14pp. & 1 pl.

E122 **Ramage, [J.] & [T.] Nelson.** 1866. A mode of producing blocks & plates for printing by means of photography. Photographic News 10: 615. Also pub. in: Journal, Photographic Society 11: 173-174, 1866/67.
The patent specification.

E123 **Dallas, D.** 1867. Producing printing surfaces by photography. Photographic News 11: 344-345.
The patent specification.

E124 **Courtenay, R.H.** 1867. Obtaining printing surfaces. Photographic News 11: 361.
The provisional patent specification.

E125 **Anon.** 1868. Photo-block printing. Photographic News 12: 389-390.
Fruwirth's process; with a specimen.

E126 **Fruwirth, D. & A. Hawkins.** 1869. Producing raised printing surfaces. Photographic News 13: 308.
The patent specification.

E127 **Anon.** 1869. The phototype. Scientific Opinion 1: 316.
Fruwirth & Hawkins's process; with a specimen.

E128 **Courtenay, R.H.** 1870. On photo-printing & heliographic processes. Photographic News 14: 136.

E129 **Denne, T.J. & H. Billingsley.** 1870. Photo-block printing. Photographic News 14: 393-394.
The patent specification.

E130 **Robinson, J.V.** 1870. Photo-mechanical printing. Photographic News 14: 90-91.
The provisional patent specification.

E131 **Roper, E. & G. Shaw.** 1870. Photography & graphotype for producing printing surfaces. Photographic News 14: 405-407.
The patent specification.

E132 **Lewis, J.** 1870/71. Printing surfaces in relief & their production. Lithographer 1: 122-123, 142-143, 154-155, 186-187.
Discussion of various processes incl. Pretsch's photo-relief, graphotype, and Lewis's own.

E133 **Anon.** 1873. The Dallastype process. Lithographer 4: 48-50.
With specimens.

E134 ----- 1874. The Dallastype process. Fleet Street Gazette 1874 (Mar.): 6, & 1 pl.
The pl. is a specimen.

E135 **Courtenay, R.H.** 1874. Photo-block printing. Photographic News 18: 340-341.
The patent specification.

E136 **Woodbury, W.B.** 1874. Photo-block printing. Photographic News 18: 329.
The patent specification.

E137 **Banks, J.H.** 1875. Photo engraving & block printing. Photographic News 19: 5.
The patent specification.

E138 **Anon.** 1875. Banks's photo-raised surface blocks. Printing Times & Lithographer N.S.1: 192-193.
With specimens.

E139 **Hornig, -.** 1875. Paniconography. Photographic News 19: 567.
Brief description of Gillot's process.

E140 **Anon.** 1876. The zincographic process. Photographic News 20: 494-495, 513-514, 523-524.
Translated from a German article.

E141 ----- 1877. Dallas' photo-mechanical process. Photographic News 21: 277; also letter from Dallas, p.299.
On Dallastint.

E142 ----- 1879. Phototypy. Printing Times & Lithographer N.S.5: 219-220.
Vidal's process of gelatine relief.

E143 **Knight, H.** 1880. Photo-engraving process for surface printing. Photographic News 24: 20-21.

E144 **Vidal, L.** 1882. Process of photo-engraving on zinc or on copper by means of bichromated albumen. Photographic News 26: 363-364.

E145 **Anon.** 1882. A phototype block for the printing press. Photographic News 26: 465-466.
Ives' method of photo-engraving, with a specimen.

E146 ----- 1882. Chemigraphic engraving. Photographic News 26: 673-674, 690-691, 706, 738-739, 770.
Zinc relief etching.

E147 **Vidal, L.** 1883. Phototype process. British Journal Photographic Almanac 1883: 71-72.

E148 **Anon.** 1883. "Processes" -- photo-engraving on zinc or on copper by means of bichromated albumen. British Journal Photographic Almanac 1883: 142-144.
Vidal's process.

E149 ----- 1883. Typographic blocks from ordinary negatives. Photographic News 27: 258-260.
Asser's process.

E150 ----- 1883. Photo-block printing 23 years ago. Photographic News 27: 385-387.
About Pretsch's process, with a facsimile of his block of 1860 (E119), hand engraved by Swain!

E151 Anon. 1883. Ives' photo-block method. Photographic News 27: 498-499.

E152 ----- 1883. Luxotype. Photographic News 27: 580.
Brown, Barnes & Bell's patent process; with a specimen.

E153 ----- 1883. Photographic blocks for the letterpress printer. Photographic News 27: 598-599.
Dallastint; with specimens.

E154 ----- 1883. Photographs transformed into typographic blocks. Photographic News 27: 676-678.
Ives' process; with a specimen.

E155 ----- 1883. Scamoni's electrotype method of reproducing photo-reliefs: The production of heliographic blocks by electrotyping in the Geographical Institute of Vienna. Photographic News 27: 705-706, 753.

E156 ----- 1883. Improvements in photo-block printing. Photographic News 27: 802-803.
Etching methods, grain production, etc. Supplementary to (E154 E155).

E157 ----- 1883. Photo-block printing from nature: The recent revival of phototypic processes. Photographic News 27: 739-740.
With specimens of Meisenbach h-tone & luxotype.

E158 ----- 1884. Zuccato's method for the translation of a photograph into lines for typographic printing. Photographic News 28: 81.
On his patents, nos. 4152-4154 of 1883.

E159 ----- 1884. The Luxotype process. Printer 1884 (Feb.): 19, & 1 pl.
With a specimen; others also appeared in Ibid. 1888 (Aug.): 55, & 1884 (Nov.): 71.

E160 ----- 1884. The Luxotype. Printing Times & Lithographer N.S.10: 32.
With a specimen.

E161 ----- 1884. The Ives process for making photo-tint blocks. Photographic News 28: 257.

E162 ----- 1884. The Meisenbach photo-block process. Photographic News 28: 275-276.
With a specimen.

E163 Lang, W. jun. 1884. Poitevin's photo-reliefs. Photographic News 28: 245.

E164 Anon. 1885. The phototype block process of Thiriet & Roux. Photographic News 29: 130.
With an example.

E165 ----- 1885. Another block process. Photographic News 29: 193.
Geo. Sutherland's process; with a specimen.

E166 ----- 1885. Direct photo-typography & photo-lithography by the chrom--albumen process. Photographic News 29: 225-226.

E167 Anon. 1885. Phototype blocks by Mr. Vero C. Driffield. Photographic News 29: 306.
With a specimen.

E168 ----- 1885. Borland's phototype process. Photographic News 29: 322.
With examples of typographic & lithographic application.

E169 Sutherland, G. 1885. Another block process. Photographic News 29: 403-404.

E170 Swan, J.W. 1885. Photography & letterpress printing. Year Book of Photography 1885: 81-82.
With a specimen of Meisenbach half-tone.

E171 Anon. 1886. Zinc etching. Printing Times & Lithographer N.S.12: 105.

E172 ----- 1886. Photo-zincotypy & similar processes. Printing Times & Lithographer N.S.12: 162.

E173 Böck, J. 1886. Zincography: Guide to the art of in connection with letterpress printing. Transl. by E. Menken. London. 2nd edn., rev. & enl., ca.1886. 55pp.; 4th edn., ca.1890; 5th edn., n.d.
First edn. not seen.

E174 Anon. 1887. Grain in photo-typographic blocks. Photographic News 31: 610-611.
Husnik's method, with a specimen.

E175 ----- 1888. Leimtypie (Husnik's new patent process for rapid reproduction of drawings etc., also called gelatinotypie). Printing Times & Lithographer N.S.14: 49.

E176 Müller, C.A. 1888. Theory of typo-photography. British & Colonial Printer 20: 129-130, 145-146. First pub. in: American Lithographer & printer.

E177 Wilkinson, W.T. 1888. Half-tone blocks for type printing. British Journal Photographic Almanac 1888: 434-436.

E178 ----- 1889. The wash-out process for photo-engraving. Photographic News 33: 760-761. First pub. in: Wilson's Photographic Magazine.

E179 Anon. 1891. Sutton's process for producing a printing block. Photographic News 35: 297-298, 313-314.

E180 ----- 1891. The Hoke engraving process. Photographic News 35: 387.
With a specimen.

E181 Anon. 1891. New zincographic process by August & Louis Lumiere. Photographic News 35: 506.

E182 Waterhouse, J. 1892. Half-tone photo-block printing. Photographic News 36: 387-389.

E183 **Calmels, H.** 1893/94. Tone etching on copper. Photographic Journal N.S.18: 284-287; also a letter, p.312.
The fish glue process.

E184 **Anon.** 1894. Photographic engraving & the work of Mr. Frederic Ives. British Printer 7: 65-68.

E185 **Kitton, F.G.** 1894. The art of photo-etching & engraving: A visit to the establishemnt of Messrs John Swain & Son. British Printer 7: 218-231.
Also pub. in: Printing World N.S.1: 470-475, 1893.

E186 **Farquhar, H.D.** 1895. The grammar of photo-engraving: With additional matter on the fish glue enamel process ... & a valuable appendix on the making of half-tone negatives. Transl. from the German by J.M. Eder. Containing instructions in drawing, chemistry & optics, as applied to photo--engraving & a practical treatise on the art of half-tone, zinc etching, swelled gelatine, lithotype & chalk plate engraving, as practised in the United States. London. 145pp.
This translation was simultaneously pub. in New York.

E187 **"Verfasser, J." [i.e. W. Gamble.]** 1895. The half-tone process: A practical manual of photo-engraving in half-tone on zinc & copper. Bradford. 126pp. & 3 pls.
Pt. I: The atelier, fittings & appliances; Pt. II: The operations.

E188 **Cronenberg, W.** 1896. Half-tone on the American basis. From the personal experience of ... Transl. by W. Gamble. Bradford. 164pp. & 12 pls.
"Chapters on photo-engraving in America" is followed by a full technical account of their methods; the suppl. plates are examples of that work.

E189 **Cheshire, W.** 1896. On the touching of half-tone process blocks. Photographic Journal N.S.20: 181-186.
With specimens of an untouched and a hand worked block.

E190 **Turati, V.** [1896.] Isotypie, a new half-tone process. London. 11pp.
First pub. in: Process Work & the Printer.

E191 **"Verfasser, J." [i.e. W. Gamble.]** 1896. The half-tone process: A practical manual of photo-engraving in half-tone on zinc & copper. 2nd edn., rev. & in great part re-written. London. 172pp. & 4 pls.
Covers all photographic and mechanical operations up to mounting and proving the block. An enl. 3rd edn. pub. 1904. 292pp. & 9 pls.

E192 **Hentschel & Co.** 1901. Pictorial reproduction & the art of process engraving. London. 24pp. & 1 pl.
A trade booklet.

Ee Photo-planographic processes: Lithographic

The practical success and popular acceptance of lithography for all kinds of line and tonal illustration ensured that it would become involved in the wave of photographic experimentation in the 1850's. Early successes were achieved and by 1860 photo-lithographs were being printed by several workable methods. The earliest method, developed in 1852, utilised a light sensitive asphalt (bitumen) coating on stone which, after exposure under a paper negative, was washed with turpentine leaving an image that was inked and printed. Paris was the home of this technique but, as Ramsay reported (E193), successful tonal prints from coarsely grained stones were produced in 1855 by a Scottish artist. In the same year Poitevin, a Frenchman, patented another direct process based on his discovery that the exposed portions of a bichromated gelatine film became insoluble such that the unexposed parts could be washed away leaving a hardened gelatine image. Furthermore, when rolled-up with a greasy litho ink, this image "took" ink. By using lithographic stone (rather than glass or metal plate) coated with bichromated albumen Poitevin worked up the inked image and, after "etching" the stone in the routine way, could print the image by normal lithographic methods. A similar process was developed by Rousseau & Masson (E194) soon afterwards.

All direct processes, however, suffered the disadvantage of allowing only a few hundred impressions before the image broke up. Asser overcame this problem in 1856 by making his photographic exposure on a sensitized starch-coated lithographic transfer paper. After developing and inking, the image was transferred to stone and was capable of printing normally long runs without deterioration (E196).

Pouncy was the first to print successful tonal photo-lithographs in England by the bichromate process and, although he kept his method secret, he probably used a transfer from the carbon pigment process that he also developed at this time (E195). Two years later, in 1859, Col. James of the Ordnance Survey Office discovered a transfer process similar to Asser's (E197-E199) and almost simultaneously Osborne in Australia arrived at the same method (E200 E205). This photo-zincographic process immediately proved itself as a commercially workable operation and an instructional manual on the Ordnance Survey methods was published (E206) and soon augmented (E214). In 1893 Pouncy improved his transfer process (E211 E212), using a mixture of oil or fat, bichromate of potash, asphalt, and spirit. After exposure the surface was washed with spirit leaving an image in a substance analogous to printer's ink, ready for transfer to a well grained stone; a process also described by Sutton (E213). Various patents for methods of transfer onto stone or zinc were taken out in the early 1860's, such as Beatty & Alexander (E201 E202), Toovey (E215 E216), and Tessie du Motay & Maréchal (E217). The asphalt and bichromate processes produced excellent results with line and dot drawing but tonal work was only achieved with difficulty, sometimes requiring hand-finishing. In 1865 the Bullock brothers produced very successful tonal prints by breaking up the image on the transfer paper into a reticulate grain. This they did by various methods including, graining the gelatine-coated transfer paper by impressing an aquatint-like texture onto it, or photographing a diapositive through a gauze or other granulate-patterned "screen" to create a tonal negative suitable for transfer to stone (E218). In the 1880's half-tone photo-lithographs were made possible by Husband's Papyrotint process which relied on the reticulation of a special formula of gelatine on the transfer paper (E240 E243 E244).

At the end of the century Waterhouse gave a detailed review of the methods for creating half-tone (E256). A variety of periodical articles and reports chronicle the developments of the medium from the 1860's onward. Cartography, which had been the chief stimulus for James' and Osborne's developments, continued to be a research field for photo-lithography and the excellent texts of Waterhouse record these developments (E223 E233 E245), together with the improved version of James' manual (E228). With the arrival of general photo-mechanical textbooks, such as Vogel (E35), Wilkinson (E47 E64), Burton (E49), and Brothers (E60), photo-lithographic methods were widely publicised. Schnauss included this medium in his treatise on collotype (E248), and in 1895 the first separate textbook on photo-lithography was produced by Fritz (E253); the translation of a German work which concentrated on Continental methods. Photographically produced images upon stone or zinc were printed by normal litho-printing methods, literature about which is included in section Dc supra.

E193 **Ramsay, A.C.** 1855. On a process for obtaining lithographs by the photographic process. Report, British Association, 25th Meeting, 1855; Notices & Abstracts: 69-70. Reported in: Athenaeum 1855 (Sept. 22): 1093.
Apropos 2 photo-lithographs shown at the Photographic Exhibition, Glasgow, Sept. 1855. "A process by which Mr. Robert M'Pherson of Rome, had succeeded in obtaining beautiful photo-lithographs".

E194 **Rousseau, E. & - Masson.** 1856. Method of reproducing photographic images on paper, stone or metal, without salts of silver. Journal, Photographic Society 3: 11-12.

E195 **Pouncy, J.** 1859. [A paper on carbon printing.] Journal, Photographic Society 5: 122-130.
Incl. a transcript of the lengthy discussion following the reading of this paper.

E196 **Anon.** 1859. Method of obtaining photographs in printing or lithographic ink. Photographic News 3: 146-147.
Asser's process.

E197 **James, Sir H.** 1860. Photo-zincography. Southampton. 10pp.

E198 **Anon.** 1860. On the reduction of Ordnance Survey plans by photography, & copying & printing by photo-zincography. Journal, Photographic Society 6: 223-225, & 1 pl.
The pl. is a specimen.

E199 ----- 1860. Photo-zincography. Photographic News 3: 360, & 1 pl.
Ordnance survey process; the pl. is a specimen.

E200 **Osborne, J.W.** 1860. On a new photo-lithographic process. Transactions, Philosophical Institute of Victoria 4 (2): 172-183. Also pub. in: Photographic News 4: 374-375, 388-389, 1860; & Journal, Photographic Society 7: 163-166, 1861.

E201 **Beatty, F.S. & S. Alexander.** 1861. Certain improvements in photo-lithography, etc. Journal, Photographic Society 7: 282-285. Also pub. in: Photographic News 5: 327-329, 1861; & editorial comment p.323.
The patent specification.

E202 **Anon.** 1861. Beatty's patent heliographic printing: For the production of photographic representations in printers' ink. Photographic News 5: 459.

E203 **James, Sir H.** 1861. On photozincography. Report, Meeting of the British Association, 31st Meeting, 1861; Notices & Abstracts: 263. Also pub. in: British Journal of Photography 7: 240.

E204 **Osborne, J.W.** 1862. On some of the difficulties connected with the practice of photo-lithography. Journal, Photographic Society 8: 160-165.

E205 ----- 1862. Details of a photo-lithographic process as adopted by the Government of Victoria, for the publication of maps. Journal, Photographic Society 8: 167-169. Also pub. in: Photographic News 6: 484-487.

E206 **Scott, A. de C.** 1862. On photo-zincography & other photographic processes employed at the Ordnance Survey Office, Southampton. Published under the direction of Col. Sir H. James. London. viiii+16pp. & 12 pls.
Pt. I: Production of the negative; Pt. II: Preparation of the positive photographic print in greasy ink; Pt. III: Transference of the print to zinc, and preparation for printing. The pls. incl. examples of photo-zincographic facsimiles of maps, MSS, early letterpress printing, an engraving, etc.

E207 **Anon.** 1862. Half tone in photolithographs. Photographic News 6: 529.

E208 **MacTear, A.** 1863. On photolithography. Photographic News 7: 41-43.
Lecture to the Glasgow Photographic Association discussing several methods.

E209 **Lewis, J.** 1863. Photolithography. The varied action of light upon bitumen & bichromates -- a new transfer process. Photographic News 7: 403, 414, 449, 499.
Several methods are discussed.

E210 **Liesegang, P.** 1863. Photolithography. Photographic News 7: 426-427.
The method of Quaglio, of Vienna.

E211 **Pouncy, J.** 1863. Specification of his new patent process for permanent printing. Journal, Photographic Society 8: 336-337. Also pub. in: Photographic News 7: 367-368.

E212 **Anon.** 1863. Photographs in printing ink. Photographic News 7: 361-363.
Pouncy's process.

E213 **Sutton, T.** 1863. Photography in printing ink: Being a description of the process recently patented by J. Pouncy of Dorchester. London. 68pp.

E214 **Scott, A. de C.** 1863. On photo-zincography & other photographic process employed at the Ordnance Survey Office, Southampton. Published under the direction of Col. Sir H. James. 2nd edn. London. viii+16pp. & 15 pls.

E215 **Toovey, W.** 1864. Improved photolithographic process. Journal, Photographic Society 9: 45-46.

E216 **Anon.** 1864. A new lithographic process. Photographic News 8: 158-159; also editorial comment, p.171, & letter from J. Lewis claiming priority for the discovery, p.177.
Toovey's process.

E217 **Tessie du Motay, C.M. & C.R. Maréchal.** 1866. Improvements in photo-lithographic transfers. Photographic News 10: 103-104.
The patent specification.

E218 **Bullock, J.** 1866. Improvements in the application of photography to the obtaining of printing proofs or impressions. Journal, Photographic Society 11: 15-17. Also pub. in: Photographic News 10: 185-186, 1866, & 1 pl.; also editorial comment p.181-183.
The pl. in the Photographic News version is a fine specimen of the process. For a reprint of the original patent specification see: Half-tone lithography & the zinc-block process, its position twenty-seven years ago; Messrs E. & J. Bullock's patent no. 2954, No. 17, 1865. British Lithographer 1 (4): 19-20, 1892.

E219 ----- 1866. Photo-lithography. Photographic News 10: 232-233.
Short lecture to South London Photographic Society.

E220 **Bolton, F.J. & H. Matheson.** 1866. Photography, photozincography, etc. Photographic News 10: 343-344.
The patent specification.

E221 **Lallemand, M.** 1868. Photolithography. Journal, Photographic Society 12: 175-176.

E222 **Griggs, W.** 1868. On the use of photography in lithographic & other modes of printing. Journal, Photographic Society 13: 21-25. Also pub. in: Photographic News 12: 199-200, with an editorial note, pp.194-195; also editorial comment pp.227, 239.

E223 **Waterhouse, J.** 1868. Photo zincography in practice. Photographic News 12: 280-281, 293-295, 306-307, 317-318, 340-342, 354-356.

E224 **Window, F.R.** 1870. A new carbon process & photo-lithographic process. Photographic News 14: 243.
The patent specification.

E225 **Schrank, L.** 1871. The asphalte photo lithographic process. Photographic News 15: 368-369.

E226 **Anon.** 1872/73. Photo-lithography. Lithographer 3: 126-127.

E227 **Slater, A.** 1874. Improvements in photo-lithography. Photographic News 18: 315-316.
Provisional patent specification.

E228 **James, Sir H.** Ed. 1875. Account of the methods & processes adopted for the production of the maps of the Ordnance Survey of the United Kingdom. London. vi+214pp. & pls.
Not seen.

E229 **Anon.** 1877. Asser's photo-lithographic process. Photographic News 21: 405.
Transl. from: Photographisches Archiv.

E230 **Duby, E.** 1878. The modern photo-mechanical printing methods. Photographic News 22: 199-200.
Deals only with photo-lithography.

E231 **Butter, H.** 1880. Modern photo-lithography. Photographic News 24: 140-142. Also pub. in: British & Colonial Printer 4: 1140-1142, 1880.

E232 **Anon.** 1881. About photo-lithography. Photographic News 25: 568-569. Use of the velvet roller.

E233 **Waterhouse, J.** 1882-85. Photo-lithography & photo-zincography. Photographic News 26: 482-484, 564-566, 587-589, 596-598, 651-652, 715-716, 748-749, 774-775, 787-788, 1882; 27: 53-55, 90-92, 122-124, 133-134, 180-182, 196-199, 267-268, 278-280, 325-326, 365-366, 397, 407-408, 428-429, 445-447, 502-503, 541-542, 548-550, 587-588, 615, 630, 725-725, 742-743, 773-775, 795-796, 830-831, 1883; 28: 29-30, 70-71, 86-87, 221, 620-621, 636-637, 780-781, 812-813, 1884; 29: 21-22, 60, 269-270, 301-302, 411-413, 444-446, 1885.
An important textbook of some 18 chapters is distributed in fragments throughout 4 years' issues of the journal. It covers preparatory manipulations, theory of photo-lithography, photo-transfer methods, direct collo-chromatic methods, asphalt process, negative transfer process, miscellaneous minor processes, and photo-lithography in half-tones.

E234 **Anon.** 1883. Asser's photo-lithographic transfer process. Printing Times & Lithographer N.S.9: 304.

E235 ----- 1883. Asser's photo-lithographic method. Photographic News 27: 433-434, & 1 pl.
The pl. is a specimen.

E236 **Laws, T.M.** 1883. Photo-lithography. Photographic News 27: 188-190.

E237 **Anon.** 1884. The velvet roller for photolithographic transfer. Photographic News 28: 162-163.

E238 **Husnik, J.** 1884. On the treatment of Husnik's photo-lithographic transfer paper. British Journal of Photography 31: 489-490, 571-572, 585, 634-635.

E239 **Asser, E.J.** 1885. Some practical hints on photo-lithography & photo-zincography. Year Book of Photography 1885: 72-73.

E240 **Anon.** 1886/87. Practical lithography in half-tone: Description of Husband's papyrotint process. Photographic Journal N.S.11: 126-127, & 1 pl.
The pl. is a specimen.

E241 **Barnes, W.M.** 1887. Printing in carbon, & oil colours, & photo-lithography. British Journal of Photography 34: 474-475, 487-489.
Lecture on Pouncy's methods.

E242 **Anon.** 1887. A visit to the Ordnance Survey Office, Southampton. Briish Journal of Photography 34: 547-548, 565-566.
Describes their photo-zincographic methods.

E243 ----- 1887. Practical lithography in half-tone: Description of Husband's papyrotint process. Printing Times & Lithographer N.S.13: 101-102, 142.

E244 **Anon.** 1888. Husband's process of photo-lithography in half-tone. Photographic News 32: 49.

E245 **Waterhouse, J.** 1889. Direct process of photo-zincography. Photographic News 33: 733-734.
Bichromate process worked out by J. Harrald, and asphalt process by A.W. Turner. Repr. from: Annual Report, Survey of India Department, 1888/89.

E246 **Wilkinson, W.T.** 1888-89. Photography & lithography. Printing Times & Lithographer N.S.14: 65-66, 87-88, 104-105, 142-143, 184-185, 202-203, 1888; N.S. 15: 6, 27, 64, 161, 181, 1889.

E247 ----- 1889. Something new in photo-mechanical work. Photographic News 33: 248-249.
Short technical note on photo-lithographic transfer process.

E248 **Schnauss, J.** 1889. Collotype & photo-lithography practically elaborated ... transl. ... by E.C. Middleton, together with an appendix on steam presses by the translator. London. 170pp. Another edn., 1895.

E249 **Gunther, H.E.** 1890. Photo-lithography & the new Albert photo-lithographic transfer paper. Photographic News 34: 147-148.

E250 **Mantell, A.M.** 1890/91. Husband's papyrotint process for lithography in half-tone. Photographic Quarterly 2: 183-186.

E251 **Anon.** 1891-95. Photo-mechanical lithographic printing processes. [Title later changed to: Photo-lithographic processes.] British Lithographer 1 (1): 3-4, (2): 24-28, (3): 2-4, (4): 27-28, (5): 2-3, (6): 4, 1891/92; 2: 2-4, 38-39, 105-106, 125-126, 159-160, 213-215, 1892/93; 3: 21-22, 84-85, 109-110, 135-136, 1893/94; 4: 15-17, 82-84, 117-119, 149-150, 183-186, 1894/95.

E252 **Debenham, W.E.** 1892/93. Photolithography. Photographic Journal N.S.17: 126-131.

E253 **Fritz, G.** 1895. Photo-lithography. Transl. by E.J. Wall. London. 92pp. & 6 pls.
Describes Continental methods, incl. 2 processes for photo-chromo-lithography.

E254 **Richmond, W.D.** 1897. Photo-lithography. Photographic Journal N.S.21: 252-261.

E255 **Gamble, W.** 1899. Direct photo-lithography on stone. Process Photogram 6: 145-146, 163-165.

E256 **Waterhouse, J.** 1900. Photo-lithography in half-tone. Penrose Annual 6: 17-24.

Ef Photo-planographic processes : Collotype

In 1855 Alphonse Poitevin's researches led him to discover that an exposed bichromated gelatine-coated plate, when wetted and rolled with greasy ink, would only accept ink on the exposed portions of the picture. But the successful commercial exploitation of this idea had to wait until the late 1860's when Josef Albert commenced production of Albertypes, or collotypes as they are now called. However, there had been some earlier trials and some experimental successes. In 1860 Joubert presented a specimen "print in permanent ink" to a photographic periodical and styled it his "Phototype Process" (E257). This was the name used by the Frenchmen Tessie du Motay & Maréchal in the mid. 1860's for their process which employed a chromated gelatine coating on a copper-plate support (E258). Although Joubert advertised his process nothing more seems to have been heard of it and his specimen survives as the earliest published collotype in England.

Albert succeeded, where others had failed, by using a plate glass support for the gelatine and also by devising a method for firmly securing it -- a problem that had defeated the Frenchmen -- with excellent results (E259 E260). In England, Edwards developed a version which he called Heliotype (E261 E262) and which enjoyed some commercial success after he formed a company to exploit it (E269 E275). He added the technique of hardening the exposed image with chrome alum, so improving its durability. Another German, Max Gemoser, was also involved with collotype developments, coining the name Lichtdruck for his version, and his firm, Ohm & Grossmann, leased the patent rights to the Autotype Co. in England. Sawyer, a principal in the Autotype Co., had previously announced a process of his own, called Sawyer's Collotype (E272), but it was dropped in favour of the more successful German patent which became known as the Autotype Mechanical Process (E277). For a short while there was vigorous competition with Heliotype but Edwards moved the centre of his operations to America.

Waterhouse, always active in photo-mechanical research, made improvements in collotype in connection with his cartographic printing duties at the Survey of India (E266 E267 E276). After the rush of developments in the early 1870's a steady stream of journal articles recorded the various minor improvements being made, particularly by German and Austrian firms. These included the use of a metal support for the gelatine printing film; Husnik tried zinc (E281) while Hodson described the Improved Heliotype which used steel plate. The first separate manual of collotype techniques to appear in England was by Schnauss (E290) and at about the same time the process was first included in Wilkinson's manual (E48) and thereafter it was also included in Wilkinson (E54 E64) and Brothers (E60). In 1895 Wilkinson produced a separate little manual (E295) and just after the turn of the century a more comprehensive textbook was prepared by Fithian (E296).

The superb tonal qualities of collotype, coupled with its high definition, generated much interest in some quarters. Although its use for book illustration was generally confined to high class work, it was very popular for postcards, calendars, and other commercial work. Power driven collotype machines had been introduced in the early 1870's in Germany but were slow in reaching England. However, as fast efficient machines became available, (the first British machine was introduced in 1893), several larger printing firms, such as Waterlow (E287) took up this branch of the trade. Instruction in the special techniques for printing collotype became a significant element in the literature, as shown by Schnauss's chapter on the steam press (E290), in lectures by Denovan (E292 E294), and in Fithian's textbook (E296).

E257 **Joubert, F.** 1860. [Letter] The phototype printing process. Journal, Photographic Society 6: 287, & 1 pl.
Relates to the specimen of collotype pub. as a suppl. to the Jan. issue: "Phototype Process. This print in permanent ink is presented by Mr. F. Joubert ..."

E258 **Maréchal, C.R. & C.M. Tessie du Motay.** 1867. Mechanical photographic printing. Photographic News 11: 260-261.
A paper read to the French photographic society.

E259 **Anon.** 1869. Herr Albert's new mechanical process. Photographic News 13: 61-62, 121-122. Also pub. in: Journal, Photographic Society 13: 236-237.

E260 ----- 1869. Our presentation print by Herr Albert's new process. Photographic News 13: 455-456, & 1 pl.
The pl. is a specimen.

E261 **Edwards, E.** 1870. Photo-mechanical printing patent. Photographic News 14: 283-284.

E262 **Anon.** 1870. Mr. Edwards's photo-collographic process. Photographic News 14: 409-410.

E263 ----- 1870. On heliotypy as a means of reproducing works of art. Photographic News 14: 538-539, 559-560.

E264 ----- 1870. Our presentation print -- Albert-Type. Photographic News 14: 289-290, & 1 pl.
The pl. is a specimen.

E265 **Jessen, C.F.** 1870. The "Lichtdruck" process. Journal, Photographic Society 15: 28-30. Also pub. in: Photographic News 14: 292-293, 1870.

E266 **Waterhouse, J.** 1871. On a new photo-collographic printing process. Proceedings, Asiatic Society of Bengal 1871: 239-245.

E267 ----- 1871. A new (photo-collographic) photo-mechanical printing process. Photographic News 15: 556-557.

E268 **Edwards, E.** 1871. On photography in the printing press, being a description of the working of the Heliotype process. Journal, Society of Arts 19: 479-485, & 1 pl. Also pub. in: Photographic News 15: 208-210, 225-226, 236-237, 248-249.
The pl. is a specimen.

E269 **Edwards & Kidd** [Firm.] 1871. The heliotype process. International Exhibition, 1871. London. 8pp.
A prospectus which incl. a rep. of Edwards' article (E268).

E270 **Edwards, E.** 1871. Improvements in photo-collographic printing. Photographic News 15: 566-567.
The patent specification.

E271 **Simpson, G.W.** 1871. On some new methods of printing. Portfolio 2: 135-138.
On photo-collography.

E272 **Sawyer, J.R.** 1872. Photography in the printing press. Journal, Photographic Society 15: 108-112. Also pub. separately, London, [1872]. 15pp. Also pub. in: Photographic News 16: 32-33, 44-45, 1872.

E273 **Anon.** 1872. Albertype, or photo-collography. Photographic News 16: 283-284, 298-299.
Lecture to the U.S. National Photographic Association, St. Louis.

E274 ----- 1872. Capt. Waterhouse's improvements in photo-collography. Photographic News 16: 471, 482.

E275 **Heliotype Co.** ca.1872. The heliotype process described & illustrated with twelve specimens. London. 16pp.

E276 **Waterhouse, J.** 1873. Notes on photo-collotype printing. Journal, Photographic Society 15: 221-223, 1873; 16: 11-13, 1873. Also pub. in: Photographic News 17: 301, 1873; 18: 4-5, 1874.

E277 **Autotype Co.** [ca.1872-76.] The Autotype mechanical process: Or, the art of reproducing photographs in the printing press. With an illustration from life. London. 16pp. & 1 pl.
Incl. a repr. of Simpson's 1871 article (E271). The pl. is a specimen of collotype.

E278 **Husnik, J.** 1875. An excellent lichtdruck process. Photographic News 19: 568-569.

E279 ----- 1877. Improvements in the production of lichtdruck printing plates. Photographic News 21: 45-46.
Repr. from Photographische Correspondenz.

E280 **Voight, M.T.H.** 1877. Photo-collotype printing. Photographic News 21: 64-65, 201-202, 212-213.
Repr. from Bulletin, Societe Francaise de Photographie.

E281 **Husnik, J.** 1879. Collotypes on zinc plates. Photographic News 23: 57-58.
Repr. from Photographisches Wochenblatt.

E282 **Anon.** 1881. New formulae for collotypic printing. Photographic News 25: 241.

E283 ----- 1881. Herr Löwy in Vienna -- the lichtdruck in detail. Photographic News 25: 590-591.

E284 ----- 1882. The collotype process in practice. Photographic News 26: 642-643.
Various methods.

E285 **Anon.** 1883. "Processes" -- collotype or lichtdruck. British Journal Photographic Almanac 1883: 124-128.
Account of Albert, Löwy, and Obernetter's processes.

E286 ----- 1887. Husnik's improved lichtdruck. Epitome of the manipulations & defects inherent to Husnik's lichtdruck. Photographic News 21: 245, 255-256, 293.

E287 ----- 1887. Printing collotypes at the machine: A visit to Waterlow & Sons Ltd. Photographic News 31: 129-130, 177. Also pub. in: British & Colonial Printer 18: 277, 293-294.

E288 **Taylor, J.T.** 1888. Practical artotype or collotype. British Journal Photographic Almanac 1888: 356-358.

E289 **Anon.** 1889. Collotype printing. British & Colonial Printer 24: 413.

E290 **Schnauss, J.** 1889. Collotype & photo-lithography practically elaborated ... transl. ... by E.C. Middleton, together with an appendix on steam presses by the translator. London. 170pp. & 1 pl. Another edn. 1895.
The pl. is a specimen of collotype.

E291 **Warnerke, L.** 1890/91. A simplified photo-collographic process. Photographic Journal N.S.15: 105-110.

E292 **Denovan, W.A.** 1893-94. Practical collotype printing. British & Colonial Printer 32: 392, 435, 457, 1893; 33: 4, 70, 105, 128, 178, 1894.
Report of lectures given in Glasgow.

E293 **Debenham, W.E.** 1893/94. A demonstration of collotype printing. Photographic Journal N.S.18: 84-88.

E294 **Denovan, W.A.** 1894. Practical collotype printing. Printing Times & Lithographer N.S.3: 312-316.
Outline of a series of lectures.

E295 **Wilkinson, W.T.** 1895. Collotype. London. 16pp. & 4 pls.

E296 **Fithian, A.W.** 1901. Practical collotype. London. 90pp.
Incl. sections on collotype presses and machines, collotype from dry plates, the Photo-Autocopyist (a simplified form of collotype), and collotype transfers to stone or zinc.

Eg Photo-pigment processes

Although not described as a "pigment process" Herschel's cyanotype shares the same virtue of permanence (E297 E298). It was a simply operated process that produced "negative" white images on a vivid blue ground and utilised paper coated with an iron compound. The process was employed for the production of at least one botanical book (E520 E520*).

In the early days photographers were dismayed to find that their silver and other prints suffered from serious fading in a relatively short time. Efforts were made to find a more appropriate "positive" pigment that shared the same degree of permanence as the cyanotype. In 1856 a competition was held in France which was to award prizes to the value of 10,000 Francs to the discoverer of a solution to the fading of photographs. In the event Poitevin was awarded the gold medal and the Dorsetshire photographer, Pouncy, won the silver. Carbon, the most stable pigment known, formed the basis of the winning processes.

Pouncy coated paper with a film of vegetable carbon, gum arabic, and potassium bichromate, exposed it under a negative and washed away the unexposed, unhardened, portions so as to leave a pigmented gum image (E300 E301). Half-tones were scarcely possible by this method since the gelatine hardened from the surface downwards and the lightly exposed portions were lost in washing. Swan devised a method which utilized a gelatine tissue coloured with carbon and sensitized with bichromate of potash that could be removed from its support and fixed face downwards onto a sheet of paper. With the hardened gelatine on the underside, washing left a print with a surface of varying thickness, the deep areas appearing black, the shallow areas light, thus presenting a tonal effect (E302 E309). This process, with modifications and technical improvements, formed the basis of Autotype. The details of Swan's carbon process and the Autotype developments and techniques can be found in several informative works by Simpson (E320), Blair (E323), Johnson (E326-E329 E332), Autotype (E330 E336), Sawyer (E340 E342), and especially Sawyer's 1877 manual (E348). Autotype was a very successful process that found considerable application in book illustration and the publication of "art prints" for framing.

Another process of equal quality and greater success was Woodburytype. Woodbury was an ingenious and industrious worker who added many patent improvements to photographic and photo-mechanical methods. He introduced Woodburytype in 1865 (E313-E315) and brought it to perfection and patented it two years later (E321). His process involved making a long exposure on a thickly coated light-sensitive pigmented gelatine film, transferring and inverting the film to another support, developing and washing it in the usual way and then allowing it to dry and contract for a while. This low-relief dried print was then placed on a steel plate with a lead plate above it and, under enormous pressure, a mould of the gelatine was obtained in the lead. To make a print an electrotype of the mould was pressed face downwards onto a sheet of paper with a pool of warm pigmented gelatine between. After being held for a while to allow it to set a low relief pigmented gelatine image was revealed and was rendered insoluble with alum. The print was a vividly well-defined grainless image with all the appearance of a photograph but incapable of fading (E315). In 1867 the inventor patented a method for printing woodburytypes on a roller press in which one roller, of softer metal, had been impressed with the image but it is doubtful whether the idea was put to practical use (E321). Woodbury later produced a modified process called stannotype which achieved similar results at even lower cost than Woodburytype by employing relatively simple machinery (E352 E356). Hodson (E44) who described stannotype methods remarks that the prints were practically indistinguishable from Woodburytype.

Another beautiful photographic process was patented by Willis in 1877, called platinotype, and was occasionally used for book illustrations (E343). It was, as the name suggests, based on the presence of pure platinum pigmentation in the final print and had absolute permanence, producing prints with dark grey tones capable of great delicacy. The best account of the process is given by Pizzighelli & Hübl (E355).

Willis's father was the inventor of the aniline process, patented in 1865 (E312), which enabled line prints to be made from drawings, plans, maps, etc.

without taking a negative and the patent was quickly taken up by a leading lithographic printer. Paper, prepared with an acid bichromate, was exposed beneath the plan, then developed with aniline vapour and fixed by washing it in a weak acid solution.

The pigment processes of the 19th century produced numerous book illustrations that have survived to this day in a brilliant state of permanence, a credit to the ingenuity of their inventors and printers. They eventually gave way to the photo-mechanical processes which generally required less skillful preparation and printing.

The literature generated by these discoveries is remarkable for its profusion, chiefly in the form of periodical articles, and indicates the extent of interest stimulated among photographers and printers.

E297 **Herschel, Sir J.F.W.** 1842. On the action of the rays of the solar spectrum on vegetable colours, & on some new photographic processes. Philosophical Transactions, Royal Society of London 1842: 181-214. Also pub. in: Philosophical Magazine 22: 5-21, 107-116, 135, 170-180, 246-252, 505-511.
Cyanotype is mentioned on pp.210-211 of the first pub.

E298 ----- 1843. On certain improvements in photographic processes described in a former communication, & on the parathermic rays of the solar spectrum. Philosophical Transactions, Royal Society of London 1843: 1-6.

E299 **Anon.** 1858/59. New discoveries: Printing in carbon, MM. Henri Garnier & Alphonse Salmon. Photographic News 1: 4-5; & letter from J. Pouncy protesting at comparison with his own invention, p.20.

E300 ----- 1858. Mr. Pouncy's carbon process. Photographic News 1: 51-52.
An editorial review of specimens just received.

A301 **Pouncy, J.** 1859. [Untitled article on carbon printing.] Journal, Photographic Society 5: 122-130.

E302 **Swan, J.** 1864. On a new method of carbon printing. Journal, Photographic Society 9: 20-25. Also pub. in: Photographic News 8: 185-187.

E303 ----- 1864. Swan's patent carbon process. Journal, Photographic Society 9: 106-108.
Extracts from the patent specification.

E304 **Anon.** 1864. Mr. Swan's carbon process. Photographic News 8: 169-170; and editorial comments, pp.181-182, 193-194.

E305 ----- 1864. The new carbon process. Exposure & development. Various manipulations. Additional hints. Photographic News 8: 217-218, 230-231, 279.
Swan's carbon process.

E306 **Cooper, H. jun.** 1864. Some remarks on the new carbon process. Photographic News 8: 245-246.
Experiments with Swan's carbon process.

E307 **Anon.** 1864. Further hints on the new carbon process. Photographic News 8: 253-254.
Swan's carbon process.

E308 **Cooper, H. jun.** 1864. Printing in carbon. Photographic News 8: 329-330, 351-352.

E309 **Swan, J.W.** 1864. Mr. Swan's patent carbon process. Photographic News 8: 437-439; and editorial comment, pp.433-434.
The patent specification.

E310 **Pouncy, J.** 1865. On photographic carbon printing. Journal, Photographic Society 9: 179-183.
Followed by a controversial correspondence relating to Pouncy's claim of priority in discovering carbon printing.

E311 ----- 1865. Photographs in printing ink. Photographic News 9: 18-19.
Lecture to the Photographic Society of Scotland.

E312 **Willis, W.** 1865. The aniline process of photographic printing. Journal, Photographic Society 10: 26-31. Also pub. in: Photographic News 9: 186-187, 196-197.
Also: Letter from Vincent Brooks announcing his acquisition of rights to exploit the patent, Photographic News 10: 378, 1866.

E313 **Woodbury, W.B.** 1865. A new photo-relief printing process. Journal, Photographic Society 10: 202-206.

E314 ----- 1865. The new photo-relief printing process in semi-transparent ink. Photographic News 9: 387-388; and editorial comment, pp.397-399.

E315 **Anon.** 1866. Our presentation print -- Woodbury's process. Photographic News 10: 37-38, & 1 pl.

E316 **Cherrill, N.K.** 1866-67. Carbon printing. Photographic News 10: 459-460, 483-484, 532, 603-604, 1866; 11: 134-135, 453-454, 1867.

E317 **Swan, J.W.** 1867. Practical details of carbon printing. Photographic News 11: 18-20.

E318 ----- 1867. Carbon process for reproduction in line or stipple. Photographic News 11: 122-123.

E319 **Anon.** 1867. Swan's carbon process. Journal, Photographic Society 12: 77-80.

E320 **Simpson, G.W.** 1867. On the production of photographs in pigments: Containing historical notes on carbon printing, & practical details of Swan's patent carbon process. London. iv+103pp. & 1 pl.
Incl. the patent specification for Swan's process and a specimen print.

E321 **Woodbury, W.B.** 1867. Photo-relief printing by machinery. Photographic News 11: 250.
The patent specification.

E322 **Autotype Printing & Publishing Co. Ltd.** [1868.] [Company prospectus.] London. 15pp.
Incl. a discussion of the background to the autotype invention, touching on Poitevin's and Swan's work, and a description of the mode of working the autotype patent. Probably by J.F. Boyes, the company secretary.

E323 **Blair, W.** 1869. Mr. Swan's patent. Photographic News 13: 41-42; also editorial comment, pp.37-38, 50-51, and letter from Blair, p.58.

E324 **Edwards, E.** 1869. Modified carbon printing process. Photographic News 13: 46.
The patent specification.

E325 **Woodbury, W.B.** 1869. Description of the Woodburytype or photo relief process. Journal, Photographic Society 14: 4-6. Also pub. in: Photographic News 13: 140.

E326 **Anon.** 1869. Mr. Johnson's improved carbon process. Photographic News 13: 157-158.

E327 **Johnson, J.R.** 1869. On a greatly simplified process of printing in carbon or other permanent pigment. Journal, Photographic Society 14: 31-33, 51-53. Also pub. in: Photographic News 13: 247-249.

E328 ----- 1869. Manipulations in carbon printing. Photographic News 13: 294.

E329 ----- 1869. Improvements in carbon printing. Photographic News 13: 474-476.
The patent specification.

E330 **Autotype Printing & Publishing Co. Ltd.** 1870. The autotype process: Being a popular manual of instruction in the art of printing in carbon or other permanent pigments. London.
Not seen.

E331 **Anon.** 1870. Manipulations in Johnson's carbon process. Photographic News 14: 224-225, 233-234, 259-260, 272-273, 286.
Extracts from the Autotype Company's manual.

E332 **Johnson, J.R.** 1870. Latest improvements in the carbon process. Photographic News 14: 124-125.
Lecture to the South London Photographic Society.

E333 **Swan, J.W.** 1870. The chemistry of the carbon process. Journal, Photographic Society 15: 21-23. Also pub. in: Photographic News 14: 234-235.

E334 **Bovey, W.T.** 1870. Printing in carbon described in two chapters. Photographic News 14: 326-328, 341-343.
On Edwards' improvements to Swan's process.

E335 **Johnson, J.R.** 1870. Improvements in preparing carbon tissue. Photographic News 14: 394-395; and editorial comment, pp.397-398.
The patent specification.

E336 **Autotype Printing & Publishing Co. Ltd.** 1871. The autotype process, [etc.] New edn., rev. & enl. London. 63pp. 3rd edn., 1873; 4th edn., 1875; 5th edn., Ed. J.R. Sawyer, 1876.
Pt. I: Its nature & history; Pt. II: Its general practice; Pt. III: Its special practice -- non inverted pictures; Pt. IV: Its special practice -- inverted pictures.

E337 **Taylor, T.** 1871. The autotype process. Portfolio 2: 53-59. Also pub. in: Photographic News 15: 173-174, 188, 198-199, 1871.

E338 **Liesegang, P.E.** 1872. Dr. Liesegang on carbon printing. Photographic News 16: 472-474, 495.

E339 **Anon.** 1873. The origin & progress of autotype printing. Lithographer 4: 69-71.

E340 **Sawyer, J.R.** 1875. Photography in permanent pigments, with recent improvements in autotype transfer. Journal, Photographic Society 16: 113-117. Also pub. in: Photographic News 19: 194-195, 206-208.

E341 **Johnson, J.R.** 1876. On some improvements in autotype or pigment printing. Photographic News 20: 10.

E342 **Sawyer, J.R.** 1876. Improved flexible support for developing carbon prints. Photographic News 20: 257.
The patent specification.

E343 **Willis, W. jun.** 1877. The platinum printing process. Photographic News 21: 41.
The patent specification.

E344 **Turner, A.W.** 1877. Carbon printing. Photographic News 21: 67-69, 91-92, 106-107, 124, 141-142.

E345 **Croughton, G.** 1877. Carbon printing. Photographic News 21: 69-70, 162-163.

E346 **Batho, W.E.** 1877. The platinotype. Photographic News 21: 266-267.

E347 **Johnson, J.R.** 1877. New carbon process. Photographic News 21: 567-569.
The patent specification.

E348 **Sawyer, J.R.** 1877. The autotype process: Being a practical manual of instruction in the art of printing in permanent pigments; with a notice of the autotype mechanical process. 6th edn., rev. London. x+110pp. & 1 pl.
Pt. I: Its nature and history; Pt. II: Its general practice -- manipulations, the final transfer, double transfer; Pt. III: Adaptation of the process of permanent pigment printing to the production of photographs on various materials; Pt. IV: Useful hints on pigment printing; Pt. V: Failures & their remedies; Pt. VI: Formulae; Conclusion (incl. an abstract of Sawyer's 1872 article (E272), describing his collotype process).

E349 **Autotype Co.** 1877. The autotype process: Being a popular manual. [7th edn.] London. vii+66pp. & 1 pl.
In 1877 the old autotype manual was re-cast. Sawyer wrote the expanded practical manual (E348) and this, the company's manual, appeared in a new, popular version. Pt. I: Its nature and history; Pt. II: Its general practice -- manipulations; Pt. III: Adaptations of the process of permanent pigment printing to the production of photographs on various materials. The pl., an autotype, shows the company's works.

E350 **Liesegang, P.E.** 1878. A manual of the carbon process of permanent photography & its use in making enlargements. Transl. from the 6th German edn. by R.B. Marston. London. viii+146pp. & 1 pl.
Historical sketch: Materials: Tissue manipulations: Negatives: Printing and transferring. Incl. a reprint of J.R. Johnson's patent specification. The pl. is a specimen of carbon printing using the Woodbury Co.'s new tissue.

E351 **Willis, W. jun.** 1878. Notes on the platinotype process. Journal, Photographic Society N.S.3: 32-34.

E352 **Anon.** 1882. The stannotype process. British Journal of Photography 29: 88-89.

E353 **Annan, J.C.** 1883. Carbon printing. British Journal of Photography 30: 32-34, 49-50. Also pub. in: Photographic News 27: 35-38, 1883.

E354 **Anon.** 1883-84. The Woodburytype process. Photographic News 27: 582, 723, 1883; 28: 177, 210-211, 226, 276, 1884.

E355 **Pizzighelli, G. & Baron A. Hübl.** 1883. Platinotype. (Transl. by J.F. Iselin; ed. by W. de W. Abney.) Journal, Photographic Society N.S.7: 67-72, 87-92, 103-108, 128-134, 146-152. Also pub. separately: London, 1886. 63pp. Repr. in: Bunnell, P.C. Nonsilver printing processes. New York, 1973.
The original work was pub. in Vienna & Leipzig, 1882.

E356 **Anon.** 1884. Stannotype. British Journal of Photography 31: 71, 87, 102-103, 134-135, 149-150, 166-167, 182-183, 198-199, 214-215, 261.
See also: Woodbury, W.B. A few further notes on stannotype, by the inventor, pp.453-454.

E357 ----- 1884. Carbon printing. Photographic News 28: 211-212, 332-333, 338-339, 359, 453.

E358 **Barnes, W.M.** 1887. Printing in carbon, & oil colours, & photo-lithography. British Journal of Photography 34: 474-475, 487-489.
Lecture on Pouncy's methods.

E359 **Bolte, M.** 1887. Carbon printing: Explicit instructions for professional & amateur photographers. Photographic News 31: 292-294, 358-359, 454-456, 555-556, 585-586.
Repr. from Anthony's Bulletin.

E360 **Sawyer, J.R.** 1887. The A B C guide to the making of autotype prints in permanent pigments. London. xiv+98pp. & 2 pls. Rev. edn., 1893. xii+99pp. & 2 pls.
The pls. are an autotype and Sawyer's collotype process. In the rev. edn. the pls. are an autotype single transfer sepia on toned etching paper and the collotype.

E361 **Willis, W. jun.** 1890/91. Platinotype. Photographic Journal N.S.15: 123-131.

E362 **James, G.H.** 1890/91. Autotype printing in pigments. Photographic Quarterly 2: 306-311.

E363 **Duchochois, P.C.** 1892. Photographic reproduction processes: A practical treatise of the photo-impressions without silver salts. Ed., with additional matter, by E.J. Wall. London. vii+122pp.
Incl. the cyanotype or blue-process, the aniline process, graphotypy, the platinotype, and the carbon process.

E364 **Wall, E.J.** 1894. Carbon printing. London. 69pp. & 1 pl.
Tissue manipulations: Printing: Transferring to various supports. The pl. is a specimen.

Eh Photo-mechanical printing in colour

Colour printing by lithographic and relief processes reached a very high degree of technical excellence in the second half of the 19th century and briliantly colourful work was available in books, magazines, fancy pictures, and stationery. The growing success of photo-mechanical printing methods in the last three decades of the century naturally led to a desire to achieve similar results by chromo-photographic processes.

Some early attempts at producing pigment printing in colours were made by Vidal (E365) and Sawyer (E366) but without any apparent commercial success. Griggs, who had been active in photo-lithography since the 1860's, was eventually to develop photo-chromo-lithography to a high degree of perfection and some of his earlier excursions into this field are included in his 1882 booklet (E367). In later years he combined photo-chromo-lithography with collotype for his best work.

Others concentrated on using collotype alone for colour work and the earliest examples reported in England were of German origin. The process was named Hoeschotype and methods for its production were described by Hodson (E44) and Richmond (E369). The first British colour-collotypes were reported by Anon. (E371) and illustrated with a specimen. Subsequent developments can be found recorded in Brothers (E60), Husnik (E381), and others. Brothers also described and illustrated photo-chromo-lithography and some Continental processes are included in Fritz (E253).

However, the most significant colour photo-mechanical developments took place in the final decade of the century and concentrated upon tri-chromatic relief printing, giving rise to a small flood of periodical articles. A key figure in this development was the American, Ives, who perfected the photochromoscope (E385) which was of importance in the development of tri-chromatic colour negative production. His several other theoretical and practical contributions are recorded in a valuable series of articles (E370 E373 E377 E384

E390 E403). Zander was also very active at this time, promoting a theoretical understanding of the new process, and published the first separate book on the subject (E388). Several other authors reported on a variety of aspects of its practical development and the printing trade journals of the 1890's presented their readers with numerous examples of tri-chromatic printing by British and foregn firms. General illustrated periodicals of the day were also beginning to adopt the process and in 1900 the first commercially published book, using tri-chromatic process engraving throughout, was published by A. & C. Black, the first of their famous "Colour Books".

E365 **Vidal, M.** 1876. Photo-polychrome. Photographic News 20: 208-209.
The patent specification for a form of carbon printing in colours.

E366 **Sawyer, J.R.** 1878. Chromotype printing. Photographic News 22: 434-436.
"Autotype notes", repr. from Anthony's Bulletin.

E367 **Griggs, W.** 1882. Illustrated pamphlet of photo-chromo-lithography. Electric & daylight studios, W. Griggs, photo- and chromo-lithographer to the India Government, Science & Art Department, South Kensington, & most of the learned societies: Inventor of the modern system of photo-lithography. Peckham. 15pp. & 11 pls.
A trade prospectus. The pls. incl. facsims. of letterpress, pen-and-ink sketches, and various photo- and photo-chromo-lithographs.

E368 **Anon.** 1884. Helio-chromic typography by the method of Ives. Photographic News 28: 561.

E369 **Richmond, W.D.** [1885?] The Hoeschotype photo-chromic printing process. In: Colour & colour printing as applied to lithography, [etc.]. pp.159-162. London.
For a fuller description of this book, see (D104*).

E370 **Ives, F.E.** 1888. Heliochromy. Photographic News 32: 789-790.

E371 **Anon.** 1890. Chromo-collographic printing: Illustrated by a pictorial supplement. Photographic News 34: 529, & 1 pl.
The introduction of colour collotype to this country by Waterlow & Sons.

E372 **Vidal, L.** 1890/91. Photographic methods of obtaining polychromatic impressions. Photographic Journal N.S.15: 146-154. Also pub. in: British Lithographer 1 (1): 23-26.

E373 **Ives, F.E.** 1892-93. Composite heliochromy. Journal, Society of Arts 40: 687-694, 1892; 41: 663-672, 1893.

E374 **Anon.** 1893. Some recent advances in colour printing. British Printer 6: 311-312.

E375 ----- 1893. Chromos in three printings: The heliochrome process of Vogel & Kurtz. British Lithographer 3: 56.

E376 ----- 1893. Photo-mechanical colour printing. British Lithographer 3: 59.
On Kurtz's patent screens for 3-colour work, each ruled at a different angle.

E377 **Ives, F.E.** 1894. Composite heliochromy by three-colour printing. British printer 7: 93-98.

E378 **Harland, J.W.** 1895. Three-colour printing, colour measurement & nomenclature. Art Printer & Lithographer 1: 75-77.

E379 **Hume, W.** 1895. Three-colour printing. British & Colonial Printer 35: 113, 209.

E380 ----- 1895. Remarks on photographic colour printing. Photographic News 39: 22-23, 35-37, 51-52.
A survey extending from basic photographic processes to the work of the Photochromatic Printing Co. of Belfast.

E381 **Husnik, J.** 1895. Collotype in natural colours. Art Printer & Lithographer 1: 126-128, 189-190.
Abstracted from Husnik's "Das Gesammtgebiet des Lichtdruckes die Email ...", 4. Aufl., Wien, 1894.

E382 **Whiston, W.A.** 1895. Photochromotypy. British Printer 8: 85-87.

E383 **Anon.** 1896. "Three-colour" up-to-date. British Printer 9: 5-8.
Its background and present level of development by the Heliochrome Co.

E384 **Ives, F.E.** 1896. Colour screen making. Printing Times & Lithographer N.S.5: 213-214, 233.

E385 ----- 1896. The perfected photochromascope & its colour photographs. Journal, Society of Arts 44: 517-525.

E386 **Wall, E.J.** 1896. Notes on three-colour printing. Also: Zander, C.G. A note on the printing inks required for three-colour printing. Photographic Journal N.S.20: 100-110.

E387 **Zander, C.G.** 1896. Half-tone & photochromic printing inks. Penrose Annual 2: 63-67.

E388 ----- [1896.] Photo-trichromatic printing in theory & practice. Leicester. 48pp. & 2 pls.
One of the pls. is a 3-col. eng.

E389 **Anon.** 1897. Three colour block printing. Process Work & the Printer 5: 181-185.

E390 **Ives, F.E.** 1897. Three colour printing. Process Work & the Printer 5: 183-185.

E391 **Nister, E.** 1897. New patent process for mechanically producing chromographs in three or more printings. Penrose Annual 3: 105-107.

E392 **Zander, C.G.** 1897. The capabilities, progress & future of three-colour printing. Penrose Annual 3: 59-63.

E393 **Anon.** 1898. Three colour process & its difficulties. Process Work & the Printer 5: 201-203.

E394 **Abney, W. de W.** 1898. Three-colour photographic printing. Journal, Society of Arts 46: 548-553.

E395 **Levy, M.** 1898. Screens for three-colour work. Penrose Annual 4: 13-15.

E396 **Shepherd, E.S.** 1898. A review of triple printing methods. Photographic Journal N.S.22: 96-107.
Dealing with the photographic basis of tri-chromatic printing.

E397 **Waterlow, P.** 1898. The heliochrome process applied to artistic & commercial illustration. Photographic Journal N.S.22: 65-69, & 1 pl.
The pl. is a specimen.

E398 **Richmond, W.D.** 1899. The limitation of three-colour printing. Penrose Annual 5: 25-30.

E399 **Zander, C.G.** 1899. Yellow, red & blue. Penrose Annual 5: 17-19.

E400 ----- 1899. The colour principal of photo-trichromatic printing. British & Colonial Printer 44: 337-338. Also pub. separately as: A lecture on the colour principal of tri-chromatic printing. [London, 1899]. 8pp.

E401 **Bolas, T., A.A.K. Tallent & E. Senior.** 1900. A handbook of photography in colours. London. viii+343pp.
This important work actually comprises three separate books in one. It is chiefly concerned with the theory and practice of pure colour photography and although it makes little direct reference to photo-mechanical applications is an important background work.

E402 **Shepherd, E.S.** 1900. The photography of colour. Journal, Society of Arts 48: 758-766, 769-776, 781-788, 793-797.
Incl. colour process engraving.

E403 **Ives, F.E.** 1901. The progress of three-colour printing. Penrose Annual 7: 85-86.

Ei Creation of half-tone grain

One of the major concerns of the inventors and improvers of photo-mechanical processes was to find some means of emulating the continuous-tone quality of the ordinary photograph. Total success was achieved in some relief pigment processes, such as Woodburytype and autotype, but the technology required for their production was quite different from any normal operation known to the printing trade. It was not a conventionally inked surface that produced the printed picture. Furthermore, the print necessarily had to be separately inserted into every copy of the printed book or else individually mounted on calendars or other items of stationery.

Since printers' ink was an opaque black and the light reflected from paper was ordinarily white, some means had to be found of breaking the inked areas into tiny islands of pigment so that some paper showed through, creating the effect of grey. Collotype, with its very subtle and irregular granulation, best succeeded in simulating the continuous tone of the photograph and could be produced on a printing machine. It was, however, a delicate and at times uncertain process to operate. The special qualities of collotype grain were discussed by Schnauss (E406) and the finer details of the possible varieties described, with the aid of photo-micrographs, by Wilkinson (E419).

Intaglio and lithographic processes had long utilised mezzotint, stipple, aquatint, and other granular effects for the creation of half-tones on hand--draughted prints. Some of the same ideas were applied to photo-intaglio and photo-lithographic printmaking. Thus, Woodbury (E90), Sawyer (E97), and Waterhouse (E407) created granulations with gritty powders, Talbot's earliest process (E75) achieved a stipple effect with a film of fine silk, his later improvement used an aquatint resin grain (E80), and various other methods are discussed by Winstanley (E404), Placet (E405), and Anon. (E409).

The granulated effect, so much a part of lithography, was exploited by Pouncy (E211) and others who relied upon a coarsely grained stone, while Bullock (E218) was one of several who preferred to use a textured transfer paper. The creation of the peculiar form of gelatinous reticulation that characterises collotype was variously employed for photo-intaglio and photo-lithographic processes such as Pretsch (E83) and Husband (E240). Waterhouse (E418) has provided us with a definitive end-of-century survey of tonal methods in photo-lithography.

Photo-relief was able to utilise many of these techniques for the creation of textured bichromate images that could be etched or electrotyped to produce half-tone printing blocks. Examples of these can be found in the work of Pretsch (E119), Woodbury (E136), and Brown, Barnes & Bell (E159). Photo--intaglio and photo-lithographic illustrations were produced by separate printing operations from the letterpress creating additional production costs and inconvenience. Great efforts were therefore directed at developing successful photo-relief blocks with the fine tonal quality of photographs that could be printed at the same "pass" as the letterpress. At a time when wood engravers were perfecting a hand-created tonal style of great delicacy others were struggling to perfect a mechanically created tonal effect for photo--relief processes.

Back in the 1860's Swan had tried the idea of ruled screens and used them in his photo-mezzotint process (E89). In the long run it was this principle that was adopted as the most efficient means of winning the battle for acceptable half-tone but only after technology had provided a means for the consistent producion of extremely fine, precisely ruled screens. Meisenbach's early cross-ruled screens earned his firm much success (E162) but it was the American, Ives (E154 E161 E184), who succeeded in achieving the desired quality with screens that allowed delicate tonal adjustment of half-tone relief illustrations. The results were so commercially successful as to secure an unrivalled position for photo-relief for decades to come. By the end of the century many books and magazines were lavishly illustrated with photo-relief blocks printed at the same operation as the text.

Half-tone screens were also vital to the production of tri-chromatic relief prints. Once again the expertise of Ives (E384) and another American, Levy (E395), helped to solve both the theoretical and practical aspects of the problem; the former coming over to England to work for a couple of years at this crucial period.

Deville's research produced the first theoretical analysis of the fine mathematical and optical niceties of the screen (E412) and his work was followed by Eder (E413), Ray (E415 E417 E422), and Wilkinson (E421) who again provided photo-micrographic enlargements. Additional information on a variety of methods for creating half-tone grain may also be gleaned from the general or special textbooks of photo-mechanical printing.

E404 **Winstanley, D.** 1866. Stippled gradation in photographic engraving. Photographic News 10: 498-500.
The patent specification.

E405 **Placet, P.E.** 1876. Improvements in photo-engraving. Photographic News 20: 196-197.
The patent specification. Naturally grained surfaces for photo-mechanical half-tone printing.

E406 **Schnauss, J.** 1878. The arguments for & against graining in the collotype process. On grained photo-lithographs. Photographic News 22: 278-279, 358-359.
Transl. from Photographisches Archiv.

E407 **Waterhouse, J.** 1880. On a new method of obtaining "grain" in photo--engraving. Journal, Photographic Society N.S.5: 20-21.
Sand and wax pressed into the gelatine.

E408 **Eggis, A.T.** 1883. The crayontype: A new photo-grain process. Photographic News 27: 789.
Use of a grained paper for transfer.

E409 **Anon.** 1885. Some easy ways of making grain plates or surfaces for photo-mechanical printing processes. Photographic News 29: 465-466.

E410 ----- 1888. Grain on copper plates for heliographic etching. Photographic News 32: 97.

E411 **Turcke, A.** 1891. Line-plates for half-tone zinc etching. Year Book of Photography 1891: 149-150, & 1 pl.
The pl. is a specimen.

E412 **Deville, E.** 1895. The theory of the screen in the photo-mechanical process. Transactions, Royal Society of Canada (2) 1, Section 3: 29-61.

E413 **Eder, J.M.** 1895. The shape of the half-tone dot. Process Photogram 2: 53-62.

E414 **Burton, W.K.** 1896. On the formation of the dots of the half-tone screen image. Photographic Journal N.S.20: 43-48; also a transcript of the discussion following his paper, pp.72-76.

E415 **Ray, U.** 1898. The theory of the half-tone dot. Penrose Annual 4: 33-40.

E416 **Lascelles, T.W.** 1898. Negative making for process work. Photographic Journal N.S.22: 242-250.
Incl. a detailed account of practical half-tone screen use.

E417 **Ray, U.** 1899. Half-tone theory graphically explained. Penrose Annual 5: 49-53.

E418 **Waterhouse, J.** 1900. Photo-litho in half-tone. Penrose Annual 6: 17-24.
Review of methods of half-tone grain production.

E419 **Wilkinson, W.T.** 1900. The collotype grain. Penrose Annual 6: 41-42, with photo-micrographs.

E420 **Cadett, J.** 1900. What is the best screen ruling for half-tone negatives? Penrose Annual 6: 53-55.

E421 **Wilkinson, W.T.** 1903. Photo-mechanical grain. Penrose Annual 8: 55-56, with photo-micrographs.

E422 **Ray, U.** 1904. More about the half-tone theory. Penrose Annual 9: 17-23.

Ej Special draughting methods

The arrival of photo-mechanical processes for practical illustration work led to the appearance of a number of explanatory manuals addressed to artists who, for the most part, had been accustomed to having their work reproduced by a wood engraver. The value of this literature today lies in the explanation it provides of the syntactical limitations sometimes placed upon the artist and also of the problems faced by blockmakers and printers when making photo--mechanical reproductions.

Pen-and ink drawing was the usually recommended style but its basic elements were supplemented by some novel techniques most of which are still in use today. Day's shading mediums, which had already secured a reputation in lithographic work, were found to be equally suitable to the production of tints and tones for photo-relief work (D116 D121-D123 D127). Other novelties of the later 19th century included the scraper board (E429 E434 E435 E442) and textured drawing boards. But perhaps the most ingenious innovation for the tonal illustrator was the air-brush, capable of producing work admirably suited to the newly sophisticated half-tone processes (D125 D128 D131 D134 D135). So far as book illustration was concerned these new materials and tools brought about a marked change in artists' draughting styles and the old conventions required for reproduction by wood engraving were swept away.

The most comprehensive of the manuals that were written to assist artists in mastering these new techniques was the cumbersome tome by Pennell (E426). Despite its inconvenient format it went through three editions in less than a decade (E433 E440). More managable handbooks were compiled by Robertson (E424), Blackburn (E430), Harper (E431), Hinton (E432), Pennell (E436 E439), and Vine (E437), their number indicating the sudden wave of interest in this subject in the 1890's. Techniques of colour illustration were also being modified by the new processes and the 3rd edn. of Blackburn's manual (E443) included a new chapter on colour methods in answer to this situation.

E423 **Hodson, J.S.** 1886. Preparation of drawings for photographic reproduction. Journal, Society of Arts 34: 569-576. Also pub. in: Printing Times & Lithographer N.S.12: 84-85, 102-103, 1886; British & Colonial Printer 16: 363, 378-379, 1886; & British Journal of Photography 33: 259-260, 276-277, 1886.

E424 **Robertson, H.R.** [1886?] The art of pen & ink drawing commonly called etching. London. ix+62pp.
Application to process work discussed on pp.45-62.

E425 **Anon.** 1889. Pen drawing for photo-engraving. Printing Times & Lithographer N.S.15: 162-163, 183-184.

E426 **Pennell, J.** 1889. Pen drawing & pen draughtsmen; their work & methods. A study of the art of today with technical suggestions. London. xxiii+318pp.
Illus. with pls., some of which are specimens of different methods of photo-mechanical reproduction.

E427 **Anon.** 1890. Drawings for process blocks. Photographic News 34: 919-920.
Brief general instructions.

E428 **Waterhouse, J.** 1890. Practical notes on the preparation of drawings for photographic reproduction, with a sketch of the principal photo-mechanical printing processes. London. viii+128pp. & 4 pls.
Deals with line and tonal drawing. The pls. incl. a photo-etching and a photo-lith. First pub. as a series of articles in the Indian Engineer, 1887.

E429 **Anon.** 1893. Another colour process. British Printer 6: 450, & 1 pl.
On Gilby & Hermann's "line cards" (textured board) for making colour separations or monochrome illus. The pl. demonstrates their application.

E430 **Blackburn, H.** 1894. The art of illustration. London. xvi+240pp. 2nd edn., 1896.

E431 **Harper, C.G.** 1894. A practical handbook of drawing for modern methods of reproduction. London. xii+161pp. 2nd edn, 1901.

E432 **Hinton, A.H.** 1894. A handbook of illustration: With reproductions from photograms & sketches by the author & other artists. London. 120pp., & 1 pl.

E433 **Pennell, J.** 1894. Pen drawing & pen draughtsmen; [etc.] 2nd edn. London. xxxvi+461pp.
Much enlarged from the 1st edn.

E434 **Vine, C.J.** 1894. Scraper boards. Photogram 1: 66-67, 107-108.

E435 **Anon.** 1894. Scraper boards. British Printer 7: 210-212.

E436 **Pennell, J.** 1895. Modern illustration. London. xxvi+146pp. "Student's edn.", 1898.

E437 **Vine, C.J.** 1895. Hints on drawing for process reproduction. London. 32pp.

E438 **White, G.** 1895. Drawing for process reproduction. Journal, Society of Arts 43: 277-291. Also pub. in: Photographic News 39: 124-126, 131-134, 156-158, 164-167, 181-183.

E439 **Pennell, J.** 1896. The illustration of books: A manual for the use of students, notes for a course of lectures at the Slade School, University College. London. xii+166pp.
Ch. III: Methods of drawing for reproduction in line; Ch. IV: The reproduction of line drawings; Ch. V: The making of wash drawings and their reproduction by mechanical process; Ch. X: Photogravure and photo-lithography.

E440 ----- 1897. Pen drawing & pen draughtsmen; [etc.] 3rd edn. London. xxxvii+470pp.

E441 **Furniss, H.** 1899. About the aerograph. Penrose Annual 5: 101-102.

E442 **Anon.** 1899. On scraper board drawing. Penrose Annual 5: 54-56.
On Angerer & Göschl scraperboards.

E443 **Blackburn, H.** 1901. The art of illustration. Rev. to date, together with a chapter on coloured illustration by J.S. Eland. 3rd edn. Edinburgh. xx+251pp.

Ek Photo-mechanical equipment & materials

The advent of photo-mechanical methods introduced new kinds of appliances and materials to the printer's world. Back in the 1860's when the Ordnance Survey introduced photo-zincography on a commercial basis it highlighted the need for a quite new printing-office department, the photographic studio (E444). By the end of the century the supply of process cameras and all the associated paraphernalia gave life to large business concerns, as revealed by the trade catalogues of firms like Klimsch (E453) and Penrose (E457).

Chemicals grew in importance for the photo-mechanical printer and articles by Anon. (E445) and Waterhouse (E455) underlined this aspect of the new technology. Special paper was required to satisfy the critical demands of the new half-tone relief processes and this led the Society of Arts to produce a report on this important topic (E456). New kinds of machinery, such as the all important router which "cleared" the acres of line blocks then being produced, were required in most printing works. The machines used for printing photo-intaglio, planographic, or relief work were, apart from their improved accuracy, basically similar to the ones in ordinary use. However, the printing of really good half-tone relief illustrations called for new levels of craftsmanship in presswork, a fact emphasised in the works of Fisher (C91), Jackson (C92), Joyner (C94), Ward (C96), Noble (C97), Morch (C98), Cox (C99), and others. The mechanisation of collotype printing in the late 1880's required the introduction of purpose designed machines, most of which were imported from France and Germany; Anon. (E446 E448-E452). The specialised kinds of equipment required for processes such as pigment printing are usually described in the instructional literature relating to each. However, most of these processes were only operated by a limited number of licence holders and were only a side issue for most of the printing trade.

E444 **Anon.** 1860. Photography in its applications (Reducing maps & plans by means of photography). Photographic News 3: 379-380, 392-394, 1860; 4: 25-26, 38-39, 50-52, 1860.
Description of the Ordnance Survey's specially designed camera and studio.

E445 **Anon.** 1879. Asphalte and its application to photo-lithography & engraving. Printing Times & Lithographer N.S.5: 75-77.

E446 ----- 1887. Collotype printing at the power machine. Photographic News 31: 242-243.
On Alauzet's machine.

E447 ----- 1891. Aids to speed in process engraving: Royle's "routing" machine. British & Colonial Printer 28: 437.

E448 ----- 1893. The first British built collotype machines; as seen at the works of Messrs Furnival & Co., Reddish. British & Colonial Printer 32: 73-74, illus.

E449 ----- 1893. Furnival's new collotype machine. Printing Times & Lithographer N.S.2: 439-440.

E450 ----- 1893. "Trade notes" [On Schmiers, Werner & Stein's collotype machine]. British Lithographer 2 (9): 112.

E451 ----- 1893. Collotype printing machines. British & Colonial Printer 31: 295, illus.
By Schmiers and Alauzet.

E452 ----- 1893. "Trade notes" [On Furnival's new collotype machine]. British Lithographer 3: 31. Also pub. in: British Printer 7: 125-126.

E453 **Klimsch, Hunter & Co.** [ca.1895.] Machinery for photo-engravers, etc. London.

E454 **Penrose & Co.** 1897. Photo process machinery & supplies. London.

E455 **Waterhouse, J.** 1898. Notes on the principal oils, fats & resins used in printing & photo-process work. Penrose Annual 4: 110-121.

E456 **Anon.** 1899. Paper in process work. Process Photogram 6: 90-93, 99-100.
Based on a Society of Arts committee report.

E457 **Penrose & Co.** 1901. Apparatus & supplies. London. 272pp. & 7 pls.
A trade catalogue from the leading British supply house for process engravers and photo-mechanical printers.

E1 Miscellaneous literature

Aside from the extensive literature describing photo-mechanical innovations and techniques there is an interesting background of comment and appraisal from which the following is selected.

The use of ordinary photographic prints as book illustrations was the subject of comment by Thompson (E460), and was also discussed by Bird (E467) and Lang (E472).

The rapidity with which new inventions and innovations appeared occasionally gave rise to disputes over claims for priority of discovery. Pouncy, for example, felt particularly aggrieved at rival claims to the discovery of carbon printing and photo-lithography. In their attempts to resolve the argument, the rival claimants Anon. (E458 E459) and Pouncy (E461), record minor incidental events of this developmental period which might otherwise have been lost to us. Dallas, who was accused of having stolen the "know-how" of photogravure from Pretsch, his former employer, stirred up some acrimonious but revealing correspondence over the issue (E462).

Griggs tells an interesting story of how he was able to substitute photo--lithography for wood engraving when pressing curcumstances demanded it (E465). Assessments of the comparative merits of the new photo-mechanical processes can be found in writings by Pritchard (E463) and Anon. (E464 E471 E476), while useful general surveys of progress are provided by Carr (E468), Taylor (E474), Blackburn (E475), White (E478), and Gamble (E479).

Technical comments on the impact of the new processes came from Anon. (E466 E473), Ward (E477), Boutall (E480), and Crowdy (A481). Pritchard made a survey of "studios" which included some photo-mechanical printing firms such as the Autotype, Heliotype, and Woodbury companies, thus giving his book a wider interest than its title might suggest (E469). A revealing turn-of-century indication of the size and variety of the photographic and photo-mechanical trade is given by the comprehensive index of trade names (E482).

A458 **Anon.** 1860. Carbon processes & their inventors. Photographic News 4: 337, 349.
Discussion of Pouncy's claims to have invented photo-zincography.

A459 ----- 1862. Photozincography, photolithography, & photo-engraving -- who are the discoverers? Photographic News 6: 541-543.
Assessment of the claims of Ponton, Poitevin, Pouncy, Osborne, James, and others.

E460 **Thompson, S.** 1862. Photography in its application to book illustration. British Journal of Photography 9: 88-89.

E461 **Pouncy, J.** 1865. Letter defending his claim to priority of carbon processes. Journal, Photographic Society 10: 46-48; & letters in reply from J.C. Crofton & others, pp.72-73.

E462 **Dallas, D. & others.** 1870. Letters on Paul Pretsch's photo-galvanography. Photographic News 14: 262, 274, 278-279, 297-299, 322, 334, 490.

E463 **Pritchard, H.B.** 1870. The Woodbury & lichtdruck processes compared. Photographic News 14: 398-399.

E464 **Anon.** 1870. Photography versus lithography. Lithographer 1: 62-63.

E465 **Griggs, W.** 1880. The extended use of photolithography to book illustration. British Journal Photographic Almanac 1880: 145-146.
In order to expedite a publication, for which there was insufficient time to prepare wood engravings, he had 52 artist's sketches "photographed, transferred to their required positions on six lithographic stones, and 120,000 double demy sheets ... printed off in six weeks". The illustrations were printed in spaces left for them on the completed letterpress sheets.

E466 **Anon.** 1877. Collotype printing. Photographic News 21: 405-406.

E467 **Bird, W.S.** 1878. Permanent photography & its relation to art & artists. Photographic News 22: 448-449.

E468 **Carr, J.C.** 1882. Cantor lectures on book illustration, old & new. Journal, Society of Arts 30: 1035-1040, 1045-1053, 1055-1062.

E469 **Pritchard, H.B.** 1882. The photographic studios of Europe. London. 280pp. Repr. New York, 1973. 2nd edn., 1883. 304pp.

E470 **Anon.** 1883. Some suggestions as to the future of photo-mechanical printing methods. Photographic News 27: 818.

E471 ----- 1887. Photogravure versus line engraving. British Journal of Photography 34: 657-658.

E472 **Lang, W. jr.** 1887. Book illustration by photography. British Journal of Photography 34: 263-265.

E473 **Anon.** 1888. Photo-engraving as observed from a printer's standpoint. Printing Times & Lithographer N.S.14: 27-28.

E474 **Taylor, J.T.** 1893. Some photographic methods of book illustration. British Journal Photographic Almanac 1893: 505-524.

E475 **Blackburn, H.** 1894. Cantor lectures on the art of book & newspaper illustration. Journal, Society of Arts 42: 93-99, 105-112, 121-127.

E476 **Anon.** 1895. Engraving; wood or process. British Printer 4: 190.

E477 **Ward, J.S.** 1895. The ideal of half-tone printing. Photographic Journal N.S.19: 268-272.
General discussion of printing, paper, electrotyping, etc.

E478 **White, G.** 1895. Some aspects of modern illustration. Photographic Journal N.S.19: 347-355.

E479 **Gamble, W.** 1897. Process in magazine & book illustration. Penrose Annual 3: 3-16.

E480 **Boutall, W.** 1898. The effect of the introduction of process engraving on the art of printing. British & Colonial Printer 44: 314.

E481 **Crowdy, W.L.** 1898. Process reproduction from an editor's point of view. Photographic Journal N.S.22: 206-215.
Comments on photographers and artists as illustrators.

E482 **Anon.** 1899. An index of photographic trade names. Process Photogram 6 suppl.: 1-24.
In addition to the list of names it provides an index of the firms and reproductions of their trade marks.

Historical

Em General history of photography & photo-mechanical printing

Most of the earlier general histories of photography give relatively little attention to photo-mechanical processes. All are more or less useful as chronicles of the invention of photographic manipulations, some of which were basic to the creation of photo-mechanical images and sometimes for the creation of the printing surface.

Davies (E483), Harrison (E486), Werge (E487), and Story (E493), although written too close to the events to achieve historical objectivity, are nonetheless useful for details of short-lived or out-of-the-way proccesses, sometimes gained first hand. By the end of the century some special historical reviews of photo-mechanical developments were compiled by Boutall (E490), Hentschel (E494), and others, and the Victoria & Albert Museum held two large retrospective exhibitions. The catalogues for these (E495 E497), both of which contain historical introductions, form unusually valuable surveys because they catalogue many early examples of photo-mechanical processes that are not listed elsewhere.

Schiendl's history, though rather close to the events it surveys, is of interest because of its attention to the work of German scientists crucial to the development of processes that were later taken up in Britain (E488). The most important general histories of our century are the scholarly works of Eder (E500) and Gernsheim (E509), the former being especially useful for its attention to photography as applied to the printing press. Crawford is unique in that he re-states all the formulae and techniques for the principal photographic processes of the 19th century (E519*).

Before the invention of photo-mechanical processes many books were illustrated by the insertion of ordinary photographs; Talbot's own "Pencil of Nature" (E20), for example. Schultze (E504 E507) (whose work was cut short by his death) and Krauss (E518 E519), discuss this kind of illustration. Recently Schaaf (E520 E520*) has drawn attention to a rare publication in which both text and illustrations printed by the cyanotype photography.

The life and work of Talbot, the creator of photography and photo-mechanical printing in England, is well recorded by Arnold (E515) and the efforts to preserve the fruits of his work are described by Ward (E516) and Lassam (E517). Specialised accounts of developments in photo-intalgio are provided by Waterhouse (E492), Talbot (E496), Swan (E498), Mertle (E502), and Lilien (E512). Photo-relief is well covered in the works of Ward (E489), Hentschel (E494), and Wallis (E508), while Gamble (E491), Kainen (E501), and Carr (E505) deal with the special history of the half-tone screen. An introduction to some of the main developments in photo-lithography and collotype is given by Wallis (E506) and the history of photo-zincography is documented by Wakeman (E511). Swan's invention of the carbon process is treated in a general biography (E499) and Mertle writes an enthusiastic memorial to Woodburytype (E503).

Recent years have seen the appearance of works by Ostroff (E510), Wakeman (E513), and Jussim (E514), which survey the overall part played by photography in nineteenth century book illustration. They are a good beginning but much remains to be done.

E483 **Davies, W.H.** 1867. Memoranda on the history of carbon printing, photo--lithography, & photo-engraving. Photographic News 11: 258-260, 270-271, 281.

E484 **Anon.** 1883. Photographic engraving. Photographic News 27: 769-770.
Short historical review.

E485 **Harrison, W.J.** 1887. Chapters in the history of photography. Photographic News 31: 35-36, 91-92, 137, 231, 282-283, 411-413, 604-605.

E486 ----- 1888. A history of photography: Written as a practical guide & an introduction to its latest developments. Bradford. vi+144pp. Repr. New York, 1973.
Incl: Ch. 11: History of photographic printing processes, pp.77-94; Ch. 12: History of photographic printing processes, continued, pp.95-105.

E487 **Werge, J.** 1890. The evolution of photography, with a chronological record of discoveries, inventions, etc., contributions to photographic literature & personal reminiscences extending over forty years. London. viii+312pp.
Incl: Chronological record, pp.126-139.

E488 **Schiendl, C.** 1891. Geschichte der Photographie. Wien. viii+380pp.
Incl: Kap. 11: Die Heliogravure, die Photozinkopie, und andere Druckmethoden der Neuzeit, pp.174-208; Kap. 12: Der Platindruck, pp.209-215.

E489 **Ward, W.H.** 1897. The evolution of half-tone engraving. Artist 1897: 113-118.
Chiefly in praise of Ives' work.

E490 **Boutall, W.** 1897. Process engraving; twenty-five years' progress. British & Colonial Printer 40: 273-275.

E491 **Gamble, W.** 1897. The history of the half-tone dot. Photographic Journal N.S.21: 126-136.

E492 **Waterhouse, J.** 1898. A history of photogravure. Process Photogram 5: 152-153, 183-186.
Condensed from an article in the "Camera Club Journal" (original not seen).

E493 **Story, A.T.** 1899. The story of photography. London. 192pp.
Ch. 11: Photographic printing processes, pp.103-113; Ch. 12: Photography & letter-press printing, pp.114-121; Ch. 13: Photo-block printing, pp.121-131.

E494 **Hentschel, C.** 1900. Process engraving. Journal, Society of Arts 48: 461-474. Also pub. in: British & Colonial Printer 46: 213-214, 226-227, 1900; & Printing World 8: 73-74, 97-98, 121-123, 161-162, 1900.
Historical study of developments by one who took part in many of them.

E495 **Victoria & Albert Museum.** 1901. Catalogue of the loan exhibition of modern illustration ... 1901. London. 152pp.
[Historical] Introduction by H.B. Wheatley, pp.9-21.

E496 **Talbot, C.H.** 1903. Some account of Fox Talbot's process of photographic engraving. Penrose Annual 8: 8-16.

E497 **Victoria & Albert Museum.** 1905. Catalogue of the loan collection of process engraving ... 1905. London. xx+64pp.
[Historical] Introduction by J. Waterhouse, pp.vii-xx.

E498 **Swan, D.G.** 1913. Pioneers of photogravure. Imprint 1: 381-388.

E499 **Swan, M.E. & K.R.** 1929. Sir Joseph Wilson Swan F.R.S., inventor & scientist. London. Repr. with a preface & appendix. Newcastle upon Tyne, 1968. 191pp.
See: Ch. III: The carbon process and other photographic inventions.

E500 **Eder, J.M.** 1945. History of photography. Transl. by E. Epstean. New York. xx+860pp. Repr. New York, 1978. Orig. edn., Halle, 1932.
The most detailed technical history of photography but with a strong continental bias and consequent omission of a number of the British workers whose contributions are recorder herein. Very good sections on all the photo--mechanical processes.

E501 **Kainen, J.** 1951. The development of the halftone screen. Smithsonian Report 1951: 409-425.

E502 **Mertle, J.S.** 1957. Evolution of rotogravure. Appearing originally in "Gravure Magazine". Private reprint. 88pp.
A series of 20 articles which first appeared between Nov. 1955 and June 1957.

E503 ----- 1957. The Woodburytype -- The most beautiful photographic reproduction process ever invented. Image (Rochester, N.Y.) 6: 165-170.

E504 **Schultze, R.S.** 1961. Books illustrated with original photographs: Notes on a collection & bibliography. In: Jubilaums-Festschrift, Hundert Jahre Photographische Gesellschaft in Wien, 1861-1961. pp.138-147. Vienna.
Some of his collection was exhibited in the following year, see (A403).

E505 **Carr, F.** 1962. An outline history of screen printing. British Printer Sept. 1962: 95-102.

E506 **Wallis, L.W.** 1962-63. A brief history of photographic reproduction processes (up to 1939). Photography's coming of age. Collotype. Photo--lithography. Lithoprinter 5: 653-654, 733-737, 1962; 6: 67-70, 105-108, 1963.

E507 **Schultze, R.S.** 1963. Scottish books with original photographs. Bibliotheck 4: 3-12.

E508 **Wallis, L.W.** 1963. Background to printing: The development of line photo-engraving. Print in Britain 1963 (July): 35-36.

E509 **Gernsheim, H. & A.** 1969. The history of photography from the camera obscura to the beginning of the modern era. 2nd edn. London. 599pp. 1st edn., Oxford, 1955. The "standard" English history of photography, replete with facts and illustrations. Not particularly strong on photo-mechanical processes.

E510 **Ostroff, E.** 1969. Etching, engraving & photography: History of photo-mechanical reproduction. Journal of Photographic Science 17: 65-80.

E511 **Wakeman, G.** 1970. Aspects of Victorian lithography: Anastatic printing & photo-zincography. Wymondham. 63pp. & 2 pls.
One pl. is a specimen of Victorian photo-zincography.

E512 **Lilien, O.M.** 1972. History of industrial gravure printing up to 1920. London. 155pp.

E513 **Wakeman, G.** 1973. Victorian book illustration: The technical revolution. Newton Abbot. 182pp.

E514 **Jussim, E.** 1974. Visual communication & the graphic arts: Photographic technologies in the nineteenth century. New York. xv+364pp.

E515 **Arnold, H.J.P.** 1977. William Henry Fox Talbot, pioneer of photography & man of science. London. 383pp.
Ch. 9: Photographs in printers' ink, pp.267-293, deals with his photo--engraving developments.

E516 **Ward, J.P.** 1977. The Fox Talbot collection at the Science Museum. History of Photography 1: 274-287.

E517 **Lassam, R.** 1977. The Fox Talbot museum. History of Photography 1: 297-300.

E518 **Krauss, R.H.** 1978. Photographs as early scientific book illustrations. History of Photography 2: 291-314.

E519 ----- 1979. Travel reports & photography in early photographically illustrated books. History of Photography 3: 15-30.

E519* **Crawford, W.** 1979. The keepers of light: A history & working guide to early photographic processes. Dobbs Ferry, N.Y. xi+321pp.
Incl. Silver processes; Ferric processes; Dichromate processes; Color technique; Photmechanical techniques (photogravure, collotype, other photomechanical processes, Woodburytype).

E520 **Schaaf, L.** 1979. The first photographically printed & illustrated book. Papers, Bibliographical Society of America 73: 209-224.
By: A. Atkins, British Algae: Cyanotype impressions, 1843-53.

E520* ----- 1982. Anna Atkins' cyanotypes: An experiment in photographic publishing. History of Photography 6: 151-172.

En History of photo-mechanical printing in colour

The invention and sophistication of colour photography has been excellently researched by Wall whose detailed history (E523), written for the photographic scientist (E523), is replete with technical and chemical data. The needs of the non-technical reader are satisfied by Coe's liberally illustrated survey (E525).

Early attempts at recording the development of British tri-chromatic photo-

-mechanical work were made by Anon. (E521) and Zander (E522). Gamble's chapter on "Modern colour processes" in Burch (A278) is written for the general reader and is largely based on personal experience. Later, more objective, histories were written by Eder and Sipley. Since some of the pioneer developments took place in America rather than England the opening chapters of Sipley's, largely American oriented, history are relevant (E524). Eder's history (E500), provides technical information on the development of various colour processes.

E521 **Anon.** 1895. Three colour process -- its history. Stationer & Fancy trades' Register 1895: 687-691.

E522 **Zander, C.G.** 1900. Modern chromo-typography. British Printer 13: 63-65.

E523 **Wall, E.J.** 1925. The history of three-colour photography. Boston, Mass. x+747pp. Repr. London, 1970.

E524 **Sipley, L.W.** 1951. A half century of color. New York. xvi+216pp.

E525 **Coe, B.** 1978. Colour photography: The first hundred years 1840-1940. London. 144pp.

Section F: Periodicals consulted

A register of contemporary and retrospective periodicals consulted in the compilation of this bibliography. A systematic search was made through most of the contemporary printing-trade titles and a selection of art periodicals down to 1900. The earliest specialised printing periodicals was not published until 1840 (F17) and other, more general, periodicals had to be searched for the preceding period. Because they were such a valuable source of information patent journals and other technical publications which specialised in reporting new inventions were also perused, (e.g. F51 F31 F28). Some general science journals of the earlier part of the century also reported news of technical developments in printing and graphic arts (e.g. F22 F30) but it was not possible, without unlimited time, to do more than a random search of the many such titles that exist. The extent to which each title was searched is indicated as a guide to what remains to be done.

For historical periodicals a much smaller number of titles was searched and there is undoubtedly much more to be added from those sources. The Art Index (F59) was the principal guide to other periodicals articles in the historical field.

Fa Guides to periodicals

In addition to the few works listed below, information on photographic periodicals can also be found in Harrison's bibliography (E1).

F1 **Bigmore, E.C. & C.W.H. Wyman.** 1880-83. Periodical publications. In: A bibliography of printing. Vol. 2, pp.153-195. London. Repr. New York, 1945; London, 1969; & London/New castle, De., 1978.
An annotated listing.

F2 **Bolton, H.C.** 1898. A catalogue of scientific & technical periodicals (1665-1895). 2nd edn. Washington, D.C. vii+1247pp. Smithsonian Miscellaneous Collections, vol.40.

F3 **Thorne, W.B.** 1901. Some English printing trade periodicals of the century. Printers' Register 40: 208-210.

F4 **Ulrich, C.F. & K. Küp.** 1943. Books & printing: A selected list of periodicals. Woodstock, Vt. xi+244pp.
A classified and annotated list.

F5 **St. Bride Foundation.** 1951. Catalogue of the periodicals relating to printing & allied subjects in the Technical Library of the St. Bride Institute. London. 35pp.
A very useful list which gives notes on histories and interrelationship of periodicals.

F6 **Gernsheim, H. & H.** 1969. The first decade of photographic journals. In: The history of photography from the camera obscura to the beginning of the modern era. 2nd edn. pp.586-588. London.

Fb Contemporary periodicals

Those with the title printed in **bold** have been systematically searched for the span of years indicated. Other titles have only been partly searched or incidentally consulted. The libraries which hold the bulk of these titles are the St. Bride Printing Library, The Science Library, and the Victoria & Albert Museum Library. However, some titles were incomplete and had to be sought from elsewhere, and we were unable to find a complete set for some titles (see item C119 for example.)

In addition to the periodicals listed below there was a considerable number of others that provided only isolated references.

F7 Art Journal. London. 1849-1900. Formerly: Art Union, q.v.

F8 **Art Printer & Lithographer.** Swindon. 1895-1896.

F9 **Art Union.** London. 1839-1848. Continued as: Art Journal, q.v.

F10 **British & Colonial Printer & Stationer.** London. 1878-1900.

F11 **British Journal Photographic Almanac.** London. 1861-1900. Only 1880-1895 systematically searched.

F12 **British Journal of Photography.** London. 1860-1900. Only 1882-1890 systematically searched.

F13 **British Lithographer.** London. 1891-1895. Absorbed into: British Printer, q.v.

F14 **British Printer.** Leicester. 1888-1900.

F15 Chromolithograph. London. 1867-1869.

F16 Collis's Journal. London. 1903-1906.

F17 **Compositors' Chronicle.** London. 1840-1843.

F18 **Etcher.** London. 1879-1882. Supplement: **Etcher Notes.** 1880-1882.

F19 **Fine Arts Quarterly Review.** London. 1863-1865.

F20 **Fleet Street Gazette.** London. 1874.

F21 Gentleman's Magazine. London. ca. 1800-1840.

F22 **Journal of Natural Philosophy, Chemistry & the Arts** (Nicholson's Journal). London. 1797-1813.

F23 **Journal, Photographic Society.** London. 1853-1900.

F24 **Journal, Society of Arts.** London. 1852-1900. Formerly: Transactions, Society (for the Encouragement) of Arts, q.v.

F25 **Journal of Typographic Arts.** London. 1860-1861.

F26 Library of the Fine Arts, or Monthly Repertory of Painting, ... & Engraving. London. 1831-32.

F27 Lithographer. London. 1870-1875. Absorbed into: Printing Times & Lithographer, q.v.

F28 London Journal of Arts & Sciences. London. 1820-1854.

F29 London, Provincial & Colonial Press News. London. 1866-1900.

F30 Magazine of Science. London. 1839-1848.

F31 Mechanics' Magazine. London. 1823-1872.

F32 Modern Lithographer. London. 1905-1910.

F33 Modern Printer. London. 1884-1888.

F34 Nature & Art. London. 1866-1867. Absorbed into: Chromolithograph, q.v.

F35 Paper & Printing Trades Journal. London. 1872-1896. Only 1875-1890 systematically searched.

F36 Penrose Annual, (Penrose's Pictorial Annual). London. 1895-1905.

F37 Photogram. London. 1894-1905.

Photographic Journal: Journal of the Photographic Society of London. See: Journal, Photographic Society.

F38 Photographic News. London. 1859-1895.

F39 Photographic Quarterly. London. 1889-1891.

F40 Polytechnic Journal. London. 1839-1843.

F41 Portfolio. London. 1870-1907.

F42 Poster. London. 1898-1900.

F43 Printer. London. 1843-1845.

F44 Printers' Journal & Typographical Magazine. London. 1867-1868. (Vol. for 1869 could not be located.)

F45 Printers' Register. London. 1863-1900.

F46 Printing Times & Lithographer. London. 1876-1900.

F47 Printing World. London. 1891-1900.

F48 Process Photogram. London. 1894-1905. Only 1894-1899 systematically searched.

F49 **Process Work & the Printer.** London. 1893-1899.

Process Year Book. See: Penrose Annual.

F50 Repertory of Arts & Manufactures (& Agriculture). London. 1794-1825. Continued as: Repertory of Patent Inventions.

F51 Repertory of Patent Inventions. London. 1834-1862.

F52 **Stationer, (Printer) & Fancy Trades' Register.** London. 1865-1900.

F53 **Stationery Trades' Journal.** London. 1880-1900. Only 1887-1898 systematically searched.

F54 **Studio.** London. 1893-1900.

F55 Transactions, Society (for the Encouragement) of Arts, (Manufactures & Commerce). London. 1789-1848. Continued as: Journal, Society of Arts, q.v.

F56 **Typographic Advertiser.** London. 1862-1868.

Wood's Typographic Advertiser. London. See: Typographic Advertiser.

F57 **World's Printers',** (Stationers' & Kindred Traders') **Effective Advertiser.** London. 1884-1898.

F58 **Year Book of Photography.** London. 1880-1891.

Fc Historical periodicals

Once again, the titles in **bold** were systematically searched, others only incidentally consulted.

F59 **Art Index.** New York. 1933+ (Covering literature from 1929+).

F60 **Baxter Times.** Leamington. 1923-1925. Continued as: B P Collector & Baxter Times, q.v.

F61 **B P Collector & Baxter Times.** Leamington. 1925-1927. Formerly: Baxter Times, q.v.

F62 Burlington Magazine. London. 1903+

F63 **Collectors' Magazine.** London. 1904-1905. Formerly: Printseller & Collector, q.v.

F64 Connoisseur. London. 1901+

F65 **History of Photography.** London. 1977+

F66 Image. London. 1949-1957.

F67 **Imprint.** London. 1913.

F68 **Journal, Printing Historical Society.** London. 1965+

F69 **Library,** (Transactions of the Bibliographical Society). London. 4th ser. 1920+

F70 Penrose Annual. London. 1895+

F71 Print. New Haven. 1940+

F72 **Print Collectors' Quarterly.** New York, London. 1911-1950. Complete index, vols.1-23, 1911-1936. London, [1936]. 95pp.

F73 Printing Art. Chicago. 1903-1941.

F74 Printing Review. London. 1931+

F75 **Printseller & Collector.** London. 1903-1904. Continued as: Collectors' Magazine, q.v.

F76 **Proceedings, National Picture Print Society** (for the Study of 19th Century Engraving & Colour Picture Printing). London. 1935-1941.

Appendix

Suggestion for a basic library

So far as we could discover, no single library contains the whole corpus of the literature recorded in this bibliography. We have both built up useful collections for our own research but only at the cost of many years of hunting and collecting. Fortunately, a number of key works have been reprinted in recent years which makes the task of putting together a working collection a little more feasible. However, there are still some items which remain distressingly elusive. For the assistance of those individuals who are anxious to keep an essential working collection, and for librarians who would like to keep the most informative books readily accessible for readers, we suggest a "one yard" bookshelf. The list is intended to cover all the major sections of the bibliography, including contemporary and retrospective titles.

Our selection is subjective and obviously open to argument, if only because some titles are hard to obtain. However, the principles we have kept in mind in making this selection are firstly, that contemporary instructional literature is likely to be more reliable than a modern re-telling of it, secondly, that contemporary books which contain comparative examples of printmaking processes cannot be bettered for the newcomer to print identification, and thirdly, that historical literature should describe the development of techniques as well as the artistic and cultural history of prints and printed pictures.

Titles which satisfy the first requirement are, happily, being reprinted and thus made readily available. Titles in the second category are all but impossible to reproduce but are by no means impossible to find secondhand. Some have been reprinted with photo-reproductions of the specimens, but reproductions can only give a shadowy reflection of the original print and are of little use for comparative identification. The third category is in a state of continuous growth and our selection may soon be rendered obsolete by new works in active preparation as we write.

A: Printmaking and picture printing in general:

A28 **Fielding, T.H.** 1841. The art of engraving. (Specimens).
A52 **Singer, H.W. & W. Strang.** 1897. Etching, engraving & other methods of printing pictures. (Specimens).
A133 **Wilson, F.J.F.** [1882.] Stereotyping & electrotyping.

History:

A265 **Harris, E.M.** 1968-70. Experimental graphic processes in England.
A268 **Wakeman, G.** 1973. Victorian book illustration: The technical revolution.
A270 **Godfrey, R.T.** 1978. Printmaking in Britain.
A271 **Griffiths, A.** 1980. Prints & printmaking.
A278 **Burch, R.M.** 1910. Colour printing & colour printers. (Specimens). Repr. New York, 1980 (but without the specimens).
A286 **McLean, R.** 1972. Victorian book design & colour printing.
A311 **Mitzman, M.E.** 1978. George Baxter & the Baxter prints.
A345 **Ivins, W.M. Jr.** 1953. Prints & visual communication. Repr. New York, 1969.
A347 **Ivins, W.M. Jr.** 1964. How prints look.

B: Intaglio plate processes

B3 **Faithorne, W.** 1702. The art of graving & etching. (Specimens). Repr. New York, 1970.
B26 **Hammerton, P.G.** 1876. Etching & etchers. (Specimens). Repr. East Ardsley, 1975.
B28 **Lalanne, M.** 1880. A treatise on etching. (Specimens). Repr. New York, 1981.
B77 **Strang, D.** 1930. The printing of etchings & engravings.

History:

B165 **Hind, A.M.** 1923. A history of etching & engraving. Repr. New York, 1963.
B174 **Hunnisett, B.** 1980. Steel-engraved book illustration in England.

C: Relief block processes

C2 **Jackson, J. & W.A. Chatto.** 1839 & 1861. A treatise on wood engraving, historical & practical. Repr. of 1861 edn., Detroit, Mich., 1969.
C6 **Linton, W.J.** 1884. Wood-engraving.
C112 **Noble, F.** The principles & practice of colour printing stated & explained. (C110, the same author's account of Block printing, is also strongly recommended).

History:

C2 (See above).
C195 **De Mare, E.** 1980. The Victorian woodblock illustrators.

D: Planographic (lithographic) processes:

D13 **Senefelder, A.** 1819. A complete course of lithography. (Specimens). Repr. New York, 1968.
D20 **Hullmandel, C.** 1824. The art of drawing on stone. (Specimens) Repr. New York, 1980.
D67* **Richmond, W.D.** 1878. The grammar of lithography.
D104* **Richmond, W.D.** [1885?] Colour & colour printing as applied to lithography.

History:

D251 **Twyman, M.** 1970. Lithography 1800-1850.
D252 **Wakeman, G.** 1970. Aspects of Victorian lithography. Anastatic printing & photo-zincography.
D261 **Twyman, M.** 1965. The tinted lithograph.

E: Photo-mechanical processes:

E61 **Burton, W.K.** 1892. Practical guide to photographic & photo-mechanical printing.
E68 **Wilkinson, W.T.** 1897. Photo-mechanical processes.
E69 **Brothers. A.** 1899. Photography: Its history, processes, apparatus & materials. (Specimens).
E443 **Blackburn, H.** 1901. The art of illustration.

History:

E500 **Eder, J.M.** 1945. History of photography. Repr. New York, 1978.
E514 **Jussim, E.** 1974. Visual communication & the graphic arts: Photographic technologies in the 19th century.
E525 **Coe, B.** 1978. Colour photography: The first hundred years, 1840-1940.

Indexes

Index of processes, patent names, equipment and materials

Index of authors, contributors, editors, and translators

Index of processes, patent names, equipment and materials

Reference is to item numbers, the prefixed letter indicating the relevant section. Asterisked numbers file after the corresponding plain numbers in the text.

The main list of references for each process includes all works known to provide some description of it. However, the sub-heading "History" only lists items solely concerned with the subject and does not include references to all general histories which mention it. Harris (A265) and Eder (E500), for example, discuss any number of individual processes but are not referenced from each one in this index. The user should always look for a "generic" heading as well as the "specific" process in order to trace all relevant historical materials.

Index of authors, contributors, editors and translators

Reference is to item numbers, the prefixed letter indicating the relevant section. Asterisked numbers file after the corresponding plain numbers in the text.